SAVING STUFF

*How to Care for and Preserve
Your Collectibles, Heirlooms,
and Other Prized Possessions*

Don Williams
and Louisa Jaggar

A FIRESIDE BOOK
PUBLISHED BY SIMON & SCHUSTER
New York   London   Toronto   Sydney

FIRESIDE
Rockefeller Center
1230 Avenue of the Americas
New York, NY 10020

FIRESIDE and colophon are registered trademarks
of Simon & Schuster, Inc.

For information about special discounts for bulk purchases,
please contact Simon & Schuster Special Sales at
1-800-456-6798 or business@simonandschuster.com.

Illustrations copyright © 2005 by Don Williams

Designed by Katy Riegel

Manufactured in the United States of America

10   9   8   7   6   5   4   3

Library of Congress Cataloging-in-Publication Data
Williams, Don.
        Saving stuff : how to care for and preserve your collectibles, heirlooms,
    and other prized possessions / Don Williams and Louisa Jaggar.
            p.   cm.
        Includes index.
        1. Museum conservation methods.   2. Collectibles—Conservation and
    restoration.   3. Heirlooms—Conservation and restoration.   4. Cultural
    property—Protection.   I. Jaggar, Louisa.   II. Title.
    AM145.W55   2005
    069'.53—dc22   2005040823

ISBN 0-7432-6416-9

To Mom and Dad
for teaching me that honest curiosity is not a sin.

—DW

To Carol Ammerman for saying "You can fly," and to
Jeff Goldstein and Robert Davis
for teaching me how when I didn't yet know I had wings.

—LJ

Acknowledgments

The content of this book reflects an ever-growing mountain of knowledge compiled by many preservation specialists over the years, whose ideas, scholarship, and writings were adapted and incorporated as bricks in the foundation of *Saving Stuff* and are featured prominently within its pages. At the Smithsonian Center for Materials Research and Education (SCMRE), where every lunch is akin to attending a conference of international experts, I learned immensely from interactions with my past and present coworkers. Studying their work added immeasurably to my knowledge about artifacts and their preservation: Harry Alden (microscopy); Mary Ballard (textiles conservation); Rae Beaubien (objects conservation); Ron Cunningham (paintings conservation and radiography); David Erhardt (preservation research); Martha Goodway (historical metallurgy); Carol Grissom (objects conservation); Walter Hopwood (analytical and organic chemistry); Mark McCormick-Goodhart (photographic preservation); Marion Mecklenberg (preservation research); Fei-wen Tsai (paper and book preservation); Jia-sun Tsang (paintings conservation); Charlie Tumosa (preservation research); Noreen Tuross (biochemistry); Pam Vandiver (ceramics); David von Endt (preservation of natural history collections); and Mel Wachowiak (furniture conservation). I hope I present their scholarship accurately. SCMRE Technical Information Specialist Ann N'Gadi was an unfailing navigator when I needed some obscure piece of information.

A special thanks goes to former SCMRE colleagues Dianne van der Reyden (paper and photographic conservation) and Mary Baker (preservation of modern polymers), who, in addition to teaching me about their own specialties, were the originators of the Time Capsule concept we jointly developed, and which is included in Chapter 4.

Former SCMRE furniture conservator Marc Williams, with whom I wrote an unpublished manuscript on furniture conservation nearly twenty years ago, encouraged me in using the written word. That inclination was further encouraged by Richard Lauchman's training on professional writing. Fifteen years ago Michele Pagan, a textiles conservator then working for the U.S. State Department, somehow managed to get me and my fellow SCMRE conservators to compile a lucid guide to preserving diverse decorative and fine arts collections. Though never published, this project provided the structure for much of what Louisa and I created in *Saving Stuff*.

Other Smithsonian colleagues of particular note include Greta Hansen (preservation of ethnographic materials), Deb Hull-Walski (collections management), Nora Lockshin (archives preservation), Peter Muldoon (furniture conservation), Rick Pelasera (exhibit design and construction), Beth Richwine (objects conservation), Sarah Stauderman (preservation of magnetic media), Carlene Stephens (clocks), Gary Sturm (musical instruments), and Polly Willman (textiles and costumes). Ellen Nanney of the SI Office of Product Development and Licensing, along with Lauryn Grant, Assistant General Counsel, and Claudia Barbieri of the Office of Contracting, all played critical roles in making this book a reality. Non-SI colleagues who provided valuable information or assistance include Mark Anderson, Martin Burke, Greg Landrey, Alan Levitan, Stefan Michalski, Karen Motylewski, Robert Mussey, Michael Podmaniczky, Victoria Montana Ryan, and Paul Storch. Mike Mascelli provided content and editorial counsel, and the rhetorical boot to the behind necessary when dealing with crossing the *t*'s and dotting the *i*'s. My dear friend Helen Stetina and I polished acres of Winterthur silver side by side, and she has remained a lifelong friend and steadfast source of encouragement, especially in my fiction writing. There is no way I can adequately express what Mitch Kohanek has taught me about formulating and presenting information to nonspecialist audiences, and he (along with Louisa) is responsible for the way the subject matter is presented. The rest are simply my own eccentricities and shortcomings.

Three men had great early influence on developing my skills in the preservation arts: my first and greatest teacher in restoration was Fred Schindler; Nicky Hlopoff, one of America's most renowned art conservators, steered me toward a career in museums while we were both working in the magnificent Palm Beach home of Charles and Jayne Wrightsman; and John Kuzma, my fellow patternmaker at Maddox Foundry, showed me what precision was all about.

This project would never have moved forward without the enthusiastic support of mentor and former SCMRE director Lambertus van Zelst and former coordinator for research, Ron Bishop, who approached me with Louisa's proposal and immediately recognized its potential benefits, and authorized organizational support for it. Assistant Director for Operations Melanie Feather, Assistant to the Director Beverly Smith, Assistant Director for Programming Mel Wachowiak, current Director Robert Koestler, and interim Acting Director Paula DePriest all worked diligently to make sure my particular deck was cleared so that the project could proceed with a minimum amount of disruption. Their unwavering faith in it has been an inspiration.

Louisa and I both offer our heartiest thanks to Ruth Anna Stolk, whose efforts to promote Smithsonian's leadership role in the "Science of Saving Stuff" led to this book.

Finally, a special thanks is given to my ladies at home, who have tolerated my distractions (and working long past midnight far too often) over the past year with good humor and loving grace, and for not making too much fun of my having twenty-three different kinds of shellac in the basement.

—Don Williams

I want to add my heartfelt thanks to Gail Ross, who I sat with in the bleachers during many a basketball game, watching our daughters play. She showed up at the hospital after my daughter had a critical asthma attack during a game and right then I knew we would be friends for life. Little did I know she would someday be my agent as well. Doris Cooper, our editor at Simon & Schuster, you are the absolute best! You have helped us make this a book we can be proud of. Heather Hunter, both Don and I are indebted to you. You are the greatest friend! Don and I both are also indebted to the staff at the Irish Inn at Glen Echo, where they have come to view us as their resident eccentrics, as we spent many lunches debating word choices. I need to thank all the readers who offered their comments and thoughts during this process. I thank Susan and Larry Mahan, for their advice, encouragement, and information. Barbara McCoy, Stephanie Havenstein, Heather Hunter, Jane Swensen, Cheryl and Robert King and their daughter Katherine, Patti Posnick, Sandy Krawitz, Joe and Dalene Dean, Cecilia and Guillermo Schultz, Debbie Benke, Pat Smith, Petr Speight: I want to thank each of you for reading this manuscript and offering your invaluable suggestions as well as support. Jody Bolz, thank you for sharing your knowledge and friendship and pointing me in the right direction. I thank also Maryann Will, Alana Pitcher, and Mary Power at Stone Ridge School of the Sacred Heart because you three have always been so incredibly supportive, and Celeste Richardson for all your wonderful ideas and vision. To Christina DiMeglio and Lonna Seibert at the Smithsonian Affiliations Office, for all your ideas and assistance: Don and I greatly appreciate every single bit of it. Bethany Haas, thank you for your research and your help with the Smithsonian stories. Jeff Goldstein and Bert Davis, for encouraging me to write way back when I was just a struggling single mom hoping to pay the rent. Thank you. And Bert, a special thank-you for the day you said, "You are a writer," before I ever received a dime for writing. And our missing but not forgotten friend Carol: though you will always be in my heart and a part of any journey I take, how I wish you were here sitting beside me, reading this. Thank you to all my students, who have supported me all these years. I thank my mother, Anne Jaggar, and my sister, Valerie Delyea, for always believing in me and encouraging me. And my most heartfelt thanks to my son, David, and my daughters, Alex and Lesley, for all their love and especially their ability to make me laugh till I cry.   —Louisa Jaggar

Contents

Introduction

Swirling black water poured through the basement door, drenching the family scrapbooks, old toys, newspaper clippings, books, and well-worn clothes. As I stood in two feet of water clutching my son's sopping christening gown, I realized that I treasured the old scrapbooks, toys, and photos more than the expensive crystal sitting safely upstairs in the credenza. Fuzzy Tail, the Steiff fox I cuddled every night as a little girl, my daughter Alex's art projects, my son David's early childhood writings, and boxes of our family's history were all gone. Devastated, I sank down onto the basement steps and wept.

When I later shared what had happened with my friend Don, the senior conservator at the Smithsonian Institution, he asked why I had stored my treasures in the basement in the first place. I responded that I didn't have an attic. It was then I discovered that basements and attics are both archenemies of valuables—both monetary and sentimental. Basements tend to flood and are often mildewy. Attics get too hot and dry. These conditions destroy the very things that people love to save.

Why didn't I know this?

Because there isn't one book that deals with saving all your treasures such as your family crystal, silver, and fine art collection as well as your child's macaroni art mosaic, the family scrapbook, and your favorite childhood stuffed animal. I decided I needed to find out how to take care of my most treasured stuff as well as

how to avoid common mistakes. Who better to ask than Don, my friend and senior conservator?
                                                                    —Louisa Jaggar

When Louisa first proposed our joining forces to write a book on saving stuff, I assumed that many books existed on the subject. After all, my colleagues and I talk about conservation all the time. To prove my point, I handed her a few great books on the subject: *Conservation Concerns, Scientific Design for Conservation,* and the great page-turner, *Deterioration of Materials.* Louisa lugged them home, and I awaited her return call, the call where she said we didn't need to write this book because many people already had.

She didn't call.

Instead, she showed up the next week, threw the books on my desk, and said, "What in the world is depolymerization, or perhaps you would care to explain the concept of microclimates? Not one of these doorstops you call a book is in English. And the fact that I spent a week of my life figuring out that moisture vapor barrier just means a good coat of wax has me fuming. I don't have the time! Your book selections only reinforce the idea that this information needs to be written in plain English and presented in a straightforward manner for people like me. And, frankly, who better to write this than us? I know nothing about preserving valuables, and you are an expert on the topic. I have made almost every mistake known to man or woman, and you have made a career of fixing those sorts of mistakes. Plus, when you use big words, I can hit you with one of those huge books you lent me!"

Preserving stuff is my passion, so Louisa didn't have to twist my arm. I have spent the better part of my life taking care of our nation's treasures, from the Wright Flyer to a Stradivarius violin, and couldn't pass up the opportunity to help you take care of yours.

Saving Stuff is about preserving and maintaining "the museum of you." This museum is made up of the objects that have special value for you. I can't stop an earthquake, flood, or alien invasion, but I can share how to prevent most homegrown catastrophes as well as how to go about saving stuff: comic books, wedding dresses, baseball cards, furniture, stamps, papers, film, pictures, records, DVDs, CDs, dollhouses, flags, and weird and wacky things like Cousin Cecil's African water buffalo head or your private collection of sheep's eyeballs kept by your grandfather in mayonnaise jars. In this book I will show you how to save almost anything you want.

THE FOUNDATION OF SAVING STUFF

This book is not meant to be read from cover to cover. Chapters 1 and 2 are essential reading, and then, you can go to the chapters that best answer your needs when it comes to preserving your stuff. The first two chapters give you the foundation for caring for your stuff.

In Chapter 1, I alert you to the critical dangers that every museum and historical society takes into account when deciding how to care for their collections. There are only a few basic dangers, but you need to know how to recognize and combat them.

Chapter 2 introduces the general principles of preserving stuff from the experts' point of view. How do you decide what is important to you and what you want to preserve? Chapter 2 helps you make those decisions using the same process that museum experts follow. Museums have limited space, money, and staff. They cannot save everything, and neither should you feel obligated to save all the stuff that comes your way. This chapter helps you decide what you want to save and how to prioritize depending on your personal resources.

Each subsequent chapter is devoted to caring for a particular category of object. I share with you the principles of saving each type of collectible so that you, too, can think like a conservator.

The easy-to-follow instructions on the care and preservation of your stuff follows. Each of these chapters also contains Don's Rules. These rules offer basic preventative measures you can take to save the things you love.

From beginning to end we have sprinkled Smithsonian Institution museum stories about preservation, which provide a sometimes funny, sometimes serious behind-the-scenes look at how the Smithsonian cares for our national treasures. These stories take you on a personal tour of my world within the Smithsonian, a world you never see when looking at the exhibits. Also, these stories often reflect the latest conservation techniques as well as point out how best to care for your stuff.

DON'S TIPS

All through *Saving Stuff*, I share my preservation tips, and they can be recognized by the suspenders icon. These tips include everything from debunking old wives' tales to novel uses of everyday materials around the house.

LOUISA'S TALES

Louisa has vignettes scattered throughout the book, and you can recognize them by the italicized font. Her experience as a saver of stuff allows her to help guide you in preserving your stuff. The stories she shares often involve common mistakes she has made in taking care of her stuff—mistakes she hopes she can help you avoid.

In addition, in the Resources section at the end of the book I provide a *Saving Stuff* Tool Kit—a list of supplies and materials you need in order to save your stuff. I list the necessary items and give a brief description of them—and a Suppliers List so you can find them.

Let the adventures begin!

PART ONE

The Museum of You

Chapter 1

Your Treasures Want to Live in an Egyptian Tomb

Everything you own and love eventually falls apart. No matter how big or how sturdy, it falls apart. Even the Roman Colosseum and the Greek Parthenon are but shadows of their former greatness. Like my colleagues, I call this process entropy; Louisa calls it "going back to dirt." Whatever the size of your collectible, the general process remains the same. What differs is the time involved. My job at the Smithsonian is to slow down this "going back to dirt" journey as much as possible.

Of course, the best way to ensure that stuff lasts is to place all your collectibles in an Egyptian tomb and then seal them in—after leaving the prerequisite deadly curse on all who dare enter. Stuff lasts for a really long time in a cursed tomb. Why? No light, no humidity fluctuation, no contaminants, no bugs, no furry friends, and no people.

But then why have stuff if you have to stash it away in order to keep it? At the Smithsonian Institution we do our best to balance the need to display with the need to preserve our nation's treasures.

The Star Spangled Banner represents a great example of the "back to dirt" journey. After being on display since 1907, this inspirational flag shows the damaging effects of exposure to light, dirt, and temperature changes. In a multiyear project, the flag is being carefully cleaned and repaired. The incredible emblem will then be remounted in its new home: a dramatic new flag room designed to minimize any future damage to this national symbol. The flag room is a sealed, four-story-tall, climate-controlled area that will protect the flag from insects, dirt, people, excessive light levels, and temperature and humidity fluctuations.

The same issues that threaten our national flag threaten your stuff: light, temperature, water, dirt, bugs, pollution, and you (yes, sorry to say, but in some cases you are the biggest threat to your stuff).

As you read through *Saving Stuff*, please remember that exceptions exist for every rule, some of which I discuss. A book including thorough explanations about each and every one of these rules and their exceptions would be thousands of pages long and cost hundreds of dollars. To save you time and money I have also included at the end of this chapter a chart giving general information about the major sources of deterioration and their effect on your collectibles.

HOW LIGHT DAMAGES YOUR STUFF

For living things, light is a necessary energy source for growth and vitality, but light makes dead stuff fall apart. Light damage can cause fading and other changes in the appearance of an object.

For example, if you remove a framed print from the wall where it has been hanging for some time, you will notice a fading pattern on the wall everywhere except for the space where the framed print hung. Congratulations! You have successfully protected a portion of your wall from the ravages of light. But what took the attack instead? The artwork, of course.

Curtains, rugs, clothing, prints (paper stuff of all kinds, actually), paintings, and furniture are all at risk of fading due to light damage. If the light levels stay high enough long enough, the light can actually go beyond changing the colors and destroy the underlying materials as well. In other words, light not only can fade your favorite rug but turn it to powder right where it lies.

The higher the light energy (intensity or wavelength), the more rapid the damage. Ultraviolet (UV) light from natural sunlight is particularly troublesome because it is the highest energy of the normally occurring light sources. The trouble is, you can't tell how much UV light is falling on your collection of stuff because by definition it is not visible to the naked human eye. Naked honeybee eyes, yes (I'm not kidding), but not human eyes. Shutters, UV filtering glaze, absorbing films on the windows or retractable UV-filtering shades (basically a clear plastic with UV absorbers or blockers in the mix) block UV light. Museums frequently employ all four methods to protect their collections.

Fluorescent lights also emit a fairly high level of UV light. In situations where museums must use fluorescent lights, a UV filter sleeve is placed over the tube and the output is monitored with special meters that measure the UV levels.

How Much Light?

When museum conservators talk about measuring light intensity, they refer to either "foot-candles" or "lux," terms used for measuring light intensity or how bright the light is on a particular surface. This does not mean how bright the light is when it leaves the source but how bright it is when it arrives at the collectible. The measurement includes both natural and artificial light. Conservators measure light levels in lux or foot-candles at the surface of the displayed object, using a light meter. If you have light-sensitive collectibles, you need a light meter, too. You can buy a scientific light meter, which can be obtained fairly inexpensively from a resource vendor listed in the back of the book. *Make sure you do not buy a photographic light meter by mistake—it won't do the job.*

A standard 100-watt lightbulb provides 60 foot-candles of illumination on an item placed two feet away and 15 foot-candles on the same object four feet away. A standard 60-watt bulb delivers approximately 36 foot-candles of illumination on an item placed two feet away and 9 foot-candles at four feet.

And what if the light is from a spotlight? That light is focused in a particular direction as opposed to a standard lightbulb's light, which is diffused equally in all directions. Spotlights can provide five times more light to a collectible than the standard lightbulb of the same wattage at the same distance. By comparison, direct sunlight outdoors can exceed 5,000 foot-candles, which is about fifty times more intense than typical indoor artificial lighting.

If a room receives no outside source of light, you can simply lower wattage to control the light levels. Most rooms in a house have windows, though, and those windows allow natural light to stream in. The beauty of a light meter is that it measures the collection of both artificial and natural light.

Here is a list of recommended extended light levels in foot-candles for many of the collectibles included in this book. Your light meter will typically give you readings in foot-candles. If your light meter measures in lux and you need to convert, it's a simple conversion factor: 1 foot-candle equals 10.76 lux. (Obviously, for brief periods of time for examination or restoration, higher levels are allowed.) Make sure you take this measurement when the light coming in from outside is at its brightest and the artificial lighting typically stays turned on for the test.

COLLECTIBLE	LIGHT LEVEL (FOOT-CANDLES)
Textiles	3 to 5
Color photographs	3 to 5
Watercolors	3 to 5
Fine manuscripts	5
Black-and-white photographs	10
Plastics	10
Ivory	10
Acrylic paintings	10
Oil and panel paintings	15
Wood and lacquer objects	15
Metal, stone, glass, ceramic *	25

Determining the Potential for Light Damage and How to Limit It

With more stable artworks, such as paintings, it may be especially difficult to observe color change (light damage) in any kind of normal time frame. In order to estimate the potential for light damage over long periods of time,

* These objects are not particularly light sensitive, but the brighter the light, the greater the risk of heat damage from the lighting source.

light intensity and exposure time need to be monitored for a shorter time—say, a month or three.

The standard tool for measuring the potential for light damage is called the Blue Wool Fading Strip, sometimes known as "British Blue Wool Standard." These disposable aids, available from archival suppliers, are fitted with gradations of blue wool fabric that can tell how much fading has taken place due to light exposure over a particular time. At the end of the exposure period, use the easy-to-follow instructions that allow you to estimate the potential for light damage. If the potential is low, you can rest easy. If it is high, you might consider relocating your collectible.

If you do not have the time to fiddle around with blue wool strips or light meters, my advice is to keep the lights turned off when you are not in the room and keep the shades drawn. Get in the habit of using lower power lightbulbs—changing from a 100-watt bulb to a 60-watt bulb reduces the light exposure by 40 percent—and draping your collection with opaque fabric when it is not being viewed. If the object you are trying to save is affected adversely by light, place it in a room where you need a flash to take a picture. In other words, if your camera snaps a picture without the need for a flash, there is probably too much light in that room for your collectible.

SETTING THE TEMPERATURE

Temperature is involved in four major mechanisms of deterioration:

1. A human-comfortable temperature is perfect for bugs and mold. Mold growth occurs between 60 and 120 degrees Fahrenheit and reaches its zenith at about 90 degrees. And bugs? They can be slowed down by colder temperatures but cannot be stopped until the temperatures get ridiculously low. It is not surprising that whatever killed off the dinosaurs didn't even touch the bugs.

2. Temperature helps determine the rate at which stuff falls apart. Louisa sums up the whole process of degradation thermodynamics by saying, "Degradation does really bad things to your stuff, and heat just speeds up the whole process."

3. As a general rule, when stuff gets colder, it becomes more brittle, and when it gets warmer, stuff turns more rubbery. Have you ever left a videocassette in the rear window of a car?

4. Thermal shock occurs when a material is either heated or cooled very rapidly. The quick change in temperature causes internal stresses that can lead to fractures. Clearly, this is most relevant with glass and ceramic objects. For example, Louisa once tried to cook with a glass bowl over an open flame. The glass heated up very quickly, the structure began to fracture, and then, *voilà*, there were glass fragments flying over the entire kitchen.

Temperature and Humidity

Finally, we have temperature and its favorite dance partner, humidity, and what happens when these two boogie together to just the right song? I call them partners in crime. Rarely is one force solely responsible for turning your stuff back to dirt (except in the case of fire or flood or pets or children). Instead, the forces of deterioration act in concert with each other. Any one of the agents that cause stuff to turn to dirt is a problem by itself, but give any of them a dance partner, and the rate of deterioration increases exponentially.

Substantial humidity (more than 70 percent) combined with high temperature (more than 80 degrees Fahrenheit) wreaks havoc on almost any collection that isn't glass. When these two start dancing together, mold and mildew appear, and your stuff turns green, sometimes black, and always yucky. Sometimes the combination of heat and humidity exacerbates an effect known as "rheology," or flow. All you need to know is that wildly fluctuating heat and humidity together can make problems of warping or cracking much worse.

Measuring temperature is fairly straightforward: Look at a thermometer or heating ventilation and air conditioning (HVAC) thermostat. But what about measuring humidity? Humidity is measured with a device called a psychrometer or hygrometer. It used to require a precision tool to measure accurately, but fortunately modern digital technology has made accurate temperature and humidity meters inexpensive (under $50), and they are easy to obtain from the suppliers listed in the reference section of this book.

Controlling the Moisture

Much like the other enemies, light and heat, moisture contributes to deterioration by following many paths. The most obvious means of moisture damage occurs when an object gets wet. Water dissolves as well as corrodes stuff. Certainly, kindergarten macaroni mosaics are really susceptible to water damage, as are watercolors and many types of old photographs. This is why you don't store your collectibles in a damp basement or next to the bathroom or swimming pool.

Water also stains (or destains) many types of objects. If the water contains any staining materials, such as Kool-Aid or even minerals if you have hard water, these materials tend to be deposited. Think about the walls of your shower. Or have you ever washed a red sock in a load of whites?

INSECTS, RODENTS, AND THE PROBLEMS THEY CAUSE

As I ponder insects, rodents, and the damage both inflict on some collections, I find myself humming the jingle from television's 60s era; "Munch, munch, munch a bunch of Fritos corn chips." (Surely some advertising exec is smiling to himself.) That's what bugs and rodents do: chomp, chomp, chomp.

Rodents chew on whatever is in their way or to gather nesting material. Most insects do a lot of chewing as well, but some actually view your collection as the buffet to end all buffets. Bugs particularly love nibbling on natural fiber textiles, book binding glue, painted gourds, and old photographs.

Insect infestation damage also takes place with furniture and other wooden objects. While termites consume the wood as a nutrient, other insects use the objects as a place to hang their hat and raise a family. They tunnel through wood to create egg chambers, and they tunnel out to escape the egg chambers once the birthing is done.

Regardless of the exact reason for the chomping, the result is the same: the loss of the object or even the loss of an entire collection. The first line of defense against insects is to make sure they cannot get in your home. Make sure there are no unsealed openings in walls, undereaves, or around doors and windows. Also be careful that your screens fit snugly, and mend any holes in them. Finally, avoid using bug zappers in the yard. All they do is attract more bugs. If you want to use a bug zapper, give it to your neighbor and have the bugs go to his house.

CONTAMINANTS

When we think of contaminants and pollution, we normally think of belching smokestacks and green pond scum. To be sure, bad things happen to stuff that is placed in such environments, but to a lesser degree our stuff is also subjected to chemical assaults and unwanted physical deposits. All too often we expose our treasures to harmful contaminants without even knowing it.

Take cigarettes, for example. My family and I recently purchased a cabin in the hills from a fellow who was an accomplished craftsman and talented artist, but he was also a heavy smoker. When we first saw the cabin, we noticed it had really neat, valuable stuff, including several of the man's marvelous paintings. We also noticed a film of brown tobacco goo everywhere. My wife, our daughters, and I repeatedly scrubbed the surfaces in our little cabin to get rid of the smoky smell and discoloration. I can only imagine what the smoke did to the former owner's wonderful stuff or what it will do to your collectibles if you allow anyone to smoke around them.

Another example of contaminant-caused deterioration is storing fine metals such as art bronzes and silverware in wool wraps. A bad idea. The sulphur in the wool tarnishes (corrodes) the silver almost immediately. The same is true for oxygen, which reacts with silver to form silver oxides (or copper oxides in the case of bronze and brass; more about that later). The other big mistake people make is wrapping silver in plastic cling wrap (the kind used to save leftovers). Most plastic cling wrap is made of a chemical called vinylidene chloride, and chlorine and all its evil chloride cousins are virulent corrosive agents for metals. These are just a few of the pollutants that seek to destroy your stuff.

The issue of contaminants looms large in the preservation world. That is why a part of almost every chapter in this book deals with contaminants: from the discoloration of good rag paper through close contact with either wood or wood pulp paper to the oily polishes you use (but shouldn't) on your furniture.

NORMAL USE

In many instances, and for a lot of collectibles, "normal use" presents no unusual risks because they are decorative. Normal use of furniture and other functional objects is a catch-22, however. The mere act of sitting on a chair places stresses on the seat, legs, and back. Repeated enough times, the chair will collapse. Whether it's burly ol' Don or spritelike Louisa doing the sitting, the result is the same, only the rate of damage is different.

Furniture eventually breaks, textiles become abraded and rapidly degraded by light, and antique radios and televisions inevitably give up the ghost. The only way to avoid these results is not to use your collectibles for anything—and that includes displaying them. And what fun is that?

The exception is musical instruments: playing them occasionally is part of the preservation process.

In *Saving Stuff*, we provide helpful advice about how to balance "use" with the preservation of your collectibles. Just keep in mind that "use" and "lose" are generally closely related. The more you use your collectibles, the faster you will lose them.

HANDLING AND MISUSE

How you handle—pick up, pack, move, and ship—your collectibles is important. The number one cause of preventable damage to stuff is handling. Carelessness or incomplete information on how to handle stuff often results in damaged goods.

Throughout the book your attention will be drawn to warnings about handling collectibles with your bare hands (oils and acids from your skin can stain paper and soft ceramics, corrode metals, and dissolve some furniture finishes) and handling with gloved hands (makes moving heavy furniture much more risky because you can lose your grip). Some advice sounds almost silly (such as how to turn the pages of a very old book), some reflects good common sense (how to wrap and store Great-Grandmother's wedding dress), and some is downright profound.

When you use something for which it is not intended—such as using a cane-bottomed chair as a step stool—damage is frequently the result.

PETS AND CHILDREN

Okay, the truth is that you love 'em. Another truth is they destroy more stuff than flood and fire combined. Louisa has two children, two cats, and a dog, which is like having her own demolition squad. Much of their developing years remains recorded on her furniture: chewed furniture legs from Frosty's puppy years, ripped upholstery courtesy of Chilli and Max's ever-present desire to scratch, Alexandra's name scrawled in kindergarten script across the kitchen's pinewood table, and the woven cane chair that David's foot went through when he stood on it to replace a lightbulb.

Dogs and cats love to mark their territory, a problem if your eighteenth-century easy chair resides in what they consider *their* territory. Removing the stench of animal urine when it seeps into porous material is almost impossible. If you own a priceless and vulnerable textile, piece of furniture, or objet d'art, please cover it or place it out of reach of pets, particularly if the pets are under the age of two. Puppies and kittens inflict 90 percent of the damage on collectibles as compared to grown-up pets. As a note of encouragement, pets' manners often improve with age. Kids' manners do, too.

THE RISK CHART AND FIGURING OUT THE RISKS TO YOUR COLLECTIBLES

Unfortunately, I cannot come to your home to tell you what the risks are to your collectibles. I can, however, give you a chart that will help you identify them. Using some common sense and your five senses, you can look at your collectibles and, with the help of the Risk Chart, figure out where the greatest threats are coming from.

Risk Chart for Collectibles

	Light	Insects/Mold	Handling	Contaminants	Normal Use	Temperature	Moisture
Rag paper	☹	☹	θ	θ	θ	θ	☹
Pulp paper	☹	☹	☹	☹	θ	☹	☹
Glass and ceramics	☺	☺	☹	θ	θ	θ	☺
Metals	☺	☺	θ	☹	θ	θ	☹
Wood and baskets	☹	☹	☹	☹	θ	θ	θ
Textiles—natural	☠	☠	☹	☹	☹	θ	☹
Textiles—synthetic	☠	☺	☹	☹	☹	θ	☹
Photos—prints (pre-1970)	☹	☹	θ	θ	θ	☹	☹
Photos—B&W prints (1970–)	θ	θ	θ	θ	θ	☹	☹
Photos—color prints (1970–)	☠	θ	θ	θ	θ	θ	θ
Photos—film (pre-1950)	☹	θ	θ	☠	θ	☹	☠
Photos—film (after 1950)	☹	☺	θ	☺	θ	θ	θ
Oil painting	☹	θ	☹	☹	θ	θ	☹
Acrylic painting	☹	θ	☹	☹	θ	☠	☹
Watercolor	☠	☹	θ	θ	θ	θ	☠
Pastels—charcoal	θ	θ	☠	θ	θ	θ	☹
Plastics	☹	☺	θ	☹	θ	☠	θ

Legend

☺   Generally no practical risk or immediate threat under normal conditions

θ   Some risk that can usually be minimized, depending on specific circumstances

☹   Fairly high risk of damage; pay particular attention

☠   Immediate risk of catastrophic damage

Chapter 2

Deciding What Stuff to Save, Give Away, or Toss

Weighing emotional versus financial importance is difficult. People often ask me whether something is important, but I can't determine what is a collectible and therefore important to save. To me, Fuzzy Tail was just a puppet, but to Louisa, it represented wonderful memories. People save stuff for sentimental as well as for financial reasons. Deciding what is a collectible is all about what is important to you.

Along with three other people on earth, I love anything and everything to do with shellac. I spend a good amount of time collecting stuff that involves shellac. Imagine my surprise and thrill when I recently bought on eBay a vintage ink blotter depicting the life cycle of the Lac beetle (which is where shellac comes from). Of course, I was the only bidder. Still, to me, my ink blotter is a collectible, and I love it.

ASKING THE RIGHT QUESTIONS: THE "WHYS" OF PRESERVATION

Most people cannot save everything; they are forced to make choices. The first step in developing a preservation strategy is deciding what stuff you want to keep and why you want to keep it, which is not always easy. If you

By going through the exercise outlined in this chapter, Louisa managed to identify the things that were truly important to her. This guided her efforts to preserve the stuff most valuable to her.

have infinite supplies of money, space, time, and energy, you can save all your stuff, but most people have limits. Maybe you live in an apartment with limited storage. Maybe you are limited financially. Maybe you do not have endless free time. Whatever the limitation, if you cannot save everything, you need to decide what you most want to preserve. And remember: It is okay to give or throw stuff away that you no longer feel is important to you.

Museums cannot save everything, either. They have staff and labor resources to consider. The staff must rank the objects in the collections with regard to the mission of the museum. The "whys" are simple: An object can be monetarily valuable, emotionally important, or sometimes both. For example, the Hope diamond has great monetary value, whereas the Declaration of Independence has tremendous emotional importance. How would you rank these? Which would you save first? These are the questions curators face daily.

As the curator of "the museum of you," you must confront the same questions. Do you first save your family photographs or the pen-and-ink drawings left to you by your grandfather? These were some of the decisions Louisa faced when I asked her to come up with a list ranking her top ten collectibles. She has limited time, money, and space, so she truly felt the need to prioritize. She first listed every item she had that she would consider a collectible. Then she narrowed them down to the top ten. Next, she put them in order of importance to her. The loss of emotionally valuable belongings in the flood changed the way she ranks her collectibles. Before the flood she would never have thought to include a stuffed toy. Now Skippy, a stuffed toy dog given to her by a close friend, is number four on the list. These are some of the questions I asked her to consider when developing her list:

Who: Who owned it? Who made it? Who gave it to you? To whom will you leave it?

What: What is its financial value? What is its emotional value? What is it made of?

When: When did the family acquire this treasure? When was it made?

Where: Where did it come from? Are there markings on it that give you clues?

Below is Louisa's finished list, a mix of items emotionally and/or monetarily valuable to her. In the end, though, only she can decide how important each object is and why. She has included the reasons that they are important to her.

LOUISA'S LIST

1. Family photograph albums.

2. Son's painting of a panda. Painted when he was five. He accompanied me every week to my college art class, and the teacher allowed him to draw along with the other students. His painting far surpassed mine, and the teacher shared that with the class.

3. Daughter's blankie. Alex carried this blanket everywhere until she was about three. It was her prized possession and evokes in me many sweet memories of her snuggled in bed, thumb in her mouth, and cuddled up with it.

4. Skippy. My stuffed toy dog, a gift from a dear friend. Take it with me every time I fly—emotionally valuable.

5. Son's christening gown. Saved from the flood.

6. Very early edition of Dickens's *A Christmas Carol*. Found while searching through a flea shop.

7. Crystal glassware. My mother brought a complete set back from Ireland.

8. Russian wedding table. Found at an antique shop, fell in love with it. Strong monetary value.

9. Collection of antique pen-and-ink drawings. Gifts from great-grandfather. Very valuable emotionally and financially.

10. Daughter's macaroni art mosaic. The only one rescued from the flood. Emotionally valuable.

From this list it becomes obvious that her first efforts should be to safeguard the family photo albums, then her son's drawing, and so on. This list cannot address how easy or difficult it is to preserve something or how much it costs to do so. Reading through the chapters related to what you want to save will give you an idea of the investment of time and money that preserving each object requires.

MAKING YOUR LIST AND CHECKING IT TWICE

These are the supplies you will need:

Scrap paper
Pen or pencil

Worksheet 1: *Why It Is Important to You*
Worksheet 2: *Everything You Know*

The worksheets are provided at the end of the chapter. Make as many copies as you need.

1. Make a list of all your collectibles on the piece of scrap paper. Don't worry about putting them in order of importance just yet. Write down every collectible you have that you want to save. If you want, go over this list with family and friends to make sure you haven't left anything important off the list. Write alongside the items the reasons why these collectibles are important to you, just as Louisa did in the example above.

2. Go over your list and choose what you consider the ten most important items. This can reveal unimportance as well as importance. You might find that this process starts a bit of spring cleaning in your home.

3. Put these collectibles in order numerically, one through ten, from most important to least.

4. In order of their importance, enter your list of stuff on Worksheet 1. In the space provided, record why you value these objects.

5. On Worksheet 2, list each object in order of importance and then enter all the information you have concerning it. This is different from "why" it is important to you: It is the total of everything you know about each item. Save both lists in a secure place. It is a great reference not only for you but also for your heirs. Someday historians will praise you for doing so.

YOUR *SAVING STUFF* TOOL KIT AND WHAT TO PUT IN IT

After you decide what you are going to save, you will need to make sure you have the necessary equipment and supplies. For your convenience, you will find at the back of the book a glossary of sorts—I call it Your *Saving Stuff* Tool Kit and Suppliers List—that lists all the products used in this book, explains what each product is used for, tells you where you can find it (most can be purchased at your local hardware or grocery store), and whether there is a preferred brand. If the item is more difficult to find, I have provided the name of a supplier in brackets or listed a website. The reference for where to purchase these items is noted by a number in brackets that corresponds to the suppliers list at the end of the tool kit.

SAVING STUFF WITHOUT CHANGING ITS CHARACTER

Fundamental to preserving your stuff is keeping it as it should be for as long as possible without changing what it is. This book is not about restoration, which involves the physical manipulation or repair of objects, it's about preserving things, and as a conservator I want them preserved to the greatest degree possible while changing the nature of the object as little as possible.

You have choices with your collectibles. You can preserve them with no changes for as long as possible, or you can choose to restore and repair them. On the plus side, restoring compensates for any damage or deterioration that has occurred. On the con side, restoration changes your object permanently and often lessens its inherent value. Can you restore and preserve? Yes. If you restore a piece, you still need to prevent any future degradation by following the preservation strategies listed in this book.

READY, SET, GO

You now know what you want to save and are ready to delve into the following chapters. You are thinking like a conservator, and you have your list in hand. My job at this point is to help you follow a path of your choosing as well as understand the consequences of the decisions you make. If you do the right thing, your treasures will be around for generations. What last-minute advice can I give? Read a chapter of your choosing and its accompanying instructions carefully before beginning any preservation strategy. Anything else? Yes. Absolutely have fun because you have just reached the best part. You are now doing what I love to do the most: saving stuff.

WORKSHEET 1: WHY IT IS IMPORTANT TO YOU

1.	
2.	
3.	
4.	
5.	

6.	
7.	
8.	
9.	
10.	

WORKSHEET 2: EVERYTHING YOU KNOW

	Who Who owned it? Who made it? Who gave it to you? To whom will you leave it?	**What** What is its financial value? What is its emotional value? What is it made of?	**When** When did the family acquire this treasure? When was it made?	**Where** Where did it come from? Are there markings on it that give you clues?	**Preservation Actions** What actions have you taken? What actions do you need to take?
1.					
2.					
3.					
4.					
5.					
6.					
7.					
8.					
9.					
10.					

PART TWO

Saving Family Stuff

Chapter 3

Preserving Your Photographs and Films

The debate started inside the Smithsonian Castle's Great Hall when Louisa stated that photos are often considered people's most treasured possessions. "People whose homes are threatened by fire often try to grab their photographs as they escape out the door," Louisa began. "That is, once they are sure the kids, pets, and other loved ones are safe." I, of course, was picturing myself fleeing with my antique varnishing books and a handful of prized tools. I was also picturing other people grabbing their jewelry, their silver, or possibly their stock certificates.

When Louisa insisted she was right despite my numerous and well-thought-out arguments, I stopped a passerby and asked, "If your house was on fire, what would you grab after you got the people and pets out?" Without even the slightest pause the woman responded, "The family photos." Louisa tried and failed not to look gleeful. Over the next two hours this scene played itself out with other tourists. The response of "photos" came back every single time. It didn't matter what part of the country—or, for that matter, what country—they were from. When I asked people why, they answered with a host of reasons, but they all boiled down to one theme: If you lose your family photos, part of your family history is lost forever. Later at home when I told my wife that I knew what she would save (after children and pets) and why, she was shocked to discover I had read her mind. I earned serious points that night.

THINK "DUPLICATION"

Washington, D.C.—where the men wear dark suits and staid ties, most women sport blue suits and sensible heels, and fancy colors are scarce—always reminds me of a color photograph that has been exposed to too much light. Faded colors, brittle edges, and a transparent look overtake the entire photograph. That is why the overarching theme for preserving photos is to think "duplication." Duplication allows you to enjoy and display the copied image while storing the original, perhaps for thousands of years.

Don's Rules for Photographs

1. *Duplicate!* If you want to display a photo, make a duplicate and display the duplicate while storing the original.

2. Avoid light. Photo albums are ideal for keeping your photos out of direct sunlight. Light is enemy number 1.

3. Keep out the critters. Keep the area around your photos and photo albums clean and food free. If you are concerned about bugs, keep your photo albums in sealed polyethylene or polypropylene storage containers.

4. Always wear clean cotton gloves when handling photos.

LOUISA'S TALE:
A Picture Paints a Thousand Words

In my dining room hangs a black-and-white 1900s hand-tinted photo of my grandmother. The original photo is magnificent, and the tinting reflects a superb example of this subtle art. My grandmother, as a teenager, had painted in her lips herself—bright red! When I had the photo duplicated, I had to decide whether to keep the deep painted-on red of grandmother's lips. I decided to duplicate the photo exactly as is, and the copy now hangs in my dining room—red lips and all. Amazingly, no one can distinguish the duplicate from the original. The photo proves that teenagers never really change. I bet Great-Grandma was furious.

5. Handle photos and films by holding the edges, never the face of the image.

6. Never bend your photos.

7. Be careful about dust because dust actually scratches old photos and emulsions. Gently blow dust particles off photos.

TELLING YOUR PHOTOGRAPHIC ARTIFACTS APART

There are two major types of artifacts to be concerned about: photographic prints and photographic film, also known as transparencies. Photographic film includes negatives, slides, and movie film.

You need to be able to identify what you have in order to determine how to take care of it. Also, there are serious safety issues with old photographic film, since film that is made from cellulose nitrate is flammable.

Metal and Glass Print Photos: Daguerreotypes, Ambrotypes, and Tintypes

The first generation of photographic technology (1839) produced direct images made on rigid supports. Usually all three types were sealed in a glass-front shadow box case to prevent corrosion and to allow for display in special frames. These items are thick enough that for preservation storage they can be placed in boxes made from archival paperboard rather than in an envelope or sleeve. Daguerreotypes and ambrotypes were one-of-a-kind images, whereas tintypes could produce multiple images. The starting date for widespread color photography began around 1935. Color glass or metal photos generally deteriorate much more quickly than black-and-white.

Daguerreotypes (1839 to about 1860): The first widely available photographs, these are positive images made from photo-sensitive emulsions cast on polished copper plates or silvered copper plates.

Tintypes (1855–1930): Technologically similar to daguerreotypes, they are positive images made from photo-sensitive emulsions cast on polished iron plates.

DON'S TIP: The Emulsion Side

The light-sensitive coatings in photography, whether on the film or the print, are called the emulsion. Identifying the fragile emulsion side is easy enough on prints (it's the side with the picture), but how about on film? Here are two good clues: (1) The emulsion side is usually matte, or has areas of matte corresponding to the image, while the other side is uniformly shiny, and (2) film almost always curls so that the emulsion is on the inside of the curve.

Ambrotypes (1850–80): Ambrotypes are glass negatives placed over black paper in order to reverse the image. Most glass plates were developed as negative images. These glass plates were the first negatives from which positive prints on paper were produced. Here is the good news: Glass plates can be negative or positive, but how you identify them and take care of them is exactly the same. How do you tell if you have a negative or a positive glass plate? A positive glass plate reflects the light and dark of the original image that was taken. The image is dark in the same places and light in the same places as the original image being photographed. A negative image has reverse tonality, meaning it is light where the photographed image is dark and dark where the original image is light.

Distinguishing Metal (Daguerreotypes, Tintypes) from Glass Prints (Ambrotypes)

To positively identify an old photo, it is best for you to take it to an expert in the subject. You can find a photographic conservator at *http//:aic.stanford .edu*. But here are some hints that will assist you. The only tools you need are one small magnet and one good eye.

First, hold a small magnet to the back side of the photo plate. If the magnet is not attracted to the photographic plate and the plate is highly polished, with an image visible only from some angles and not others, like a modern holographic image, odds are good you have a copper plate Daguerreotype. If the metal plate photograph is not reflective but the magnet is attracted to the plate, it is iron and therefore a tintype. Also, if the tintype has a chocolate brown tone to it, the print was produced after 1870.

If the rigid photograph is reflective and visible from all angles and yet does not hold the magnet, it is probably an ambrotype (glass print). Another clue that it is an ambrotype is that glass prints are usually backed with a dark background and the overwhelming majority of ambrotypes are negative glass images.

PAPER PRINTS: ALBUMIN, GELATIN, AND RESIN-COATED

Albumin: These prints were popular between 1860 and 1890. They are coated with an emulsion of egg whites (which is where the name *albumin* comes from) and then immersed in a bath of silver nitrate. They fade to browns and yellows with faint traces of purples and reds. The surface is very glossy, and the prints are often also mounted on paper or cardboard to prevent curling.

Gelatin: From 1890 to around 1960 the standard for photographic prints was gelatin emulsion on paper. These prints provide true black-and-white tone, with bluish, greenish, and even brownish tints. These prints may be mounted or unmounted.

Resin-coated: These became popular around the 1970s, and unless you develop your own pictures or use a professional photographer, the recent photos you have of your family vacations are on resin-coated paper.

Identifying Types of Paper Prints

If you had to describe an albumin print as compared to a gelatin print, the word you would use is *warm*. The colors of an albumin print are warm and sepia-colored and can be recognized by a reddish brown or purple image tone. A gelatin print's overall tone is cool. Gelatin prints tend to "silver" with age, particularly at the edges. Albumin prints tend to yellow as they age. Art photography is almost always a gelatin print on high-quality paper, usually linen rag paper.

Resin-coated prints are easily recognizable because they have a plastic look and feel about them. Also, they are typically printed with a thin white border. The early resin-coated prints also show an unnatural orange-red discoloration as they age.

FILM: CELLULOSE NITRATE, CELLULOSE ACETATE, AND POLYESTER

Cellulose nitrate: Unfortunately, around 1890 the notoriously unstable cellulose nitrate plastic film replaced glass plate negatives. This film is highly explosive, because it is functionally similar to gunpowder. Degradation of this film leads to a chemical reaction that can cause it to ignite spontaneously. It does not burst into flames immediately, however, because a fair amount of degradation has to occur first. If you own this type of film, which includes both photo negatives and early movies, you need to be very cautious. Do not leave this film lying around your house; if you do, it won't just go bad, it will eventually burn down your house. The only safe way to prevent it from bursting into flames is to store it in a sealed container in the freezer. If you cannot do that, then you need to get rid of it.

Cellulose acetate: Cellulose nitrate film was replaced by the almost equally notorious cellulose acetate "safety film" in the 1930s for both photographic negatives and movies. Cellulose acetate "safety film" actually gives off acids as it degrades. Among its degradation by-products is acetic acid, or vinegar. This problem is aptly called the Vinegar Syndrome. If you open a movie-film canister and smell coleslaw, your film is on the fast track to Gonesville. To halt this degradation process, this type of film should be stored in the freezer.

Polyester film: Finally, the film we are most familiar with made its debut in 1960. Polyester film is much more stable and reliable. It doesn't go up in flames and it doesn't turn to vinegar. All you need to do is be a little sensible and follow good housekeeping and storing rules: Keep it clean, dry, and cool. (Detailed instructions follow later in this chapter.)

Distinguishing Polyester from Cellulose Nitrate or Cellulose Acetate Film

You can see why you need to know what type of film (slides, negatives, or movies) you are preserving. Until recently the only way to tell what type of film you had was to snip off a tiny piece, go outside, and light it on fire. If it burned with a burst, it was cellulose nitrate and had to be placed in deep-freeze storage immediately, away from the rest of the collection. If it just smoldered or melted, it was either cellulose acetate or polyester, and the risks were not as immediate, especially in the case of polyester. I do not recommend this method. It involves destroying part of the very thing you are trying to save, and it can be dangerous.

I recommend a much safer, simpler test for narrowing down the type of film you have. Find two lenses from a cheap pair of "polarizing" sunglasses. Take the two lenses, lay them flat, one on top of the other, and then rotate the top one 90 degrees. Place your film in between the two sunglass lenses and shine a bright light through the sandwich of lenses and film. If the result is a darkened light with no rainbows, you have one of the bad films—

DON'S TIP:
Preserving
Color Slides

Color slides for the most part are modern enough that you really do not have to worry about spontaneous combustion or Vinegar Syndrome. If, however, you have some very rare film slides predating 1960 (such as those film strips we endured in elementary school), you need to store them in a sealed container in the freezer. Glass projection slides never combust regardless of how old they are.

cellulose nitrate or cellulose acetate. If you have a rainbow effect, you have polyester. Since the preservation of both cellulose nitrate and cellulose acetate films are the same (and dramatically different from polyester), this should tell you all you need to know before progressing further. If the film is one of the dangerous films, store it in a sealed container in the freezer or get rid of it. If it is polyester, follow the instructions provided later in this chapter.

DUPLICATION OPTIONS

Photos present a perplexing problem: Preserving them usually means not enjoying them, at least not enjoying the original. Continued handling and exposure to light causes long-term degradation. In order to preserve photos, you should make copies for your family and friends' enjoyment and put the original in an appropriate storage place for permanent preservation (see below). There are two general but distinct methods of duplication: photo-

LOUISA'S TALES:
Always Make Copies When Storing Photos

I started storing pictures on my hard drive about two years ago. It is a wonderful way to preserve photographs. As an added benefit you can purchase computer programs that allow you to manipulate your photos. Putting mustaches on several family members is almost as much fun as taking out blemishes, wrinkles, and red eye. Adobe PhotoShop is excellent, as is Corel PhotoPaint and many others from Kodak and Polaroid. I was exceptionally proud of my computer savvy, but out there a danger lurked that I was blissfully unaware of.

Alex, my daughter, used our computer during a thunderstorm. The next thing I knew, Alex was yelling that the computer was on fire. The computer smoked and sparked and then, in a final burst of flames, died. Up in a blaze went all my stories and all my photos. I ended up having to pay more than $500 to retrieve the files on the hard drive (the computer itself was dead). I have since learned that if you store your photos in a digital format, always, always back this up by copying them onto a CD or DVD. I now make two copies on CDs of my digital photos, and this also frees up my hard drive. Don goes a step further. He actually keeps three copies of his computer files, each one in a separate location, one of them undisclosed.

graphic replication and digital replication. Each is a valuable and widely used method for preserving photographic collections in museums, although they are usually referred to as reformating.

Photo replication is pretty much what it sounds like: using a photographic method to reproduce the material being preserved. Digital replication involves changing your photographic information into a format that can be stored on your computer's hard drive or on a CD or DVD or zip disks (floppies just don't have enough storage space to make them practical).

There are a number of things to consider before you decide which process to use:

1. How do you normally like to view your images? Do you prefer 4-by-6-inch photos in an album with an occasional 8-by-10-inch on the dresser? Or do you like to carry "albums" on your computer or laptop and email them to family and friends?

2. Are the photos you want to preserve already damaged or faded?

3. Do you want the copies you make to last forever like the images from your parents' wedding day, or are they less memorable but still amusing like your college-age son's Friday night out?

4. What is the original format? Do you have the original negative, or is it digital?

5. Do you want to deal with computers at all (not everyone is a computer fanatic) when duplicating photos?

These and other considerations will help you decide which process is best for you. The decision tree that follows will help you determine your best option.

Remember: Decide which of the family treasures are worth investing the time and money it takes to restore and preserve them. A casual photo is easily relegated to a nice 4-by-6 print or two along with its well-stored negative, or to a digital file stored on a CD or DVD. One trip to a good one-hour photo store can typically help you duplicate your photos whether they are on a CD or DVD, you have the negatives, or you simply have an old print. The cost of turning negatives into photos is negligible. Creating a print from a print without its negative is expensive.

It is common practice nowadays for photo stores to create a companion CD of digital file duplicates from your original negatives or the prints if you ask for it. If you want to be sure to preserve your photos, I strongly recommend this.

Illus. 3-1. Steps for deciding how to duplicate your photographs. Looks complicated? It's not. Just follow the arrows.

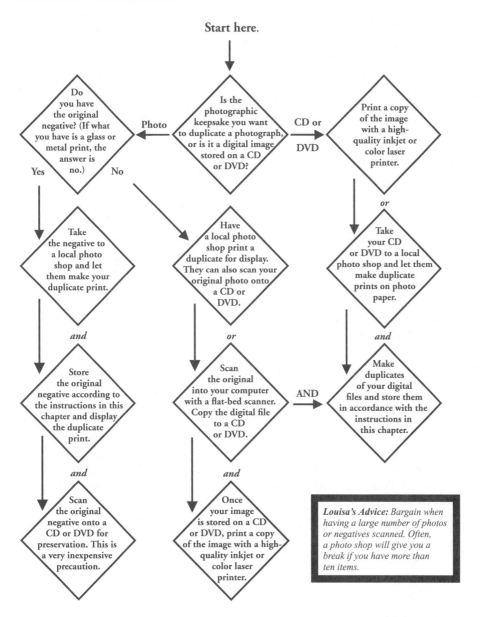

The permanence of such digital image files and how to save them is addressed in Chapter 10: Preserving Entertainment Memorabilia and Media.

PRESERVING BLACK-AND-WHITE AND COLOR PHOTOS PRINTED ON RESIN-COATED PAPER

Photos on resin-coated paper, which was developed around 1970, are the black-and-white and color snapshots you have. "Resin-coated" is somewhat misleading because the paper is actually coated with polymers and resembles a sheet of plastic.

These images are essentially plastic. They are not quite as permanent as older photos because plastics are not as stable as linen rag paper, but they are much more durable and sensible for the casualness of our modern lifestyles. Fortunately, the photographic industry craves permanence and spends billions of dollars to make sure your pictures last a very long time. All you have to do is take care of them.

These are the supplies you need:

Cotton gloves
Photographer's compressed air can
Archival photo envelopes
Graphite pencil
Archival boxes

1. Put on your cotton gloves. Even though these are plastic artifacts, they are sensitive to the oils and acids on your skin. Always handle photographs with clean cotton gloves.

2. Use the compressed air to blow away all traces of dust. Storing dust with your photographs is like tossing a handful of gravel in the washing machine when washing your delicates—not that I have any delicates.

3. Record identifying information about the photograph on the archival envelope with either a graphite pencil or an indelible ink pen.

4. Record the same information with a graphite pencil on the back of the corresponding photo. Always a great idea to write all names, as well as the year the picture was taken, on the back of your photograph.

5. Carefully slide the photographs into the archival plastic or paper envelope.

6. Record on the outside of the archival box what photos you will be storing inside.

7. Place these envelopes in the archival box according to the organizational scheme you have chosen, such as date, person, or place. Make sure the photos lie flat inside the box. You do not want to cram them in because bent photos are damaged photos.

PRESERVING PRE-1970 GELATIN AND ALBUMIN PRINTS

Understanding the history and materials of photography is important, especially when you have to distinguish between modern resin-coated paper prints and older gelatin emulsion prints on real paper. The latter requires a bit more attention.

The "gelatin" on gelatin prints is really gelatin, the same ingredient you use in your dessert creations (although much purer than food gelatin), and the "paper" is really paper, not something that feels like plastic food wrapping. The gelatin used on photographs is remarkably sensitive to moisture. If it is too dry, gelatin shrinks and causes the photo to curl; if it is dry enough, it will crack and almost literally break a paper photo in two. With gelatin you are on a mission to keep the balance of dryness and humidity just right. The paper itself is usually high quality, such as linen rag paper, so the paper's longevity is not in question.

**DON'S TIP:
Saving Your
Polaroid Prints**

Instant, self-developing color prints known as Polaroids are hopelessly short-lived. My sister and nephew work in a restaurant that posts instant photos of anyone who can finish their two-pound burger in one sitting. These prints have faded noticeably in just a few years. Treat these images as you would resin-coated paper prints, with the knowledge that Polaroids are truly fleeting images if you display them.

Albumin prints can be preserved by following the same strategy as for gelatin prints with the warning that the older the photograph, the more fragile it is. While the steps for preservation of these photos is similar, you must pay particular attention to the final four entries, which I call the Goldilocks Effect. As Goldilocks says, "Not too hot, not too cold, not too damp, not too dry. Where, oh where can my photos go?" If there is severe curling, which occurs when the print has not been mounted, do not attempt to fix this yourself. Take the print to a professional conservator.

These are the supplies you will need:

Cotton gloves
Photographer's compressed air can
Archival photo envelopes
Graphite pencil
Indelible ink pen
Archival boxes

1. Put on your cotton gloves. Even though these artifacts are quite robust, especially black-and-white prints, they are sensitive to the oils and acids on your skin, and particularly to the warm moisture coming off of you. Always handle photographs with clean cotton gloves.

2. Use the compressed air to blow away all traces of dust.

3. Record identifying information about the photograph on the archival envelope with either the pencil or pen.

4. Record the same information with a graphite pencil on the back of the corresponding photo.

5. Carefully slide the photographs into the archival plastic or paper envelope.

6. Record on the outside of the archival box what photos you will be storing inside. Place the envelopes in the archival box according to whatever organizational scheme you have chosen, such as date, person, or place. Make sure the photos lie flat inside the box. You do not want to cram them in because bent photos are damaged photos.

7. Store the box of photos in a place that will not get too damp. The gelatin emulsion is bug food, as is the paper; plus, the gelatin gets sticky when damp.

8. Store the box of photos in a place that will not get too dry. If the photos get too dry, the emulsion will shrink, and they will want to curl. If restrained

by being placed snugly in a storage box, they may crack or even break instead of curling.

    9. Store the box of photos in a place that will not get too cold. In Chapter 2 I mentioned that some materials become brittle as they get cold.

    10. Store the box of photos in a place that is not too hot. In Chapter 2 I also mentioned the unholy alliance between moisture and temperature.

PRESERVING REALLY OLD PHOTOS ON METAL: DAGUERREOTYPES AND TINTYPES

The goal with metal prints is to prevent corrosion.

    These are the supplies you will need:

Soft lint-free cloth
Distilled water
Mild dishwashing soap (if a tintype)
Hair dryer
Cotton gloves
Photographer's compressed air can
Archival boxes
Graphite pencil
Indelible ink pen

SMITHSONIAN STORIES:
The Cracked Lincoln Photograph

Alexander Gardner took a photograph of Abraham Lincoln using a large glass negative. The glass broke before the photo could be processed. Gardner did, however, make one print before destroying the negative. The photograph is famous because the crack has been said to foretell the assassination of the president, as the crack runs through Lincoln's forehead just as Booth's bullet did. A Polaroid copy of Gardner's original albumen silver print of President Lincoln went on tour as part of the exhibit to mark the Smithsonian's 150th anniversary. Go to *http://www.150.si .edu/150trav/remember/r313.htm* and view the photograph courtesy of the National Portrait Gallery and the Polaroid Corporation.

Illus. 3-2. Even though this glass plate photographic portrait of Abraham Lincoln was damaged and discarded by the photographer, it remains one of the most important images of its era.

1. If it is a daguerreotype, clean the glass case (the cover plate) with a cloth slightly dampened with distilled water. Do not attempt to clean it any further. Only a professional conservator should ever clean a daguerreotype itself. Why? Because one mistake can easily destroy the object.

If it is a tintype, clean with a mild soap solution and rinse with distilled water. Do not ever soak. Then dry gently with a hair dryer set on low and cool.

2. Put on your cotton gloves. These old plates may be in cases, but almost certainly the cases are sensitive to the chemistry of your skin and particularly to the warm moisture coming off you. Always handle photographic artifacts with cotton gloves.

3. Use the compressed air to remove all traces of dust.

4. Record on the archival box identifying information about the photograph with either the pencil or pen.

5. Carefully place the photograph case into the archival box.

6. Store the box in a place that is environmentally moderate: cool but not cold, dry but not parched.

PRESERVING REALLY OLD PHOTOS ON GLASS: AMBROTYPES

Have a professional conservator clean these prints because it is easy to rub off the photographic image if you make a mistake. The goal with glass prints is to store them in such a way that the glass is safe from breakage. Careful storage is crucial to the preservation of these photos.

These are the supplies you will need:

Cotton gloves
Photographer's compressed air can
Archival paper or photo envelopes
Graphite pencil or indelible ink pen
Archival boxes

1. Put on your cotton gloves. Even though these are glass artifacts, they are coated on one side with some fairly sensitive photo emulsion materials that could easily be damaged by the oils and acids on your skin. Always handle glass plates by their edges and with cotton gloves.

2. Use the compressed air to remove all traces of dust. Often the photographic part of glass plate artifacts is fragile and without any additional protective coating, which makes it all the more necessary to clean them before proceeding.

3. Take the archival paper and make a custom envelope for the glass plate. Since the surface of the plate is so delicate, unless you can find an envelope that fits it exactly, make your own custom envelope as illustrated on the next page. You do not want any "wiggle room" inside it.

4. Record on the archival envelope identifying information about the photograph with either the pencil or indelible pen.

5. Carefully place the glass plate in an archival box that fits the plates so that the plates stand on edge. Place these envelopes in the archival box according to whatever organizational scheme you choose, such as date, person, or place. Do not cram them, but make sure they fit snugly against each

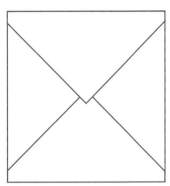

Illus. 3-4. A completed custom-fitted archival envelope.

Illus. 3-3. To make a custom-fitted archival envelope for any flat artifact—whether photo, paper artwork, or similar—lay the artifact diagonally on the piece of acid-free paper you are using for the envelope. Fold it (dotted line) and notch it at the corners as shown here.

other in a sideways stack. If there is extra space, fill it with a spacer made from a folded piece of archival paper to make sure the plates do not bounce around when the box is handled.

6. Record on the outside of the archival box what photos you will be storing inside. Store the box of glass plates in a cool but not cold space with low-to-moderate relative humidity—60 degrees Fahrenheit and about 35 percent relative humidity is fine.

A WORD ABOUT PHOTO ALBUMS

Perhaps the most popular format for saving a collection of family or personal photos is the photo album. For the most part this is a good compromise between keeping your favorite pictures forever and having them at your fingertips for occasional journeys down memory lane. Certainly the album protects photos from light and handling, but other dangers can be present. Water, bugs, and mold are still hazards you need to watch out for. If your photo album is made from acid-free pages and covers and is stored in a dark, bug-free, dry place, your collection is well cared for. If, though, you are in any doubt about the quality of the album materials, replace your current album with a good-quality new one.

Don's Rules for Choosing a Photo Album

1. Make sure the pages are acid free. Believe me, the "archival" quality of photo albums is a strong marketing tool. If it is acid free, it will say so. If it doesn't, it isn't.

2. Check that the plastic sleeves into which you slide the photos are made from polyethylene, polypropylene, or polyester rather than polyvinyl chloride. Polyvinyl chloride emits contaminating substances that will damage your photos. You may have to ask a salesperson to find out or call the manufacturing company.

3. Be careful when purchasing one of the popular magnetic-style albums where the photos are held under sheets of transparent plastic. These can be a real problem because the plastic is often polyvinyl chloride and is held to the page by an unstable adhesive. Also, the paperboard is probably wood pulp, which is acidic and degrades, and may contribute to the deterioration of other things in contact with it. A triple-header of bad news. The only good news is that modern resin-coated photos are pretty tough, so the album itself is likely to disintegrate before the photos.

FILM: SLIDES, NEGATIVES, AND MOVIE FILM

Unlike photographic prints, which are comfortable when you are comfortable, film such as slides, negatives, and movies want things as cold as you can get them. The term *cold storage* is the mantra of the film preservationist. So, whenever possible, store your film in a frost-free freezer or, if that is not feasible, the coldest place you can. If your freezer is in the basement, you have my

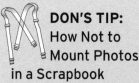

DON'S TIP: How Not to Mount Photos in a Scrapbook

Do not glue your photos in the album; use corner mounts (see page 42) on pages of plain rag paper or archival buffered paper (the package will identify them as such). Glue can harm your photos and also make them difficult to remove. Trying to unstick a glued-on photo usually results in a torn, damaged photo.

Illus. 3-5. Photos should always be mounted in albums by first attaching corner mounts to the page and then gently sliding the corners of the photo into the corner mount. Mylar corner mounts can be attached with double-sided tape, and paper mounts come with glue on the back side.

blessing to place your film collection inside it. Additionally, when you remove your film from the freezer, be sure you follow "Don's Tip: Taking Film out of Cold Storage" on page 46.

Slides

These are the supplies you will need:

> Cotton gloves
> Photographer's compressed air can
> Graphite pencil or indelible ink pen
> Archival polypropylene or polyethylene slide holders
>   (8 by 11 inches)

Archival boxes
Heavy-duty zippered plastic bags
Frost-free freezer or the coldest place possible

1. Put on your cotton gloves. Even though slides have a frame (the "mount") around them, it's best to develop good habits. The transparency in the center is easily smudged and is sensitive to the oils and acids on your skin, and particularly to warm, moist hands. Always handle slides with clean cotton gloves.

2. Use the compressed air to remove all traces of dust.

3. Record identifying information about the slide on the mount with either the pencil or pen.

4. Carefully insert the slides into plastic archival slide holders. Make sure you do not bend or force the slides into their new home. They should go in smoothly.

5. Record on the outside of the archival box what slides you will be storing inside. Make sure the slide holders are flat inside the box. You do not want to cram them in because bent slides are damaged slides.

6. Place the archival box containing the slide holders in a heavyweight archival zippered plastic bag to protect them from moisture.

7. Place the zippered bag in *another* archival zippered bag. That's right: You want all your film going into the deep-freeze to be double bagged. It is additional protection from moisture if the first bag gets snagged or punctured accidentally.

8. Place the package in the coldest freezer you can find. It can survive there for centuries.

Negatives

You will need the same supplies as for slides (above).

1. Put on your cotton gloves. Film negatives are sensitive to the oils and acids on your skin, and particularly to warm, moist hands. Always handle negatives with clean cotton gloves, touching only their edges.

2. Use the compressed air to remove all traces of dust.

3. Record identifying information about the film negatives on the archival film sleeve with the pencil or pen.

4. Carefully insert the film negatives in the archival film sleeves.

5. Record on the outside of the archival box what film negatives you will be storing inside.

6. Place the film sleeve sheets in the archival box according to whatever organizational scheme you choose, such as date, person, place, etc. Make sure the sheets are flat inside the box. You do not want to cram them in because bent film is damaged film.

7. Place the archival box containing the film sleeve sheets in a heavy-weight archival zippered plastic bag.

8. Place the zippered bag containing the box of film sleeve sheets in another archival zippered bag.

9. Place the package in the coldest freezer you can find.

Polyester Movie Film

Movie film is technologically identical to slide film in that it possesses a transparent image emulsion on a plastic backing. The difference is that movie film is assaulted with an entirely different level of stress and contamination since it runs through a movie projector, which exposes the film to tension, contamination, heat, and light. Each of these contributes its own dynamic to the degradation of the film. Together they mean that you must be much more aggressive in the care of movies as opposed to slide film or photographic negatives.

Cleaning Polyester Movie Film

Hand-painted or artfully scratched films should be treated with extreme delicacy and labeled clearly. Refer these problems to an expert. Specialists in these art forms will have a much better idea about caring for the film and can prevent you from damaging it by attempting an inappropriate procedure.

Movie film should be cleaned only by blowing it off with compressed air as it is transferred from one reel to another. Do not try to remove dust with soft, lint-free cloths, as *even this* will cause problems by running dust over the film and scratching it. For more complex cleaning problems, consult a conservator.

To store polyester movie film these are the supplies you will need:

Cotton gloves
Photographer's compressed air can
Graphite pencil or indelible ink pen
Archival boxes
Heavy-duty zippered plastic bags
Frost-free freezer or the coldest place possible

1. Put on your cotton gloves. Even though movie film is on a reel, the film is extremely sensitive to the oils and acids on your skin, and particularly to the warm moisture coming off you. Always handle movie film with cotton gloves.

2. Use the compressed air to remove all traces of dust.

3. Record identifying information about the movie film on the reel with either the pencil or pen.

4. Record the same information on the archival box.

5. Place the reel of movie film in the archival box.

6. Place the archival box in a heavyweight archival zippered plastic bag.

7. Place the plastic bag in *another* archival zippered plastic bag.

8. Place the package in the coldest freezer you can find.

Larger-Format Movie Film (16, 35, and 70 Millimeter)

In addition to the supplies listed for polyester movie film (above), you will need archival paper core.

Follow the instructions given above for storing movie film and then do the following:

1. Wind the film on the archival paper core rather than a movie reel.

2. Store the film "tails out" under even, gentle tension. In other words, run the movie all the way to the end and then store it.

3. Never pull the end of a reel or core of film to tighten it up. This will scratch and may break the film, or put stresses on it that will cause breakage in the future.

4. Leave 8-millimeter film on plastic reels. If your movies are on the little reels, splice them together so you can store them on larger reels. The larger the reel hub, the less likely there will be permanent distortion (curling).

Don's Rules for Preserving Movie Film That Is Not in Cold Storage

For films in regular use, where long-term cold storage is not an option, careful handling and storage is still a critical part of their care.

1. Do not store films in an attic. The temperatures vary too much throughout the seasons and in the summer it is too hot.

2. Do not store film near heaters, plumbing pipes, radiators, sprinklers, windows, electrical sources, or sinks.

3. Do not store film in direct sunlight. Avoid exterior, south-facing walls or locations that receive direct sunlight.

4. Avoid high humidity: Do not store in a basement. Most basements are quite humid and perfect for mold. Also, there is the danger of flooding.

5. For films with magnetic sound tracks, keep away from magnets such as those found in stereo speakers as well as heavy-duty electrical cables.

6. Unlike in most sections of this book, here I am going to recommend that you repair any film breaks with film splicing tape that is available from the suppliers listed in the back of the book.

7. When handling film that is in good condition, wear cotton gloves.

8. If film has lots of taped splices or frayed edges, cloth gloves may cause further damage. In that case wear vinyl or nitrile gloves.

9. Never touch the front or rear faces of the film with bare hands. Handle only by the edges.

DON'S TIP:
Taking Film out of Cold Storage

When you retrieve film from the freezer, it has to be warmed very slowly. Take it out of the freezer and keep it in the refrigerator for at least twenty-four hours, then move it to an insulated cooler until it reaches the same temperature as the room, usually another twenty-four hours. The combination of a slow warming period and a heavy paper box inside the zippered plastic bag will reduce and possibly eliminate the moisture in the package. Moisture and photographic artifacts are not a happy couple.

Chapter 4

Archiving Toys
for Young and Old

MY PARENTS TIPTOED IN, *kissed us on the cheek, and tiptoed out. The hall light went off. Their bedroom door shut. My sister and I then sat up in bed, grinned at each other, and, it is true, all our stuffed animals came to life. Fuzzy Tail, my puppet fox, reigned as leader of all the other stuffed animals. Actually, her full title was Fuzzy Tail, Empress Fox, Ruler of All Domains throughout the Magic Animal Kingdom.*

Woe to any toy or puppet who failed to acknowledge her rightful place, especially my sister's stuffed animals. Unfortunately, her animals were sometimes woefully arrogant. Empress Fuzzy Tail would then decree the presumptuous toy suffer through a ceremonial dehairing. This necessitated cutting off a lock of the animal's hair with the ceremonial scissors we kept hidden under the bed. Not one of my sister's animals survived our childhood with all its hair intact. I often wonder how our parents slept through all this and why they never noticed that Valerie's stuffed animals looked as if they had mange. Dehairing ceremonies aside, my sister and I spent many happy nights throughout our childhood imagining and dreaming with the help of our toys.

The love I lavished on Fuzzy Tail finally began to show. Fuzzy Tail became not so fuzzy and her ears not so perky, and she eventually went to reside in my childhood box of memories. On days when adulthood seemed a touch overwhelming, I would escape to the basement and retrieve Fuzzy Tail. Once she was out of her box, the nights of imagination and fun my sister and I shared would come back to life: the laughter, the jokes, the magical kingdom, the dehairing ceremonies. The sight of Fuzzy Tail evoked all these memories and quickly placed me back in a time when fantasies were real and Empress Fuzzy Tail reigned over all she surveyed.

When Fuzzy Tail was lost in the flood, I felt a real sense of loss. Old toys embody the memories of our childhood. These memories are held in the tattered ears, the rubbed-off fur, the ripped-out stuffing, and the overly loved, worn-out fabric. Preserving these valuables for ourselves and future generations is how we save our childhood memories.

—Louisa Jaggar

THINK "USE IT AND LOSE IT"

If your child is still sleeping and playing with a beloved toy, its retirement years obviously remain a way off. Still, well-loved toys or brand-new collector toys all share a basic truth in preservation: If you want to save a toy, you have to think "Use It and Lose It."

STUFFED TOYS: PRESERVING, CLEANING, DISPLAYING, AND STORING

Teddy bears and other stuffed toys are loved with an affection that extracts a great deal from them because they are used as play companions, pillows, and comforters. Aside from the cloth covering, these toys are made of the wildest range of fillers imaginable: felt, rags, shredded wood, confetti, dried beans, sawdust, and plastic beads. All these materials deteriorate either in conjunction with, or independent of, the outer covering.

In every technical respect the preservation lens sees teddy bears as an upholstered pillow, and the rules and instructions for handling, exhibiting, and storing them apply here.

Don's Rules for Preserving Stuffed Toys

1. Always wear clean white fabric gloves when handling a stuffed toy. Natural oils from your hands attach themselves to the fabric and will serve to attract and hold on to dust.

2. Make sure your clothing cannot snag and rip a stuffed toy. Remove bracelets, necklaces, or anything that could catch on the stuffed toys.

3. Store stuffed toys so that they are isolated from other materials except for acid-free tissue paper, prewashed muslin, polyester batting, or Pellon interfacing.

4. Expose stuffed toys to as little light as possible. If you can't keep the stuffed toy in a dark place, cover it with a cloth slipcover when not in use.

5. Keep stuffed toys clean.

6. Keep cool and dry. A perfect temperature is 45 degrees Fahrenheit and 35 percent relative humidity. I know that is a bit cold for folks, but keep them as cool and dry as possible, such as 70 degrees Fahrenheit with low humidity.

Cleaning

In most cases light vacuuming in the manner of vintage upholstery is required. Keeping stuffed toys clean helps reduce the risks from their other enemy: bugs. Bugs actually view them as potential dinner as well as a home.

You will need these supplies:

Vacuum cleaner with brush attachment
Masking tape
Vinyl window screen or a piece of coarse linen (about a square foot)

1. Cleaning stuffed toys can be accomplished with a vacuum cleaner as long as you don't vacuum directly on the fabric.

DON'S SPECIAL NOTE ON REPAIRING STUFFED TOYS

While I make a point of avoiding discussions about repair in this book, I realize that oftentimes damaged stuffed toys need repairs to prevent further deterioration. Leaking seams, in particular, should be sewn shut to prevent any more stuffing from falling out, and loose components, such as eyes and buttons, should be resewn with a fine needle and cotton thread.

2. Tape the edges of a square foot of vinyl window screen or sew the edges of a square foot of coarse linen.

3. Place the screen or fabric against the stuffed toy and run the vacuum brush attachment across the screen. The dust and dirt travels through the screen or fabric openings as you vacuum, and you avoid the risk of abrading or snagging the fabric.

Displaying

Stuffed animals and related toys should be handled with clean white cotton gloves to prevent any further dirtying, and they should be kept in a dust-free place. For display, that usually means a glass-front cabinet.

Keep the light low, less than 15 foot-candles, and filter out all ultraviolet light.

Make sure you don't eat or drink around your stuffed animals. Even the smallest dropped morsel can attract critters.

Generally, you do not want the temperature warmer than 70 degrees Fahrenheit.

Storing

You will need the following supplies:

Acid-free tissue paper or prewashed unbleached cotton muslin
Archival storage box or tub

DON'S TIP:
Stuffed Toys and Bugs

If a stuffed toy is infested with insects, it will be necessary to either fumigate the toy (fumigation should always be left to the professionals because lethal poisons are involved) or even open it by snipping a seam with embroidery scissors, removing and replacing the stuffing, and sewing it back up. Unless you are accomplished with embroidery scissors, needle, and thread, this is probably best left to an expert such as a textiles conservator. If historical accuracy is paramount, replace the infested stuffing with new versions of the same material. From a preservation perspective, polyester batting or polyethylene beads are the preferred new stuffing.

1. Wrap the cleaned item in the tissue paper or muslin.

2. Place it in the acid-free cardboard or polyethylene or polypropylene box or tub.

3. Place in a clean, stable, bug-free environment.

PUPPETS

To preserve puppets, follow all the instructions for caring for stuffed toys with the additional instruction of filling your puppet with polyester batting or acid-free tissue in order to help maintain its youthful figure.

CLOTH DOLL PARTS: CLEANING AND STORING

Because the torsos of many vintage dolls are made of a fabric cover stuffed with fiber, you might be tempted to toss a dirty vintage doll into the washing machine. *Don't!* This treatment is usually destructive for vintage dolls be-

SMITHSONIAN STORIES:
Kermit Gets Ready for a Trip

Several years ago the Smithsonian Institution commemorated its 150th anniversary with a huge party on the Washington Mall where my colleagues and 200,000 visitors celebrated the magnificence of the Nation's Attic. I'm betting some of you enjoyed the same commemoration at the traveling exhibition, *Smithsonian's Treasures,* that was touring twelve cities of our great land. One of those treasures was Kermit the Frog. To get Kermit ready for his adoring public, conservators carefully vacuumed him exactly as I described in this book. Once he was clean, they stuffed him with polyethylene foam so he could sit up on his own. (He is a hand puppet, after all, and without the hand inside him, he looks kind of like a weird sock.) Smithsonian conservators built a fitted case for him out of acid-free cardboard and polyethylene foam, and kept him wrapped in acid-free tissue paper to preserve his green coat and all his stuffing. After two years of touring like a rock star, he came home. Thanks to the diligent preparations for his handling, exhibition, and storage, he returned home in the same condition he had left in.

cause the dyes can run and the fabrics are degraded and weakened. Clean cloth dolls as you would other stuffed toys (see pages 48–50).

To store and display cloth dolls, follow the same rules as you would for other stuffed toys (pages 50–51).

PLASTIC CAR, SHIP, AND AIRPLANE MODELS

Plastic models are primarily made from polystyrene and acrylics because these plastics lend themselves to a multitude of manufacturing processes, especially molding and die stamping. They are soluble in acetone and toluene, and glues containing these solvents allow easy assembly of the new model. While acrylics are more stable than styrene, as a practical matter you should care for all plastic models by following the rules as outlined in "Vintage Plastic and Rubber Stuff" in Chapter 7, Sorting and Preserving the Family Trash.

PLASTIC ACTION FIGURES

These are the ones that turn from a butterfly into a flame-throwing pterodactyl. Preserve as you would plastic in the "Vintage Plastic and Rubber Stuff" in Chapter 7, Sorting and Preserving the Family Trash.

METAL AND PAINTED METAL TOYS

Metal cars and tractors are rarely all metal, and not all metal toys are made from the same metal. Often the metal body is covered in paint and the suspension is augmented by rubber tires. Metal construction toys may be connected with plastic or even paper or leather parts. Metals such as aluminum are comparatively easier to preserve because they do not corrode as aggressively as iron or steel, while zinc toys tend not to corrode much at all but are brittle and easy to break. Plated steel, as in erector sets, are at risk only if the plated surface is scratched or cracked—for example, if they get bent—providing a foothold for corrosion to the underlying steel.

Although metal toys can be made from a variety of materials, the rules for their preservation remain the same.

Don's Rules for Handling Metal and Painted Metal Toys

1. Protect from pollution and contamination. Salts and acids from skin contact or other sources of pollution lead to corrosion because they actually eat away the metal.

2. Always wear clean white cotton gloves when handling collectible metal toys.

3. Do not take metal toys directly from a cold environment to a warm environment because this will cause moisture to condense on the object and risk oxidation on any unpainted or unplated surfaces. Make sure to slow down the warming-up process by wrapping in a blanket and leaving it wrapped until it reaches room temperature.

4. Do not drop or crush. Toys tend to be made from cheaper, low-quality metals, which are often more brittle and susceptible to breakage than you might think. It is always best to handle these objects while sitting at a table that is covered with a soft cloth.

Cleaning

If the surface is not intact—in other words, if there is actively flaking paint or corrosion—do not clean at all. Contact a specialist. If the surface is intact, proceed as instructed below.

You will need the following supplies:

¾-inch artist's brush
Cotton swabs, litho pads, or clean lint-free cotton rags
Distilled water
Triton 100 detergent
Fan or hair dryer

1. Gently brush the surface with a fine artist's brush to remove all particles of dust.

2. Gently wipe the surface with either cotton swabs or litho pads moistened with distilled water.

3. If dirt remains, wipe the surface with cotton swabs or litho pads moistened with a solution of 1 percent Triton 100 detergent and 99 percent distilled water.

4. Rinse the surface with swabs or litho pads moistened with distilled water only. Distilled water does not leave behind any chemicals or residue.

5. Dry the toy completely with either a fan or a hair dryer set on low. Towels often snag on surfaces and they cannot get into crevices, so avoid them.

Displaying and Storing

Since metal toys frequently contain other materials, most notably paint, plastic, and rubber, there is no single perfect storage or preservation environment. The best you can do is compromise by keeping them in a clean, dry, moderate-temperature environment.

You will need these supplies:

Polyethylene zippered plastic bags
Original packing or polyethylene or polypropylene foam
Acid-free tissue paper
Silica gel packets
Archival storage boxes

1. If you have the original fitted packing for the toy, first place the toy in a new polyethylene zippered bag and then in its original fitted packing. The zippered bag protects the toy from contaminants and dust. The original packaging creates the perfect-size shelter for storage. If you do not have the original packing, take an archival storage box of the appropriate size and cut fitted padding from polyethylene or polypropylene foam.

2. Wrap the toy in acid-free tissue paper and place it in the cavity of the fitted padding.

3. Place one sugar-pack-sized silica gel per 200 cubic inches in the storage box.

4. Close the archival storage box and place it in a polyethylene zippered plastic bag or an appropriately similar container, such as a polyethylene box (Rubbermaid or Tupperware, for instance), and seal.

5. Store the box in a cool environment.

SLOT CARS AND TOY TRAINS

These are the toy world's versions of the electrical appliances covered in Chapter 7, Sorting and Preserving the Family Trash. While being concerned with the multitude of materials from which the sets are made, there is the

Rubber is a particularly challenging preservation problem. While it seems tough and stable, it weakens and loses its shape over time with exposure to light, moisture, and oxygen. For toys with a sizable portion of rubber, the storage steps mentioned previously need to be enhanced by including an appropriately sized packet of oxygen scavenger to reduce the oxidation deterioration of the rubber, plus a canister or sheet of activated charcoal chemical scavenger to absorb any rubber degradation by-products that might either further degrade the rubber or cause deterioration of other toy elements. And if you can avoid it, do not let the toy rest on rubber parts.

added consideration that you are dealing with a motor run on an electrically charged circuit.

These items should be preserved as you would plastic artifacts. See "Vintage Plastic and Rubber Stuff" in Chapter 7, Sorting and Preserving the Family Trash.

Painted metal cars and trains should be preserved as you would any painted metal toys (see pages 52–54).

PAPER DOLLS

Despite the fragility of paper, the instructions for preserving paper dolls are easy. Preserve them as you would the paper artifacts described in Chapter 11, Saving Your Books, Comic Books, Newspapers, Magazines, and Letters. Which of the section's rules should you follow? If your paper doll has a shiny surface, like the cover of a magazine, look at "Taking Care of Magazines" in Chapter 11. If your doll has a matte surface, look at "Old Letters" in that same chapter.

3-D DOLLS

Dolls have a long history and have been made from a wide variety of materials: textiles, plant fibers, wood, wax, ceramics, leather, metal, plastics, and concoctions that defy easy identification. Each presents a challenge to the collector. Nevertheless, the preservation strategy is the one given in the first two chapters of this book: You must mitigate the destructive agents found in the environment such as temperature, moisture, light, insects, dirt, dust, and people.

As with any collection made from a combination of materials, identifying what was used to construct the doll is difficult. I've offered clues, but they are not definitive. You will need scientific analysis. You can also check the dozens of useful books on the history and materials of dolls and might even recognize your own doll in one of the illustrations.

Don's Rules for Preserving Dolls

1. Wear clean cotton or nitrile gloves when handling dolls. Remember, the oil from your hands will attract and retain dirt and other contaminants, the acids will attack the materials, and skin flakes will attract bugs and fungi.

2. Never clean a doll until you have determined that the surfaces are intact and can withstand the contact required. In other words, never clean a doll whose surfaces are heavily fractured or flaking. In such cases seek the advice of a conservator.

3. Clean the doll only with materials and techniques you have tested in an obscure area, and make sure the materials do not leave any residue. (Do not use baby wipes or "conditioning" wipes because these leave a residue.)

4. Keep food and drink separate from dolls.

5. Avoid using chlorine bleach or other harsh cleansers—period.

Low-Fired Ceramic Dolls: Cleaning, Storing, and Displaying

Dolls made of material such as bisque or terra-cotta are essentially ceramic pots in the shape of a doll. Made of soft, fine-grained ceramic, bisque is a reddish tan much like a clay garden pot. You need to get a little more involved in caring for these dolls because they usually have suffered at the hands of loving admirers. Ceramic dolls that have been carried around by little girls often are plagued with chipped, cracked, and dirty parts. Cracks and chips need to be fixed by a professional, but the dirt is something you can tackle. Ceramics can be very porous, meaning that they often have microscopic openings in the surface that collect dirt.

How do you clean them? The answer is not easy because almost anything you might try can drive the dirt further into the surface. So please follow these instructions very carefully.

You will need the following supplies:

¾-inch artist's brush
Distilled water
Cotton swabs
Triton 100 detergent or conditioner-free liquid dish detergent
Litho pads

1. With the artist's brush gently dust off any loose dirt from the surface—and I mean *gently*. Low-fired ceramic can be as soft as a stick of chalk.

2. Test a tiny area of the surface or any painted area with one drop of distilled water to make sure it is not sensitive to water. If all is well, proceed.

3. If the surface is grimy, clean it very gently with a cotton swab moistened with a cleaning solution of distilled water and 1 percent detergent. Do not scrub the surface. Repeat as necessary to get the surface clean.

4. Rinse by dabbing the surface with swabs or litho pads moistened with distilled water. Do not rub the surface because bisque is very soft and you will simply rub it away.

5. Dry by blotting—not rubbing—the surface with litho pads.

To store the dolls, treat them as you would soft pottery. See "Ceramics, Art Glass, and Stained Glass" in Chapter 13, Taking Care of Fine Art.

To display the dolls, place them behind glass and protect them from light.

Celluloid Doll Parts: Cleaning, Storing, and Displaying

Dolls of early entertainment figures (Shirley Temple, Charlie Chaplin, Popeye) were sometimes made of molded celluloid, a hard, shiny material that was among the first synthetic plastics. Please pay attention to this warning:

Recently, I had the good fortune to work on a fascinating project, creating an exhibition with my good friend Jia-sun Tsang, SCMRE (Smithsonian Center for Materials Research and Education) senior painting conservator. Through a series of happy opportunities she began researching the creation and preservation of small wooden sculptures known as *santos*. While these beautiful carved wood figurines can easily be mistaken for dolls, they are in fact something very different.

Portraying the Virgin Mary or one of the many saints, these figures were carved in great detail, painted, and then often adorned with glass eyes, wigs, and real clothes. Because they are used in private devotion, especially in the Hispanic Catholic community, these statues require a completely different level of preservation because it is crucial to remember that for the faithful, *santos* are integral expressions of religious devotion and righteousness. My favorite is of Saint Peter of Alcantara; it was carved out of South American citrus wood, and the detail is so fine that I had to use a magnifying glass to view it.

The oldest *santos* that we worked on were over 300 years old. In order to preserve these statues for future generations, we cleaned them carefully, glued any flaking paint back onto the surface, and placed them in sealed exhibit cases that protected them from fluctuations in relative humidity. You can see the sculpture of St. Peter and other unbelievably beautiful *santos* as well as learn more about history and preservation of *santos* at *www.si.edu/scmre/educationoutreach/santos.htm.*

Vintage celluloid (used to make dolls between the 1870s and the 1950s) is extremely unstable because the basic material is flammable. As it degrades, it can become self-igniting, at worst, or increasingly brittle through the oozing loss of camphor plasticizer, an additive that makes the plastic less brittle.

One of the degradation by-products of celluloid is nitric acid, which accelerates degradation of the film itself. As a result, celluloid needs to be cleaned to slow down this speedy back-to-dirt process. The good news is that nitric acid is completely soluble in water. The bad news is that degraded celluloid is very sensitive to water. *Never ever use a strong detergent or cleaner on celluloid!*

To clean celluloid doll parts you will need the following supplies:

Cotton swabs or litho pads
Distilled water

1. Dip a swab or litho pad into the distilled water, getting it damp but not soaking.

2. Gently roll the swab or dab the litho pad on the surface of the doll part.

3. Immediately dry by dabbing with a clean litho pad.

Celluloid is going to go bad. It is an inevitable result of what celluloid is and how it is made. The best you can hope for is to slow down the degradation somewhat, but stopping it even temporarily is not a likely goal. That said, here are a list of rules for providing the best possible environment for celluloid dolls, whether in long-term storage or on display.

1. Keep your doll in an environment of fairly low relative humidity to reduce the rate of water-induced chemical degradation. A relative humidity of 20 to 40 percent is recommended.

2. The colder the better. Remember that I recommend celluloid photo film be kept in the deep freeze.

3. Keep away from any and all sources of heat because they can ignite.

4. Keep celluloid dolls isolated from other collectibles and even from other celluloid dolls so that they do not contaminate other objects. As celluloid ages and degrades, it oozes or even evaporates camphor that can be redeposited on other things in the same environment. It can also emit nitric acid—nasty stuff.

5. Never forget that celluloid is extremely flammable, so keep it in a fireproof space. I would store celluloid objects in an explosion-proof chemicals cabinet with an acid-resistant paint coating. I am not kidding. Or you can keep them in a clean, well-ventilated space so that the degradation by-products can be "ventilated away." One example of this is metal shelving with powder-coating paint; the shelves should be lined with polyethylene or polypropylene foam, and the doll should be draped with a piece of disposable acid-free paper (and you will need to dispose of and replace the dust cover periodically).

6. Do not keep celluloid dolls in paper or cardboard boxes because the

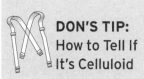

DON'S TIP:
How to Tell If
It's Celluloid

A definitive identification of celluloid requires sophisticated analytical tests, but here are some things you can do yourself to help you determine the material.

Unless it has degraded to the point of oozing, celluloid is hard at normal room temperature, and softens with moderate heat. Warm the surface for a few seconds by holding it about 3 inches from a bright light. If it is celluloid, the doll's surface should be soft enough to leave a tiny fingernail imprint. Rub it with a soft cloth. If it is celluloid, it will give off the odor of camphor.

degradation by-products will cause the boxes to degrade and, more important, increase their risk of igniting as well.

7. Keep light levels as low as possible and eliminate ultraviolet light to the greatest degree possible.

Painted Wooden Dolls: Cleaning, Storing, and Displaying

Wooden doll parts are susceptible to all the problems endemic to wooden objects described elsewhere. They do not respond well to light, heat, or humidity and are a feast for many bugs. It is best to keep wooden dolls out of the sunlight and in a cool, dry place.

To clean wooden dolls you will need the following supplies:

Artist's brush
Distilled water
Cotton swabs or litho pads
Triton 100 or similar mild nonconditioning liquid dish detergent

Reminder: If there is any flaking or heavy fracturing of the paint film, do not clean!

1. Surface dust can be removed with a soft artist's brush.

2. Test a tiny area of the surface or any painted area with one drop of distilled water to make sure it is not sensitive to water. If all is well, proceed.

3. Wipe the surface gently with a cotton swab or litho pad dampened with distilled water.

4. If the surface is grimy, swab it gently with a cleaning solution of distilled water and 1 percent detergent. Repeat as necessary to get the surface clean.

5. Rinse by dabbing the surface with swabs or litho pads moistened with distilled water.

6. Dry by blotting the surface with litho pads.

To store the dolls be sure to think of them as special forms of panel paintings and treat them accordingly. Follow the instructions for panel paintings in Chapter 13, Taking Care of Fine Art. In addition do the following: Wrap the doll in acid-free tissue paper or clean, unbleached, fine cotton muslin, place in an archival box, and store in a cool, dry space.

To display the dolls, place them behind glass with insect traps placed nearby because bugs love wood. Their environment should have stable humidity since humidity fluctuation can cause wood to swell and shrink, which leads to cracking and flaking of the paint (while the wood is swelling and shrinking, the paint is not).

Composition Dolls: Cleaning, Storing, and Displaying

Composition is the name given to a plasterlike material made from various recipes but usually containing water-soluble glue, plaster, chalk, felt or pulverized cloth or wood flour as a filler, and sometimes even some linseed oil and resins. This collection of materials is mixed together under various conditions, almost always starting with warm or hot water, until the consistency is like dough. This molding material is less prone to breaking than ceramic or porcelain. The finished parts are then painted and assembled into a doll.

The composition resembles a hard tan plaster and is denser than most other materials from which dolls are made, and therefore the dolls tend to be heavier than other dolls of the same size. Fine cracks are normal in composition dolls and are part of the general aging process. Some composition recipes include papier-mâché.

Dolls made of composition do not break as easily as do ceramics, but they are extremely sensitive to moisture, as you might imagine. The behavior and structure is actually very similar to the ground and paint layers of an oil painting as described in Chapter 13, Taking Care of Fine Art. While they are not so fragile as to prevent being handled, they need extreme care in designing their storage environment.

Composition dolls should be cleaned and stored in the same manner as painted wooden dolls on the previous page.

They should always be displayed in a area where there are no extreme temperature or humidity fluctuations. Avoid displaying them in a room with high humidity because of their extreme sensitivity to moisture of any kind.

DON'S TIP:
Polishing
Wooden Dolls

Just as oil polishes are bad for wooden furniture, they are also bad for wooden dolls. If you feel the need to provide some additional surface protection, follow the rules and instructions for waxing furniture in Chapter 8, Preserving Your Furniture, and always keep in mind the warning that overly aggressive polishing of delicately decorated painted surfaces can remove those decorations.

Ceramic and Porcelain Dolls

Ceramic dolls are really nothing more than dinner plates in the form of miniature people or creatures. If the doll looks like your everyday dinner plate, it is probably glazed ceramic. If it is more like the really good china (translucent and with a sharp ringing sound when tapped with your fingernail), the odds are good you have porcelain.

When cleaning and storing ceramic and porcelain dolls you should refer to the rules and instructions for china in "Dinner China and Crystal: Cleaning, Storing, and Displaying" in Chapter 6, Saving Your Family Treasures.

Always display ceramic and porcelain dolls out of direct sunlight, preferably behind glass.

Plastic Dolls and Doll Parts: Hello, Barbie and G.I. Joe

Many modern dolls are made from a variety of synthetic plastics, most prominently polyvinyl chloride (PVC) for hollow and articulated dolls (Barbie, etc.) and polyethylene for solid molded figures.

Display them away from direct sunlight as well as any heat sources. Remember that plastic warps when exposed to heat and is easily stained once it begins to age. For cleaning and storing instructions, see "Vintage Plastic and Rubber Stuff" in Chapter 7, Sorting and Preserving the Family Trash.

DON'S TIP:
"Green Ear"—Learn to Love It

Whenever you have chloride touching copper, such as a degrading polyvinyl chloride doll (Barbie) with brass jewelry, you get copper chloride corrosion—green ear—also known to artists as green copper pigment. The green corrosion penetrates and stains degraded plastic and cannot be removed short of truly heroic and esoteric chemical means. Your only practical alternative is to turn necessity into virtue: Think of green ear as "patina" for vintage plastic dolls.

Leather Dolls

For preserving and displaying leather dolls, please refer to "Baseballs, Gloves, Footballs, Basketballs, Saddles, and Cleats" in Chapter 9, Preserving Your Sports and Political Memorabilia.

DOLL CLOTHES

Doll clothes are a specialized form of vintage textile art and attire. Follow the rules and instructions for preserving textiles as found in Chapter 14, Taking Care of Textiles.

DOLLHOUSES

Dollhouses face a high risk of deterioration because they are big and take up a lot of space. They are essentially large boxes and are easily smashed. Make sure your strategy takes their physical size and fragility into consideration for their long-term storage packaging. In addition, as a practical matter doll houses are boxes made from one of four major materials: wood, cardboard, plastic, or painted metal. You need to make sure the information about those materials is integrated into your thinking, planning, and execution for their preservation.

Wood: Preserve your dollhouse by following the guidelines under "Wood Furniture" for cleaning and waxing in Chapter 8, Preserving Your Furniture.

Cardboard: Preserve it by following the guidelines for wood pulp paper in "Old Letters" in Chapter 11, Saving Your Books, Comic Books, Newspapers, Magazines, and Letters.

Plastic: Preserve it by following the rules in "Vintage Plastic and Rubber Stuff" in Chapter 7, Sorting and Preserving the Family Trash.

Painted Metal: Follow the guidelines listed earlier in this chapter for painted metal toys.

Chapter 5

Saving the Stuff Only a Parent Could Love

I picture the swirling water pouring through Louisa's basement door. She is soaked and desperately trying to salvage boxes filled with memories. In my mind's eye she stands in two feet of water clutching her son's sopping christening gown, realizing she treasures the old scrapbooks, toys, and her children's macaroni mosaics more than she values the expensive crystal that is sitting safely upstairs. The stuff only a parent can love is irreplaceable; you can always buy more china.

Who knows how many families have suffered the heartache of losing precious belongings? Over the years I have fielded hundreds of letters, phone calls, and conversations revolving around this very issue: "What do I do with stuff that is important to me but to no one else?" "Where can I find information on taking care of fragile macaroni art and seashell mosaics?" Or *"Help!* I saw a mouse nibbling on my box of kindergarten treasures. How do I save them?"

Nothing reflects the love and intimacy of a family more than our "useless" treasures. They identify us and our relationships, and the attention we pay to their preservation needs to reflect the importance we place on them.

This chapter deals with everything a parent keeps to remind him or her of their children's early years. A number of teachers requested this section as well because, to be honest, how many books deal with preserving macaroni art?

THINK "PLASTIC"

The most important step you can take to preserve your child's artistic creations is to put them in a place where bugs cannot get to them. The second biggest danger to these objects is water, which rots paper collages, dissolves macaroni art, and causes bean mosaics to sprout suddenly. Plastic tubs, such as large Tupperware storage containers, not only keep out pesky bugs but also double as protectors from water. So think "Plastic" when preserving childhood treasures.

Don's Rules for Preserving Craft Projects Only a Parent Could Love

1. Store craft projects in sealable plastic (polypropylene or polyethylene) containers such as Rubbermaid or Tupperware.

2. Never store art projects in cardboard boxes because cardboard wilts when wet, attracts bugs when wet or dry, and collapses when sat or stepped on.

3. *Keep an inventory list* of what you have and where it is. Put a copy of the list inside as well as outside the plastic container. Lists on the outside of containers can be ruined. The list on the inside of the container is protected and can give you a quick reference for the items inside, especially if they have been lovingly wrapped.

4. Try to avoid storing stuff in your basement or attic. Attics are too dry; basements are too wet. But if these are the only spaces you have, take some precautions. In a basement, store containers high up on a shelf if possible or stack on wood planks—anything to keep the containers off the damp floor. Run a dehumidifier to keep moisture levels low. In an attic, make sure it is ventilated with an automatic fan. This will help keep the heat down.

5. Display craft projects on a stable surface. Do not display them on the refrigerator door because a swinging door offers no stability.

6. Frame favorite pieces of your children's art in order to save

If your stuff gets damp, you have only a few hours before the beans sprout, the glue loosens, and the pasta dissolves. Get it dry as soon as possible. Otherwise, you might as well plant the beans and eat the pasta. To dry wet artifacts of almost any kind, place them in a plastic tub or bucket with plenty of silica gel and cover with an airtight lid. Make sure the tub is big enough that you can lay your treasure flat on the silica gel. Silica gel absorbs moisture and will dry out everything inside. You can usually find silica gel in craft stores because it is used for drying flowers and leaves. It begins working immediately. How wet your stuff is will determine how long it will take to dry.

them. If your craft project is three-dimensional, then frame in a shadow box. The directions for this are included in this chapter.

YOUR CHILD'S THREE-DIMENSIONAL ART PROJECTS

These projects include popsicle art, ornaments, decorated Easter egg shells, and so forth. Storing bulky, large kid sculpture is one area where most families throw in the towel and simply cram the artistic oddity from kindergarten craft time into the nearest (or sometimes farthest) niche they can find in the attic, basement, or closet. Once again high-quality plastic containers ride to the rescue.

You will need the following supplies:

Clear plastic bags large enough to hold the art
Sturdy, good-quality sealing polyethylene plastic containers (such as Rubbermaid and Tupperware) large enough to hold the bagged artwork
Confetti from quality paper (shredded photocopy paper is fine)
Polyethylene foam (if the artwork is heavy)

1. Place the artwork in an archival zippered plastic bag. Clear bags are best because they allow you to see what is inside, reducing the amount of rummaging you have to do to find what you are looking for.

2. Set your sealable, sturdy plastic container in a place where you can fill it without any danger of knocking it on the floor.

3. Place a bed of shredded photocopy paper on the bottom to provide padding for the artwork. If the artwork is so heavy that it will crush the confetti, you may have to switch to polyethylene foam.

4. Gently place each piece of artwork in the container, allowing at least two inches of space between them. Fill the container with as many artworks as can fit with the "two-inch spacing" requirement. Use the paper confetti to fill the space between artworks.

5. Gently stuff confetti around and on top of the artwork or wrap completely in polyethylene foam.

6. Place the lid on the top and seal.

7. Put the container where you will be storing it.

DON'S TIP:
Where to Display Art Projects

Place weekly art projects on a wall or a bulletin board where they cannot be jostled and knocked off. Make sure the art is up high enough so that young children cannot touch and accidentally rip the work.

FLAT ART

The best method for preserving paintings, collages, and drawings is to frame them. They can then be hung just like grown-up flat art. Whether displayed in the kitchen, your child's bedroom, or the family den, children's art often adds a whimsical touch to any decorating scheme. Chapter 13, Taking Care of Fine Art, discusses exactly how to save art.

DON'S TIP:
Displaying Three-Dimensional Craft Projects

If you want to display your child's sculpture or craft project, it is important to consider the risks it will face. One sensible way to display smaller sculptures is to put them inside a glass cookie dome that keeps out bugs, mitigates moisture problems, and, if placed in the right niche, remains virtually smash free.

MACARONI/BEAN MOSAIC ARTWORK

To save this artwork, follow the instructions for the three-dimensional art projects with one additional caveat: Store it flat inside the plastic container and make sure not to place anything heavy directly on top of it.

SHADOW BOXES

One of the best methods for displaying art that is not quite flat but not quite round, such as macaroni art or collages that include Styrofoam balls, is to place them in a shadow box. A shadow box is really just a deep frame or shallow box the size of the artwork and with a glass or acrylic window on the front. Many local craft stores, and certainly e-commerce sites, sell shadow boxes in a variety of styles and sizes for displaying dried flower arrangements and similar arts and crafts. Or you can make your own.

Making a Shadow Box

If you are experienced in woodworking and would prefer to make your own, you can construct a shadow box large enough and deep enough to hold the art, glass front, and backing board.

SMITHSONIAN STORIES:
The Headache of Warhol's Collage

If Andy Warhol is known for one thing, it's the statement: "In the future everyone will be famous for fifteen minutes." My former colleague Tim Vitale, who is a paper conservator, worked on a small collage by Warhol that was assembled from pieces of torn paper (so far so good) and glued together with rubber cement and cellulose nitrate adhesive (not so good). Over the years the collage had become badly stained by the degrading adhesives. The biggest problem involved taking the collage apart, removing the stains from the paper using various methods, and then reassembling the collage exactly as it had been. Tim used an archivally sound adhesive to reassemble the collage and, thanks to his efforts, the Warhol collage will last a lot longer than a mere fifteen minutes.

Fifteen years ago I worked with a colleague on a number of fabulous paintings by the prolific modern American artist William H. Johnson. Though academically trained, Johnson had embarked on a "primitivistic" artistic path to reflect the experience of his youth as a rural black southerner. He had diverged from traditional, classical techniques and instead focused on using whatever materials were at hand. The paintings I worked on were painted on cheap shipping crate plywood. In the course of the project I learned a great deal about this fascinating artist and his tragic life. One of the more entertaining episodes involved his work as an art teacher of schoolchildren. Johnson frequently took the kids' artworks, presumably the ones they were not happy with, and used the back sides as his own canvas. Smithsonian collections include a number of artifacts that are kindergarten splashes on one side and studies by this famed artist on the other. So if you see kid's art at the flea market or in a yard sale, make sure to check the back side. It just might be an original William H. Johnson.

You will need the following supplies:

⅛-inch-thick glazing (acrylic, polycarbonate, or tempered glass)
    of the appropriate size
Safety glasses
1- by 4-inch lumber (length is determined by the size of the box)
Table saw or router
Masking tape
Carpenter's glue
¼-inch plywood the same size as the glazing
Small nails or screws
Screwdriver or hammer

1. Determine the size of the box—height, width, and depth.

2. Cut or obtain the glazing—to the height minus 1 inch and the width minus 1 inch. In other words, for a 24- by 30-inch box the glazing should be 23 by 29 inches.

3. Put on your safety glasses.

4. Cut two lumber pieces exactly to the height measurement and two pieces exactly to the width measurement.

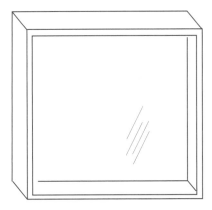

Illus. 5-1. A typical shadow box for displaying three-dimensional children's art (and other art, too). All materials should be archival (see instructions). Normally a shadow box is 3 to 5 inches deep.

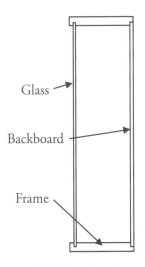

Illus. 5-2. Side view of a typical shadow box.

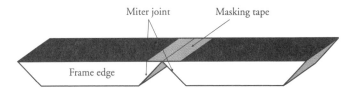

Illus. 5-3. "Dry-fitting" the shadow-box frame. Lay out the frame pieces so that the necessary miter joints are formed at the corners. Place a piece of masking tape over each joint to hold it together. This will not only allow you to "test-drive" the joint but the tape will serve as the clamping system when you put it together for real.

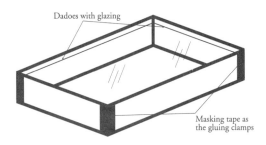

Illus. 5-4. Gluing the shadow box together. Because of the mitered corners the box can be glued together with white glue and masking tape. By "wrapping" the box frame around the glazing, you are assembling the whole box in one step.

5. Miter the ends of each board with a 45-degree angle so that the four pieces form a perfect rectangle when placed together.

6. Mark one long edge of each board with an "F" for the front and one long edge with "R" for the rear.

7. With a table saw or a router with a guide fence, cut a dado groove $\frac{1}{8}$ inch wide and $\frac{5}{16}$ inch deep, $\frac{1}{4}$ inch from the front edge.

8. With a table saw or router cut a rabbet joint on the inside of the rear edge of the box boards. The rabbet should be $\frac{5}{16}$ inch deep and $\frac{5}{16}$ inch wide.

9. "Dry-assemble" the box using masking tape to make sure the whole thing fits together properly. Line up two adjacent miter corners and run tape along their length to hold the corner together. If the fit is good, undo the box.

10. Apply glue to the miters and reassemble the box with the glazing in

DON'S TIP:
About the Shadow Box Contents

If the artwork medium (macaroni, beans, Styrofoam, etc.) is light and on a fairly stiff support (for example, if it is on poster board strong enough that it does not tend to fold over on itself due to its own weight), you can mount the artwork to the back mat and then assemble, seal, and hang the shadow box.

If the artwork is heavy, however—that is, if it has lots of beans, macaroni, or other materials—and is not on a stiff support but is instead stuck to something like construction paper, you may have to provide additional strength by mounting the artwork on a piece of rigid board. This is probably the only time in this entire book where I recommend gluing an artifact completely to a support.

You can accomplish this by cutting a piece of heavyweight (4-ply or more) acid-free mat board to fit into the shadow box. Spread methylcellulose wallpaper paste over the entire surface of the mat board and press the artwork onto it while it is lying on a flat horizontal surface.

You may need to provide a little weight on the artwork to make everything lie properly and in the right place. You can do this, provided that the artwork will not be damaged by gentle pressure, by *temporarily* covering the front side of the artwork with plastic cling wrap and placing a bed pillow or two on top.

Once the glue is dry, remove the pillows and plastic wrap, place the mounted artwork in the shadow box, and seal and hang it in a safe place.

place. Tape the corners together and allow the glue to dry according to the instructions on the glue bottle.

11. Once the glue has dried, remove the tape that served as the clamps while the glue was drying.

12. For placing the artwork on the shadow box, follow the instructions in step one of "Matting and Framing Art on Paper" in Chapter 13, Taking Care of Fine Art, using the $\frac{1}{4}$-inch plywood sheet as the mounting board.

13. Nail or screw the mounting board with the mounted artwork into the rabbet at the rear of the shadow box.

SCHOOL PAPERS

Follow the rules for "Old Letters" in Chapter 11, Saving Your Books, Comic Books, Newspapers, Magazines, and Letters. *Note:* Mimeograph paper and thermal fax paper documents need to be photocopied onto linen stationery as soon as possible. Enjoy the originals quickly because the words will disappear off the pages.

TIME CAPSULE

A terrific way to preserve your children's treasures and teach them preservation at the same time is to create a museum-quality time capsule. Surprisingly simple to assemble and make, our time capsule encapsulates a period in your child's life. My colleagues and I at SCMRE developed a how-to guide for putting together a time capsule as a tool to preserve family memories and teach preservation because it is important to foster budding conservators.

There are five steps to creating, completing, and storing a time capsule:

1. Deciding what to put inside the time capsule
2. Choosing the container
3. Preparing and placing the objects in the time capsule
4. Sealing the time capsule
5. Storing the time capsule

CAUTION: If you are going to make a time capsule, it is critical for you to read each step before buying or putting together any part of the capsule.

Why? Because what you decide to save in your time capsule determines how big the container will need to be. In addition, some things store well for years and other stuff doesn't. You need to know what you can save and what type of container you need to save it in before you go to the store to gather supplies.

Step 1: Deciding What to Put Inside the Time Capsule

Steps 1 and 2 actually occur simultaneously. You must choose your container based on the size of the stuff you want to save, and you must choose what to save based on the size of the container you are placing them in. As you begin to load up your time capsule, you will notice that your choice of contents and your choice of container must match. You are not going to be able to put a basketball in a peanut butter jar. If you have already chosen your container, measure the diameter of the hole at the top so that you know what will fit inside before you begin to choose what you want to save. If you do not already have a container, remember that the largest opening available for a recommended container is typically four inches in diameter. So whatever you choose must be able to fit through that size opening.

Remember also that the contents of your time capsule need to last as long as possible. If you put in the wrong stuff, the time capsule and its contents will change over time (in color, texture, composition, and strength), perhaps to the point of being unrecognizable. Because of this I have created a master list of good and bad stuff to place in your time capsule. When choosing what stuff to save, remember that the two major considerations are size and stability.

Here are some examples of good and bad stuff to put in a time capsule:

DON'S TIP:
Opening Your
Time Capsule

A word about opening your time capsule: *don't*. At least don't do it unless you are done with it. A sealed time capsule is a one-time thing. Once you open it, the seal is broken. Decide in advance when you are going to open it, and stick to it. Are you saving it for an infant's twenty-first birthday? A youngster's fiftieth? For your grandchildren's seventy-fifth wedding anniversary?

GOOD (DETERIORATES SLOWLY)

Black-and-white photos
   (great)
Books on rag paper
Color photos (good)
Copper, brass, and bronze
   items

Currency
Dirt
Glass and ceramic
Hair, fingernails, teeth
Laser prints or photocopies
   on buffered paper

Lead, silver, and gold items
Macaroni art with either clear glue (methylcellulose) or starch glue
Pencil drawings on good paper
Rag paper (fine stationery, also known as "good paper")
Seeds
Stable plastics (polyethylene, polypropylene)
Stable textiles such as cotton or linen (badges, ribbons)
Stamps
Stones and gems

BAD (DETERIORATES QUICKLY OR CONTAMINATES OTHER ITEMS)

Acidic wood products (particleboard, fiberboard)
Artwork on construction paper
Books on wood pulp paper
Collages with rubber cement or Elmer's (PVA) glue
CDs and DVDs
Electronics
Inkjet prints
Newspaper clippings (must be photocopied to be saved in time capsule)
Photo negatives, slides, and movie film
Rubber
Unstable fabrics such as burlap, jute, silk, and rayon
Unstable plastics (polyvinyl chloride; most toys are PVC plastic)
Videotape or audiotape cassettes

Sadly, you should not save your child's newspaper clippings in the time capsule. Newsprint is essentially an unstable vegetable product, but high-quality photocopies on linen stationery are just about perfect. Yes, you can save your child's teeth, baby photographs, and, if it's the right fabric, his or her blankie in the time capsule.

Step 2: Choosing the Container

Once you have decided what to put into your time capsule, you must find a container to house it. There are two main choices: glass and plastic jars. Glass is stable and prevents oxygen from entering, but it also breaks far too easily. But there is the polyethylene terephthalate (PET) jar. What the heck is PET? It's a special plastic developed as a near perfect unbreakable oxygen

One of the ways to develop a time capsule is to choose a theme. You do not need to save only childhood memories. Maybe you want a time capsule of your daughter's wedding, or maybe you want to save reminders of your first anniversary. Create a time capsule using any theme you want.

barrier. Oxygen increases the rate of deterioration, so the time capsule must be able to keep all oxygen out.

Fortunately, it is easily available to you as peanut butter and pretzel jars (two foods notoriously oxygen sensitive—the former goes rancid and the latter stale). This jar is available from larger scrapbook suppliers, or you can simply buy a jar of peanut butter or pretzels from your local grocery store and enjoy the contents first. Again, make sure the stuff you have chosen to save will fit through the opening of the jar you have chosen. Also make sure you choose a jar large enough for everything you plan to put inside.

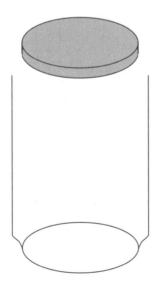

Illus. 5-5. A polyethylene terephthalate (PET) plastic food jar makes an almost perfect time capsule. It is chemically tough and an excellent oxygen barrier. They are typically used for peanut butter and pretzels.

CAUTION: Make sure the plastic is not polyethylene or polyvinyl chloride. Polyethylene allows moisture in as it ages, and polyvinyl chloride jars release contaminants into the contents. These jars hold everything that is not peanut butter, cheese puffs, bread sticks, pretzels, or nuts, so be careful.

Step 3: Preparing and Placing the Objects in the Time Capsule

You will need the following supplies:

Pencil
Linen stationery
Polyethylene Terephthalate (PET) plastic jar with lid (referred to as a time capsule)
Cotton gloves
Acid-free tissue or polyester batting for wrapping and padding
Polyethylene zippered bags
Acid-free paper boxes or PET plastic boxes to hold the fragile stuff (make sure they will fit through the hole on the top of the jar)
Coin sleeves
Polyethylene laboratory vials
Envelopes—Mylar sheet sleeves or acid-free paper (also known as photo and/or stamp sleeves)
Acid-free glassine wrapping paper
Acid-free buffer board

As a general rule, items placed inside the jar are actually in more than one container. Most stuff goes in an individual envelope, and several envelopes containing the same type of material are then placed in a sturdy inert container (acid-free box). This is then placed inside the time capsule (PET jar). It provides the safest conditions for your stuff. The supplies listed above include everything you need to save a variety of stuff. Purchase the supplies when you know what is needed. Newsprint requires a buffer board, but none of the other items do, so if you are not saving newsprint, you do not need a buffer board.

1. Using a pencil and writing on linen paper, make an inventory of the contents. Place one copy outside and one copy inside the time capsule. This should be a detailed list of everything you are placing inside, including why

you chose each item. You know each item and you know all the reasons for choosing them, but the person opening this time capsule tens or hundreds of years from now will not know.

2. Prepare the items to be placed inside the time capsule. When you are done, place each item inside the time capsule. Here are the instructions for preparing each item:

Baby shoes and other cloth objects that need to maintain their shape: Baby shoes deserve a special mention because almost all new parents save their child's first baby shoes, but other cloth objects also need stuffing to retain their shape. Stuff the shoes or other items with acid-free paper or polyester batting and place in a zippered plastic bag.

Books on rag paper: First box the book in a snug but not tight archival box and then place it in a zippered plastic bag. Remember, this has to fit through the opening.

Currency: Place in archival coin sleeves; these are widely available from coin and stamp shops. If you are saving more than one coin, place each one in a sleeve and then place the sleeves together in an archival box.

Dirt: Wrap in acid-free paper and place in a zippered plastic bag. Place the bag in an archival box.

Glass and ceramic: Individually wrap in soft acid-free tissue or clean polyester cloth and then place in a sturdy container made from PET or acid-free paper.

Hair, fingernails, and teeth: Place individual items in tiny polyethylene laboratory vials with snap caps and then place in a larger PET or archival paper box.

Laser prints or photocopies on linen paper: Treat as you would photographs.

Lead, silver, and gold items: Individually wrap metal objects such as jewelry and class rings in soft acid-free tissue. Place in an archival zippered plastic bag and then in its own sturdy box made from PET or acid-free paper.

Macaroni art with either clear glue (methylcellulose) or starch glue: Wrap in acid-free paper and place in a zippered plastic bag and then in an archival box.

Pencil drawings on good paper: Prepare nearly identical to rag paper objects, except that the drawing side of the paper should be protected by a sheet of acid-free glassine to provide further protection.

Photographs: Place photos in a photo sleeve, which is really an envelope

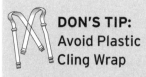

DON'S TIP:
Avoid Plastic
Cling Wrap

Make sure you do not wrap metal items, or any items for that matter, in plastic cling wrap. Disaster results if you do. Cling wrap is bad, bad, *bad*. It emits harmful chemicals that erode almost any article wrapped in it.

made from either high-density polyester (Mylar) or archival paper. Place only one photo in each sleeve so the photos will not rub against each other. If you have several photos in sleeves, it would be best to put them in an archival paper box before placing them in the time capsule. Remember, though, that everything has to fit through the mouth of the jar.

Rag paper (fine stationery, also known as good paper): Treat paper the same way you treat photographs. Folded paper is a special problem because creases are weaker than flat paper and tend to tear more easily, so avoid folding paper whenever you can.

Seeds: Air-dry and place inside tiny archival zippered plastic bags and then in their own archival box. Be sure to include a slip of linen paper in each bag with a penciled note identifying the seed.

Stable textiles such as cotton or linen (badges, ribbons, etc.): Much like paper, folding is a problem for textiles for any long-term storage. The best way to handle the problem is to pad the textile with inert materials such as polyester batting or acid-free tissue. Chapter 14, Taking Care of Textiles, discusses how to prepare textiles for storage. Once prepared, place the textile in an archival zippered plastic bag, and if it is small enough, place the wrapped textile in an archival box.

Stamps: Fortunately, almost any stamp-collecting shop will provide the necessary archival housings for stamps. They are called stamp sleeves rather than photo sleeves.

Stable plastics (polyethylene, polypropylene): Place in a zippered plastic bag and place the bag into an archival box.

Stone and gems: These should be treated like metal items. Wrap in acid-free tissue and place in a zippered plastic bag and then in an archival box.

Wood pulp paper (also known as newsprint or bad paper): You really should not include wood pulp paper in the time capsule. A better alternative is to photocopy it on good linen stationery and place the copy in the capsule. If you feel compelled to include pulp paper, be advised that its chances of survival are not very good and may very well contribute to the degradation of the capsule contents. If you still feel compelled to save the newsprint, place the paper between two sheets of acid-free buffer board and then place it inside an archival zippered plastic bag.

Step 4: Sealing the Time Capsule

You will need the following supplies:

Silica gel packets (must be prepared several hours in advance); also
found in granular form in art supply stores, hardware stores,
scientific and laboratory supplies, and some department store
closet shops

Unscented and uncolored candle

Ageless oxygen scavenger

Once your time capsule has been filled it needs to be sealed perfectly, a process that must be executed carefully and rapidly. I cannot overstate the importance of a perfect seal: It is what will make your time capsule last for many decades rather than months or a few years.

1. Condition the packets of silica gel by placing them in a very warm environment for several hours—on top of a heating vent in the wintertime or in a toaster oven at about 110 degrees Fahrenheit will work just fine. This dries out the silica gel. Once it is dried out, it is ready to gather up all the moisture inside the time capsule. You will need about six sugar packs' worth of silica gel for a two-pound peanut butter jar.

2. Calculate the space inside the container (see the instructions with the Ageless oxygen scavenger) and select the appropriate number of packets. *Warning:* Carefully read the following directions in their entirety before proceeding. *From this point on you have to work extremely quickly and make no mistakes.*

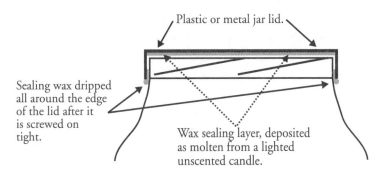

Plastic or metal jar lid.

Sealing wax dripped
all around the edge
of the lid after it
is screwed on
tight.

Wax sealing layer, deposited
as molten from a lighted
unscented candle.

Illus. 5-6. Detailed cross section of the time capsule lid, sealed with candle wax.

3. Prepare the lid by lighting a candle and dripping hot wax on the inside of the lid, coating the entire flat surface (coating the threads comes later). You will need that candle for steps 6 and 7, so keep it burning.

4. Insert the silica gel packets.

5. Make a small tear in the Ageless packet(s) and place them in the container. You have only ten or fifteen seconds to get through steps 4 to 6 because the Ageless begins reacting immediately with the air inside the container.

6. Drip molten candle wax on the threads of the container lid and immediately, before the wax hardens, screw the lid on tight. If you work too slowly, warm the wax on the threads with a hair dryer until the lid screws on tightly.

7. Once the lid is on tightly, drip molten candle wax around the complete outside edge where the lid and the container meet. You are done!

Step 5: Storing the Time Capsule

You should place your time capsule in a cool, dry, dark environment. If possible, the location should be vibration-free. In short, the top shelf of your closet is just about the perfect place to put your time capsule.

If you prepare it properly, leave it alone, and do not damage it, the time capsule you make will survive for generations until it is opened.

REMINDERS OF YOUR CHILD'S DEVELOPMENT

Children grow up so quickly. Saving mementos of the important milestones is one way to temporarily stop the clock.

Christening gowns and other special clothes: Follow the directions found in Chapter 14, Taking Care of Textiles.

Diplomas: Diplomas need to be framed in order to be preserved. Follow the directions given in "Matting and Framing Art on Paper" in Chapter 13, Taking Care of Fine Art.

Varsity letters: Wrap in acid-free tissue and place in an acid-free archival box. Make sure the box is large enough to lay the letter down flat. Folding or bending the letter will weaken the material.

DON'T BURY YOUR TIME CAPSULE

Historical accounts of storing time capsules provide an important lesson as you prepare your treasures for the future. The popular (mis)conception is that burying time capsules is the best thing to do with them. This may or may not be the most common response to the question, "Now what the heck do we do with this thing?" but burying it is probably the worst alternative. It exposes a time capsule to a whole host of unnecessary risks, most notably ground water encroachment. Then there's my all-time favorite—suffered by both George Washington and the cast of *M*A*S*H*: they forgot where they buried their treasures!

Chapter 6

Saving Your Family Treasures

SHEBA WAS BORN *a mass of nervous excitement, always barking, leaping, and completely immune to the charms of obedience school. She was the type of dog that gives dogs a bad name. When I went on a business trip, my friend Barbara agreed to keep an eye on Sheba.*

When I left, Sheba became fixated on a stunning octagonal China plate, depicting a quaint village scene, that Barbara's grandmother had left to her. This nineteenth-century German plate was hand-painted in blue and white. Barbara displayed it proudly on a small round table in the living room. I remember its beauty, the eggshell of the china, and the delicacy of the painting.

Maybe Sheba thought the plate was a Frisbee. As Barbara describes the infamous incident, Sheba placed her paws on the table, turned her head sideways, grabbed the plate between her teeth, and took off. As Barbara careened around the corner trying to catch Sheba, she screamed, "Sheba!" Recognizing a death cry when she heard it, Sheba became even more worked up. She ran right between the slats of the stair banister, her head became stuck, and the plate soared through the air as if propelled by a NASA rocket. The fire department had to come to grease Sheba and pull her out.

Sheba emerged unscathed. The plate never had a chance. Barbara's plate had survived a transatlantic voyage, light, heat, bugs, the humidity of the South, the cold of the North, but not my dog. I can't replace it, though I have looked in an-

tique stores for a similar plate. The truth is, the biggest danger to china is not light, bugs, heat, cold, or any of the regular villains. The biggest danger to china is children, people, and pets—especially my pets. —Louisa Jaggar

THE BASICS OF PRESERVING: THINK "HANDLE WITH CARE"

Nothing is more dangerous to your good china and crystal than your family and pets. That's the bad news. The good news is that with these treasures you do not need to worry about light, water, bugs, or temperatures—with the exception of extreme hot and cold. Go ahead and store these treasures in your attic or basement. Southerners went so far as to bury their silver at the end of the Civil War when the Yankee troops were coming. When the silver was dug up afterward, it was in fine condition.

What is the most important consideration for preserving these treasures for generations to come? Treat them the way you would an unboiled egg—"Handle With Care."

SILVER

The strategy for preserving artifacts made from silver or gold (or plated with silver or gold) depends on the answer to the following question: How often do you intend to use or handle the collection? Fine silver objects that are rarely used require a different strategy from silver objects that you use regularly for serving or consuming food. A silver service that is used regularly does not tend to tarnish, but one that is used seldom does. Also, silver that never holds food should be coated to help preserve it, but you should never

DON'S TIP:
How to Tell Gold from Copper or Brass or Bronze

Gold or gold-plated artifacts such as dinnerware do not tarnish. Ever. If your treasure looks like gold and tarnishes, it is probably a copper alloy such as polished bronze or brass. If it looks like gold and does not tarnish, it is probably gold.

coat silver that you use with food. If you use your treasured silver service on a daily basis, you have already made the decision to consume rather than preserve it.

The main components in the deterioration of silver are corrosion and mechanical damage such as scratching, denting, and breaking. The latter concerns are easy enough to deal with.

Silver does not necessarily need to be treated with kid gloves. Clean cotton gloves will do. The greatest damage comes from clanging metal. When you hear your family treasures clanking together, damage is lurking just around the corner.

Don's Rules for Saving Your Family Silver

1. Never place silverware in the dishwasher.
2. Use padded mats on the table or counters when handling silver.
3. Never, ever wrap your silver in plastic cling wrap or wool cloth. Both cause the silver to tarnish.
4. Always remove jewelry from your hands before handling because jewelry can scratch the surface.

Preserving Your Special-Occasion Silver Service

This is the silver you use only when the family visits for Thanksgiving or you are celebrating a new job. Tarnish is a problem that all silver owners complain about. Tarnish is proof that the atmosphere is eating away at your

DON'S TIP:
Never Wrap Silver in Plastic Cling Wrap

Louisa pulled out a gray metal urn that had resisted her attempts to make it beautiful. She thought it was a common metal because someone in the past had probably wrapped it in plastic cling wrap and nearly destroyed the surface of the object. The cling wrap had etched the surface with chlorine. A beautiful mid-1800s piece of artistry had been camouflaged by tarnish (a common word for corrosion). The urn was actually silverplate. By using the proper polishing steps, the urn was transformed from a dull, grungy bowl into a piece of glistening silver artwork.

silver, turning the pure metal into corrosion through chemical reactions with pollutants such as oxygen, chlorine, and sulfur.

The traditional way to deal with tarnish has been to use abrasive polishes, such as commercially available silver polishes, an onerous task. I know: I spent my college years in the Objects Conservation Laboratory of Winterthur Museum caring for one of the finest silver collections in the universe.

Your special-occasion silver needs to be both cleaned and polished, very different endeavors. Cleaning silver removes food particles, oily deposits from your skin, and other yucky stuff, while polishing removes tarnish.

The greatest temptation in cleaning and polishing silver is to rush through it, doing what is easiest rather than what is best for the silver. Coarse abrasives get the tarnish off in a hurry, but they take off the silver, too. You run the risk of cutting through the silver if the object is plated, or wiping out the delicate details of engraving and chasing. The polish that I suggest is a gentle alternative that can add years to the life of your silver.

You will need the following supplies:

Organic solvent mask
Paint-stripping gloves
Soft bristle brush, such as a toothbrush or an artist's oil painting
    brush
Three lint-free cloths (flannel or similar fabric)

Don's Cleaning Solution:

- One cup of acetone
- One cup of alcohol (hardware-store grade is fine)
- Small plastic funnel
- Polyethylene or polypropylene squirt bottle

Don's Silver Polishing Slurry:

- One teaspoon of ultrafine polishing abrasive (pulverized limestone, also known as powdered chalk, from the garden supply or hardware store, or "whiting" from an art supply store)
- One tablespoon of alcohol or mineral spirits
- Small, shallow bowl

1. Put on the mask and gloves. This will not only protect the silver surface from the oils and acids on your skin but will also protect your skin from the cleaning solution, which is a mixture of organic solvents.

2. Prepare the cleaning solution. Mix equal portions of the acetone and alcohol together and pour through the funnel into the squirt bottle.

3. Clean the silver surface with the cleaning solution using a soft brush. Scrub the surfaces to remove any dirt and residue, being sure to clean the back- and undersides.

4. Dry the silver with a lint-free cloth.

5. Prepare the polishing slurry. (Remember that cleaning and polishing are very different.) Mix the polishing abrasive and alcohol or mineral spirits together in the bowl. You may have to make several batches depending on the amount of silver to be cleaned. One reason the polishing slurry is made in small amounts is that the alcohol evaporates quickly. (Remember that Don's Polishing Slurry is best for your silver. Commercial polishing agents and silver dips often contribute to the deterioration of the object because they frequently contain harsh chemicals that corrode the metal or coarse abrasives that leave the surface badly scratched. Anything with ammonia, acids, or salt eats the metal.)

6. Dip a clean lint-free cloth in the slurry and begin polishing the silver. You only need to rub gently with the cloth in order for the abrasive to remove the tarnish. Continue until the silver is as shiny as you want. Pay particular attention to areas of wear because you might be polishing the underlying copper if it is a plated piece. Be extra careful not to go too far.

7. Rinse the slurry off with the cleaning solution and a soft brush until all the residue is gone.

Way back in the Dark Ages, I paid for college by working in the Objects Conservation Laboratory of Winterthur Museum, alongside my dear friend and coworker Helen Stetina. Our main task was to keep the metal collections of the museum in good condition. Mostly, we carefully polished brass, iron, steel, and especially silver by the hours, though by the acre might be more accurate. Perhaps the most memorable event came when we walked into the museum pushing our padded cart and loaded up the prized Paul Revere silver set: a matched group of six exquisite silver tankards by one of the greatest revolutionary heroes and artisans of his time. We polished and coated them exactly as I describe in this book: cleaning with an acetone/alcohol solution, polishing with clean flannel cloth and a whiting slurry, and coating with spray lacquer. If it's good enough for real-live Revere ware, it's good enough for your silver too.

You are now done with museum-quality silver polishing. Take a breath and relax. If this silver is used for food, you are finished. If the silver you have just finished cleaning and polishing is decorative only, you should also coat it. The instructions for this are below.

Coating Nonfood Service Silver After Polishing

All nonfood service-related silver should be coated. This helps preserve the display silver as well as the silver you have stored away. To make sure your efforts to remove the corrosion from the silver do not go to waste, to prolong the polishing effect, and to add further protection to the metal, the silver can be coated with a spray lacquer such as Krylon acrylic or a similar product available at hardware stores. This coating isn't permanent, but done properly it can last for several years. Until it wears off or degrades, you will not have to polish your silver. You're welcome!

You will need the following:

Nitrile gloves
Clean piece of cardboard, butcher's paper, or other clean work
    surface

Spray filter mask
Can of spray lacquer

1. Put on the gloves.

2. Place the newly polished silver in the center of the work surface. Be sure to work in a dust-free, well-ventilated space.

3. Put on the spray mask.

4. Spray a thin layer of lacquer on every polished silver object. Every surface will need to be sprayed—back, front, top, bottom, inside, outside, etc. Because of this you will need to spray one portion at a time, wait an hour, then spray the remaining portion. Important: Spray all the silver evenly and be sure not to miss any area.

5. Allow the spray to dry for an hour or so. If it is still sticky, it is not dry; wait a little longer. Turn it over or rotate it and spray the next section the same as the first.

6. Repeat steps 4 and 5 until all surfaces are covered.

7. You want to double-coat the silver just to make sure, so repeat steps 4, 5, and 6 until you have two complete thin coats of lacquer on each piece of silver.

8. Once the lacquer is completely dry you can handle the silver carefully. The lacquer is not going to be "rock hard," so be careful about scratching it. That will lead to localized areas of tarnish where the lacquer has been scratched off.

Preserving Your In-Use Silver

Because of the slight buffing of the silver that occurs through normal use and cleaning, in-use silver generally needs no "polishing." All it needs is good care and storing between uses. Do not leave food residues on the silver. Wash right away!

You will need the following supplies:

Soft sponge
Mild liquid dishwashing soap
Soft cloth for drying
Anti-tarnish-cloth lined fitted silverware box

1. If you wear jewelry, take it off before cleaning the silver so you do not scratch it.

2. Wash by hand using a soft sponge and mild liquid detergent. Do not ever wash in the dishwasher.

3. Dry with a clean soft cloth immediately. Water spots can help tarnish get a foothold.

4. Place in an antitarnish cloth–lined fitted silverware box. It not only helps with tarnish, but the separate holders for each piece of silver prevent the pieces from knocking against each other and leaving scratch marks. *The sound of clanking silver is a really bad sign!*

Storing Uncoated Silver After Polishing

The more carefully you store your silver, the less frequently you will have to grind off microscopically thin portions of the surface with an abrasive polish. Given enough time, polishing will rub the surface details away even with the mild abrasive. Wrapping your silver in any old cloth will not do the trick for preserving that glistening surface.

You will need the following:

Anti-tarnish cloth (Fitted anti-tarnish-cloth bags are readily available for most silver objects from suppliers listed at the back of the book. You can even order cloth bags with little pockets for a complete setting.)
Archival sealable polyethylene bags
Ageless oxygen scavenger
Archival protective box large enough for the silver object(s)

1. Wrap the cleaned and polished silver in antitarnish cloth in preparation for storage.

2. Place the wrapped silver in a polyethylene bag.

3. Take a sugar-pack-sized envelope of Ageless, tear one corner slightly, and place it inside the polyethylene bag but outside the antitarnish cloth wrap or bag and zip it shut *immediately.*

4. Place it in a protective archival box.

Displaying Silver

You can display your silver almost anywhere provided it will not get bumped into or knocked down. The exceptions are damp places such as a bathroom or a spa. With enough time, moisture will penetrate even a perfectly applied lacquer coating, and moisture contributes to tarnishing. Even more important, never place silver near a hot tub or pool because chlorine actually eats away at both the lacquer and the metal.

DINNER CHINA AND CRYSTAL: CLEANING, STORING, AND DISPLAYING

China and crystal made for typical dining is pretty tough stuff. If you do not break or chip it, you are good to go for centuries.

Don's Rules for Preserving Dinner China and Crystal

1. Don't drop or throw (easy to say).
2. Place out of reach of children and pets.
3. Prevent heat damage by keeping china and crystal out of direct sunlight.
4. Use padded mats on the table or counters when handling china or crystal, especially if you have the increasingly popular marble or granite countertops.
5. Wash by hand, not in the dishwasher. Put a rubber mat or pad at the bottom of the sink to prevent damage from the china bumping against the hard surface of the sink.
6. Dry by hand.
7. When storing plates, stack with padding in between each piece. A cloth napkin works perfectly. You can also place paper plates between each piece. Automatic-drip coffee filters also work well. The tinkling of china pieces against each other is not good!
8. Do not overstack the shelf. Shelves can buckle under excessive weight and collapse.
9. Do not stack too many plates on top of each other. Too much weight can cause old, delicate china to crack or break.
10. Always pick up china and crystal with two hands.
11. Do not carry more than one or two pieces at a time. If you slip or lose your grip with one or two pieces, you will be sad. If you are carrying a whole stack and lose your grip, no amount of super glue will solve the problem.

Cleaning

Once you are done eating, wash off the foodstuffs immediately because dried or caked-on food requires more force to remove. Always think to handle with care. Also, never clean your crystal or china in the dishwasher.

You will need the following:

Soft sponge or cloth
Mild liquid detergent
Soft dishcloth for drying

1. If you wear jewelry, take it off before handling china or crystal so you do not scratch it.
2. Wash each piece separately by hand, using the sponge or cloth and detergent. Never use the abrasive side of a sponge.
3. Dry with the dishcloth immediately.

Storing

Store in the original packing. If the packing is not available, invest in storage boxes designed especially for china and crystal because the biggest danger stored china and crystal face, besides being dropped, is cracking and shattering if the separate pieces touch with enough force. The good news is that you can store these items in your attic or basement as long as the temperatures in these places are not extreme.

Displaying

The best choice for these delicates is a glass cabinet because it will protect them from being knocked into or dropped. You can also display plates and cups on the wall using plate and cup brackets as long as you place them high enough so that children cannot reach them and where people cannot knock into them accidentally. Be sure to avoid placing china or crystal in an area where there is extreme temperature fluctuations or in direct sunlight.

If you live in an earthquake zone, it is best to secure your crystal and china in the cabinet or on the wall or table with Quake Hold Gel or Quake Wax, or firmly attach the pieces with plate and cup brackets.

CHANDELIERS

Sometimes all a chandelier needs is a light dusting, which must be done with a fine brush. Never use a vacuum directly on a chandelier. Sometimes, however, a simple dusting will not do the job.

While I worked my way through college polishing silver, a friend of mine did pretty much the same but with crystal chandeliers. Usually far above the table and out of reach except for the most enthusiastic revelers, chandeliers are generally immune to damage other than the catastrophic failure of the bolts or hooks holding it to the ceiling. In that case the chandelier comes crashing down, smashing itself and anything or anyone between it and the center of the earth.

Cleaning chandeliers is not conceptually complicated, but it does help quite a bit if you are persnickety about keeping track of hundreds or even thousands of nearly identical parts.

You will need the following:

Needle-nose pliers
Huge piece of kraft paper (size depends on the chandelier)
Triton 100 detergent or nonconditioning liquid detergent
Distilled water
Small plastic pan or bucket
Clean lint-free cloths (towels and worn cotton T-shirts are perfect)
Artist's paintbrush
Polyethylene squirt bottle

Hair dryer
Clean white cotton gloves
Brass wire

1. Unhook the crystals one at a time by loosening the attached wires using the pair of needle-nose pliers. Some of the wires may break, but don't worry about that.

2. Arrange the crystals on a huge piece of kraft paper in the exact order they come off the chandelier. If you get the order mixed up, no amount of aspirin will help. Count all the crystals and remember that they have to be taken down in a specific order and placed back in the exact same place. You might want to trace the crystal pieces onto the paper to help you remember where they go in case they are knocked out of order.

3. Once the crystals have been removed from the metal base, you can decide whether or not the brass needs to be cleaned or just the crystal. If the brass needs attention, treat it as you would brass furniture hardware. See the brass section of "Cleaning Removable Metal Hardware" in Chapter 8, Preserving Your Furniture. If the brass does not need polishing or cleaning, proceed to step 4.

4. Put about 1 inch of a 1 percent Triton/distilled water cleaning solution in the plastic pan.

5. Unfold a towel next to where you will be doing the washing.

6. Choose a piece of crystal, gently place it in the cleaning solution, and brush the surface with the artist's brush until it is clean. Change the solution as often as necessary to keep it clean.

7. Rinse the crystal thoroughly with distilled water from the squirt bottle.

8. Place the crystal on the towel to sop up the water.

9. Holding the crystal in a clean cloth, dry it completely with a breeze from the hair dryer set on cool. Be sure you get the wire holes dried completely.

10. Place the newly cleaned crystal piece back in its spot on the kraft paper.

11. Repeat steps 6 through 10 until each piece of crystal is cleaned and dried.

12. Put on your white cotton gloves and wear them while handling the crystals and their wires so that your fingers won't get them dirty all over again.

13. Replace each crystal in the proper place. If a crystal's wire has broken,

cut a new piece of wire and bend it to the proper shape with the needle-nose pliers. Be sure to use the correct size of wire. It's a good idea to take a piece of the wire to the hardware store and to get the correct diameter.

HOLIDAY ORNAMENTS: CLEANING, STORING, AND DISPLAYING

Holiday ornaments, especially the glass and ceramic ones, are among the most fragile items in our homes. Preserving them revolves almost entirely on how we handle and store them. Never forget that they are fragile. Don't drop them or step on them, and don't let pets or children climb the Christmas tree. They are really, really fragile.

You will need the following supplies to clean your ornaments:

¾-inch artist's brush
Photographer's compressed air can
Cotton swabs
Distilled water
Hair dryer

1. Gently remove any dust with a soft artist's brush immediately after removing the ornament from display. If the surface cannot be safely brushed, gently blow the dust off using the compressed air can.

2. If something has been spilled on the ornament, gently clean the affected area with a cotton swab moistened with distilled water. Do not immerse the ornament in water.

3. If you have to clean the ornament with distilled water, you will have to dry it. Turn your hair dryer on cool and low air. Hold it at least a foot away to gently dry the surface of your collectible. A dryer reaches those hard-to-reach places a towel cannot. Also, a towel or cloth can snag and thereby damage your ornament.

You will need the following to store your ornaments:

Photographer's compressed air can
Fitted packing (the best packing provides the exact negative of the

space occupied by the ornament. If this is not possible create your own version by following the instructions below.)

1. Don't remove ornaments from their place of display until you know where their containers are.

2. Blow all dirt and dust out of the ornament's fitted packing using the photographer's compressed air can. This prevents abrasion while in storage!

3. Place each clean ornament into its fitted packing (see below).

4. Double-case the ornaments. In other words, place them in their own box and then place that box or even several other boxes in a larger, more sturdy carton.

5. Store the ornaments in a cool, dry area.

Displaying Your Ornaments

1. If your ornaments are always on display, make sure they are in a glass-front cabinet to keep dust off them. A glass cookie dome can be a good alternative for individual ornaments.

2. Avoid placing any ornament in direct sunlight.

3. Display in a cool, dry place—70 degrees with humidity at 40 percent or less is best.

4. When displaying an ornament on a Christmas tree, secure it to the tree with thin floral wire. This wire can be purchased at any craft shop as well as most plant and flower shops. This prevents the ornament from being jostled and possibly falling to the ground.

5. Don't overextend your reach when installing them. Use the appropriate ladders or ask taller relatives to help you. Losing your balance while leaning into a tree full of irreplaceable ornaments is not a good thing.

Making a Fitted Packing for Ornaments

You will need the following supplies:

Ruler
Utility knife
Polyethylene 1-inch foam sheet

Archival box at least ½ inch larger than the ornament in every
   direction
Fine-tip permanent marker

1. Using the ruler as both a measuring tool and a straight edge, cut the
polyethylene foam with the utility knife into the shape of the bottom of the
archival storage box.

2. Repeat until you have enough layers of foam to fill the box from top to
bottom.

3. Remove the polyethylene foam from the box.

4. Using the ornament as a guide, cut openings in the layers of polyethylene foam so that they fit around the ornament. You may need to sketch the
outline with a fine-tip marker to guide you, and you may need to cut the
openings at an angle to accommodate the shape of the ornament.

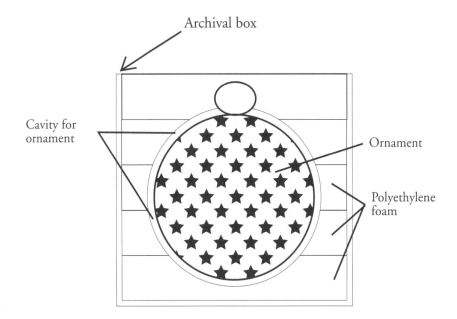

Cross section of a fitted storage box for ornaments.

Chapter 7

Sorting and Preserving the Family Trash

I recently returned from a solemn gathering where my siblings and I divided up some of our late father's stuff. As a craftsman, one of the things I value most is his shop apron. I therefore made it clear that this was my number one choice. A somewhat ragged piece of cloth made from cast-off upholstery fabric, this apron was sewn by my dad's own hand. My love of preserving stuff started at my father's side as we spent scores of evenings together hammering, sanding, and gluing in our cramped little plywood shed, which, by the way, we remodeled on an almost yearly basis to accommodate all the junk acquired over the previous year. He was a special man, and he instilled a love for puttering and tinkering that will be with me until my last breath. So, yes, his shop apron holds many special memories for me.

Each of the five siblings selected different possessions to take with us. What everything had in common was that it had little or no monetary value but great emotional value—for to us our dad's stuff is all about him and us.

Sometimes this inventorying occurs after the death of a parent, but just as often it occurs when parents downsize and move to a smaller home after retirement or move from one house to another for whatever reason. In my case, my wife and I moved twenty years ago after getting jobs in the same town and then found ourselves with so little time that we didn't sort through the stuff before we moved and expected to do it after we moved. To this day that is an unfulfilled expectation. Fortunately, we will be moving again in a few years and will have the opportunity once again to turn our attention to those forty boxes of stuff untouched since the move in 1984. I'll bet you think I'm kidding.

The collection of family trash runs the full gamut of materials and artifacts so that formulating a universal set of rules is nearly impossible. This chapter is almost the demented grown-up version of Chapter 5, Saving the Stuff Only a Parent Could Love, except that now the things we are saving can sometimes border on the bizarre. Kid's art reflects a short life span of experience; family collectibles can be the accumulation of generations of your family's interests, pack-ratting, and eccentricities.

THINK "STABILIZE"

For the most part the real challenge in preserving household artifacts is that preserving them may not be the only consideration. You might actually want to use your antique lamps as well. Fortunately, most of the stuff in this chapter is fairly durable, so your most important task is to think "Stabilize."

VINTAGE ELECTRICAL DEVICES

Preserving electrical devices, whether vintage lights, fans, or kitchen or other household appliances such as toasters, mixers, and electric razors is a ticklish issue. On one hand, as a conservator, I would like to see them maintained without any changes in the original materials or construction whatsoever. On the other hand, I recognize the inherent risks to people and homes in keeping unsafe electrical devices lying about.

Vintage electric devices of all kinds require special attention due to the deterioration of their components, many of which may have been made from extremely unstable materials that have now almost completed their trek back to dirt. This is especially true of electric cord coatings and insulation for both cords and components. Think about these two considerations:

• Rubber, a common early insulator for power cords, becomes brittle with age, will crack, and often falls off altogether. Without insulation you can have short circuits. Jolts of electricity will start a heart that has stopped, and will stop a heart that is running.

• Switches, sockets, and plugs have changed dramatically over the decades, both in terms of materials used and configuration. They can degrade at an alarming rate and become unfunctional or extremely dangerous.

Have a professional electrician replace all old wiring with new wiring. If you want to retain the form of an antique lamp but have it function safely now, you almost certainly will have to get its inner components replaced with new ones.

Place the removed electrical wiring and parts in a zippered plastic bag along with a note describing what they are and where they came from (a wiring diagram would be even better). These parts can be historically important. If you care about this, you should save these items.

Lamps and Shades

Lamps are not made of just wiring and switches but also have bases and lampshades that come in a multitude of shapes, sizes, and materials. For taking care of the nonelectrical parts of vintage lamps or lighting, consult the following sections of this book:

Wooden bases: Follow the instructions in the cleaning and waxing sections of "Wood Furniture" in Chapter 8, Preserving Your Furniture.

Brass bases: Follow the instructions in the "Cleaning Removable Metal Hardware" in Chapter 8, Preserving Your Furniture.

Ceramic bases: Follow the instructions in "Dinner China and Crystal: Cleaning, Storing, and Displaying" in Chapter 6, Saving Your Family Treasures.

Fabric shades: Follow the instructions in "Preserving Draperies and Curtains" in Chapter 14, Taking Care of Textiles.

Paper shades: Follow the basic instructions in the "Artwork on Paper" sections in Chapter 13, Taking Care of Fine Art.

Glass shades: Follow the instructions in "Ceramics, Art Glass, and Stained Glass" in Chapter 13, Taking Care of Fine Art.

Metal Chandeliers

After rewiring by a professional electrician, follow the instructions in "Chandeliers" in Chapter 6, Saving Your Family Treasures, or in "Cleaning Metal Hardware" in Chapter 8, Preserving Your Furniture, for the particular metal of your chandelier.

Electric Fans and Other Devices with Moving Parts

You should treat vintage fans with the same care and concerns as any electrical device, as described above, but also add the care and maintenance of the moving parts. For metal-to-metal parts, lubricate with lightweight machine oil. For all other moving parts lubricate with dry graphite powder. Whichever material is used for lubrication, apply a small dot of the lubricant at the point where the turning parts meet the static parts. The lubricant will work its way into the places it is supposed to be all by itself.

CAST IRON

Pots and pans, cookware (including enameled pots and iron skillets), doorknobs, locks and hinges, and andirons—the common thread of this disparate group of artifacts is that they are mostly made from iron, which has been around for several thousand years, or steel, the most common alloy of iron. (For artifacts made from copper or copper alloys such as brass or bronze, follow the instructions in "Sculpture and Objets d'Art" in Chapter 13, Taking Care of Fine Art, and in "Cleaning Metal Hardware" in Chapter 8, Preserving Your Furniture. Iron is the most common metal in museum collections and is almost certainly present in your own collection, whether fireplace tools, kitchen pots, doorknobs, or locks. The challenge of preserving iron is to keep it from rusting. Iron and other metals want to go back to dirt in a hurry. All that is required for the trip is moisture and oxygen. To slow down this trip, many of the steel and iron objects you see in stores were plated with tin or zinc, or painted with enamel.

Don's Rules for Preserving Iron and Steel Collectibles

1. The perfect environment for iron and steel is 0 percent relative humidity. As a practical matter, iron will not aggressively corrode indoors at less than 50 percent relative humidity.

2. Protect iron and steel from pollution and contamination. For example, always wear clean white cotton gloves when handling iron and steel artifacts to protect them from the salts and acids from skin contact.

3. Do not take iron collectibles directly from a cold environment to a warm environment because this will cause moisture to condense on the object and cause oxidation.

4. Iron is not light sensitive to any noticeable degree.

5. Iron can pretty much withstand any temperature less than 1,000 degrees. If the environment you are in exceeds this temperature, you have much larger problems.

6. Contaminants from cooking, such as salt, garlic, and tomato sauce, when left in iron or steel containers can also cause corrosion.

7. Iron tends to be more brittle than steel, so handle with care—don't drop it!

Cleaning

Getting rust and other contaminants off the surface of iron is critical for its long-term survival. Here are the rules for cleaning and coating intact iron and steel objects. For items that are not intact, either from breakage or extreme deterioration, consult an objects or metals conservator.

CAUTION: Work in a well-ventilated space with no flame source.

You will need the following supplies:

Organic solvent filter respirator (mask)
Safety glasses
Nitrile gloves
Two polyethylene squirt bottles
Acetone
Alcohol
Large plastic or rubber tub
Coarse bristle scrub brush
Fine steel wool or abrasive cleaning pad
Litho pads
Pumice powder

1. Put on the mask, safety glasses, and gloves.

2. Fill one polyethylene squirt bottle with a fifty-fifty mixture of acetone and alcohol.

3. Fill the second squirt bottle with alcohol only.

4. Place the object to be cleaned inside a rubber tub (or similar) to contain the activity.

5. Squirt the surface of the object with the acetone-alcohol mix and scrub with the stiff brush to remove any surface contaminants.

6. Rinse the surface with the alcohol-acetone solution until all loosened contaminants are washed away.

7. For light surface rust go to step 8. For heavy rust or texture surface go to step 10.

8. Dampen fine steel wool or abrasive pad with alcohol and *gently* scrub off the rust.

9. Rinse with alcohol until all loosened particulate matter is washed off.

10. Blot dry with litho pads. If the surface is clean and rust free, you are done. Do not continue on to step 11.

11. Squirt the object with the alcohol solution and sprinkle with pumice powder.

12. Scrub the surface with the stiff brush to loosen the corrosion and clean the surface.

13. Rinse with alcohol until all loosened particulate matter is washed off.

14. Allow to air dry.

15. Properly dispose of the dirty cleaning solutions.

Coating

Do not coat cooking utensils. Coat only decorative pieces. If you are going to use your cast iron pots and pans to cook with, go to the section below on seasoning.

Supplementing the cleaning process with a protective coating is a standard protocol when preserving iron-based artifacts that will not be used in food preparation. You should work in a well-ventilated space, and you will need the following supplies:

Solid paraffin wax (or paste wax)
Pyrex double boiler saucepan
Hot plate
Disposable cotton gloves
Paintbrush
Hot air gun or hair dryer
Nylon hosiery
Clean soft flannel cloth

1. Gently warm the object by placing it in the sun (or in an oven at low temperature) to a temperature slightly higher than the melting point of the wax (between 120 and 150 degrees Fahrenheit).

2. Place the wax (if solid paraffin) in the Pyrex double boiler on the hot plate, warming it to the melting point.

3. Put on the gloves to protect the object and keep your hands from getting coated with molten wax.

4. Using the paintbrush, spread the molten wax on the surface of the object, making sure it is fully saturated.

5. Take the hot air gun (set on low) or a hair dryer (set on high) in one hand and a wad of nylon hose in the other and wipe off the excess molten wax with the nylon while warming the surface with the hot air gun.

6. Continue to wipe off the excess wax, folding and refolding the nylon to make sure the surface is being wiped with a clean portion, until no more wax is being removed. The wax forms a protective barrier around the iron, guarding it from pollutants and contaminants.

7. Let the object cool to room temperature.

8. Buff with the cotton flannel.

DON'S TIP: Adding Pigmented Shoe Wax When Coating Iron and Steel

Coating iron and steel objects can be done with either molten block paraffin, or a good-quality paste wax, including pigmented shoe wax. Shoe wax is especially helpful if you are trying to impart some color to the surface. The best approach is to complete the paraffin treatment and then apply the pigmented shoe wax. In that way you get the benefit of full saturation of the surface by the molten wax as well as the visual enhancement by the pigmented wax.

Seasoning Cast Iron Cookware

Some of you may not hold preserving of iron pots in the highest regard. You might actually want to use them for food preparation. To make sure you do as little damage as possible until you decide to preserve your cookware, you must "season" it. Seasoning cast iron cookware creates a nonstick surface. You will need the following supplies:

Vegetable shortening (such as Crisco)
Oven
Aluminum foil

1. Apply a thin coat of shortening and use your fingers to rub the entire surface of the pan, including the handles and back.
2. Line the lower rack of the oven with foil.
3. Place the pan upside down in the oven and then turn on the oven. Set the temperature to 350 degrees to warm the pan slowly.
4. After the oven reaches 350 degrees, set the timer for one hour.
5. When an hour has passed, turn off the temperature and allow the pan to cool inside the oven.
6. Season again only if the pan gets a major scrubbing.

Don's Rules for Caring for Cast Iron Pots and Pans That Are Used for Cooking

1. Never wash the pan with soap! Clean your pot or pan while it is still warm, wiping it out with paper towels. This leaves only the oil behind, and the oil is what maintains the nonstick surface. Do not worry about sanitation because when you heat your pan, that heat will kill off bacteria.
2. To remove residue, use hot water and a non-soapy scouring pad or steel wool. Dry immediately and then apply a little cooking oil to the inside.
3. Never let it soak.
4. Never leave it wet.
5. Never boil water in it.
6. Never put it in the dishwasher.
7. Never store food in it. Food contains moisture, and moisture contributes to rust.
8. Hide your pan from children and babysitters.

9. When cooking, always preheat the pan slowly.

10. Use plenty of butter or oil when cooking.

11. Store in a cool, dry place with a paper plate or towel between each pan. Cast iron needs circulation.

Preserving Enamelware

Clean with soap and water and treat as you would china.

For enameled ironware or steel, there is only one preservation rule: Don't drop or clang against anything hard. As long as you do not fracture or chip the enameled surface, these things are practically indestructible.

BASKETS AND GOURDS

Baskets are woven from a nearly endless variety of mostly plant-based fibers. Grass, straw, bamboo, twigs, roots, rush, split wood, and bark have all been used. In the wrong conditions these materials can degrade in a matter of weeks, months, or years.

Gourds are raw vegetables that have been dried.

Preserving

1. Handle baskets about the same way you would handle sculpture: Cradle from the bottom and do not grab by appendages such as handles or loops.

2. Since the surfaces of baskets can be rough, do not handle with cotton gloves but instead use clean bare hands or vinyl or nitrile gloves.

3. Never stack baskets because this will cause distortions or breaks. Instead, display and store upright, sitting on their base.

4. For delicate baskets loosely stuff the inside with wadded acid-free tissue paper to make sure the shape is retained and the basket does not collapse.

5. Store and display in a clean, stable, dark environment of moderate temperature and humidity (about 70 degrees and 50 percent relative humidity). The exact numbers are less important than the stability and cleanliness.

6. If you do not have a clean dedicated space for baskets, keep them either in a closed container, such as a high-quality plastic tub, wrapped in a clean polyethylene bag, or in a glass-front cabinet.

Cleaning

One of the real trials of collecting and preserving baskets and gourds is that the surface texture is usually extremely irregular and absorbent, making cleaning them a real test of patience. Always be very careful when handling baskets. They can sometimes be deceptively robust-looking, holding their shape very well but having none of their earlier strength and flexibility. Old baskets tend to be brittle and inflexible, and it is easy to damage them by careless handling.

You will need the following supplies:

Soft artist's brush
Vacuum
Distilled water
Cotton swabs or litho pads
Triton 100 detergent (if necessary)

1. Use the artist's brush to gently brush the surface in the direction of the vacuum nozzle. Be especially careful around any areas of frayed or broken fibers.

2. If this is not sufficient, most baskets and gourds can be cleaned by swabbing the surfaces with distilled water.

3. If distilled water alone is not sufficient, use swabs or litho pads moistened in distilled water and 1 percent Triton 100 detergent. First test-clean an obscure area to be sure you are doing nothing destructive or removing something you do not want to remove. For many types of artifacts, especially utilitarian ones, the dirt or debris is the point of the artifact.

4. Rinse the surface by swabbing with distilled water alone to remove any detergent residue.

5. Be sure to keep your basket or gourd in a space where it will not get dusty.

VINTAGE PLASTIC AND RUBBER STUFF

Old costume jewelry, vintage radios, and even some art deco furniture are made of early synthetic plastics. Plastics are everywhere, from punch lines in famous movies to checkout lines in every store in the modern world. Because they are ubiquitous and because as a rule most people don't know exactly what plastic is or how it is made, they do not understand fully what makes plastic degrade. My task is not to explain that to you here (did I hear a sigh of relief?) but to help you figure out what your plastic is and how to keep it around if that's what you want. Degradation of plastics is always under way, unstoppable, and permanent.

Cleaning and Handling

1. Handle carefully with clean cotton or nitrile gloves.
2. Don't clean plastics with solvents or other cleaners unless their long-term effect on that particular plastic is known.
3. If the plastic needs cleaning, use distilled water on a soft sponge.
4. Inspect regularly for any signs of deterioration such as discoloring, warping, fading, cracking, or crumbling.

Displaying

1. Display plastics in the lowest light possible.
2. Display in cool, dry, clean, ventilated spaces.
3. Be sure to provide support for soft or flexible objects such as aged Tupperware or other polyethylene artifacts in order to retain their shape.

Storing

1. Store plastics in the dark. Most plastics are sensitive to light, and some are extremely sensitive to ultraviolet light.
2. Store in cool, dry, clean, ventilated spaces.
3. Isolate degraded and degrading objects from the remainder of your collection.
4. Be sure to provide support for soft or flexible objects to maintain their shape.
5. Wrap objects in acid-free tissue paper. Do not use newspaper because the ink is likely to transfer to the object.
6. Store objects either on open shelving or in archival cardboard boxes with ventilation holes covered by inert fabric. Or store in a sealed environment with both oxygen and chemical scavengers (Ageless and activated

DON'S TIP: Plastic Costume Jewelry

Plastic jewelry has been made from dozens or even hundreds of different plastics. The main concerns in caring for and using vintage plastic jewelry are that they tend to become increasingly susceptible to scratching with age and might be sensitive to organic solvents, water, and detergents.

charcoal) to reduce oxidation reactions and to remove from the atmosphere any contaminants emanating from the object due to degradation.

7. Inspect regularly for signs of deterioration.

The world of plastics is a complicated one populated by thousands of materials, each with its own idiosyncrasies. For a detailed review of them please refer to the *Saving Stuff* Tool Kit list at the back of the book. From a preservation perspective, there is little I can recommend that you do to your plastics other than cleaning and careful handling, and putting your energies into controlling the environment around them. The rules listed above are generally applicable for preserving all plastics regardless of what they are.

TOOLS

Both woodworking and gardening tools can be made from a variety of materials, especially wood and steel. Wood is primarily used for handles, while steel is the material of choice for the business end of most tools. Brass, ivory, and leather are often employed for bindings and decoration. Since these materials have different preservation needs, it is often difficult to design a perfect preservation response. The best we can do is figure out what compromises work best for these composite objects. Specific information about wood is found in Chapter 8, while more information about metals can be found in Chapters 6, 8, and 13.

Cleaning Wood Tools and Tool Parts

Most old tools that have not been used for a while will be covered with dust at the very least and perhaps other environmental contaminants as well. Actually, that is true for tools even in everyday use if my basement studio is any example. To clean these tools you will need the following supplies:

1-inch artist's brush
Vacuum

Clean lint-free cloth or soft paper towels (litho pads are my
favorite)
Distilled water
Nitrile or similar protective gloves
Mineral spirits
Paste wax

1. Brush off the loose dust with a soft artist's brush into the brush nozzle of a vacuum.

2. If the wood elements are varnished or painted, and the tougher dirt and grime are still in place after the brushing, clean by wiping with the lint-free cloth dampened with distilled water. For stubborn oily dirt or waxy residue, put on protective gloves and dampen a lint-free cloth with mineral spirits.

3. Once the cleaning is complete, apply a few coats of paste wax as described in the cleaning and waxing sections of "Wood Furniture" in Chapter 8, Preserving Your Furniture. Linseed oil mixed with turpentine is one

DON'S ADVICE:
Be Careful When Cleaning Any Old Tools

Many times the presence of an original surface elevates an antique tool from the designation of "family trash" to the "you can put your kids through school" category. Despite my several cubic yards of tools I am not a "tool collector" even though I go to antique tool auctions occasionally—okay, frequently, but I am still not a collector. You should go, too, just for the cultural experience. I once sat behind a guy who looked like he mistakenly wandered in from the rehab house down the street. In a little over two hours he dropped almost $200,000 on a handful of tools. I asked him, "Why were these tools so valuable?" "Original surfaces," he growled. In other words, though used heavily, the tools retained the original character their maker intended. Not only were these raggedy old tools rare and in some cases unique, but they were "untouched." In other words, they had never been repaired or otherwise modified.

Sometimes an old tool is just an old tool, but other times it might be worth an incomprehensible amount to somebody. Characteristics such as blue or brown coloration on steel blades as part of the forging and original painted "japanning" on the body of metal planes can make the difference between a $250 tool and a $25,000 tool.

traditional concoction for keeping the wooden parts of planes, chisels, and
screwdrivers in good condition. I do not recommend it because it does not
protect against moisture. (Research indicates it actually makes wooden objects even more susceptible to water vapor.)

Cleaning Metal Tools and Tool Parts

The care and preservation of cast iron and steel are addressed earlier in this
chapter and in "Cleaning Metal Hardware" in Chapter 8, Preserving Your
Furniture. Follow the instructions there for caring for metal tool parts in the
same manner. Be sure to read the sidebar above about cleaning wooden
tools and tool parts. The same principle applies to metal tools as well.

Storing Antique Metal and Wooden Tools

The preservation needs of collectible tools are usually simple: Keep dry
(metal), keep stable (wood), and keep your hands off (all). The sharp edges
of tools should be wrapped with polypropylene foam. Lay the tools neatly
and avoid piling them in a toolbox or other closed space. Try to prevent their
rolling or bumping each other when drawers are opened and closed. A layer
of soft, stable foam plastic or a gripper mat made specifically for toolboxes
should be placed under the tools.

For complex tools made from several pieces, it is often necessary to disassemble the tool to clean it properly. This is especially true when you are cleaning a tool with components made from different materials, such as a wood-handled plane with an iron body. They need different cleaning procedures (especially if the iron is rusty) that could be harmful to each other.

Be careful when you are disassembling. Don't force anything (fine machine oil or penetrating oil is a constant friend here) and be sure you are using the right tool. Do you have the wrench that fits the nut? Does the screwdriver match the slot *exactly*? If not, stop until you have the right tool or you will risk inflicting permanent damage. Make sure the tool comes apart without too much force. Always remember that big steel screwdrivers are stronger than little brass screws. Trust me on this.

If you have a set of tools that came in a pouch or other dedicated container, store them together unless there is a good reason not to. These pouches and containers usually provide excellent protection for the tools, and there is great historical (and collectible) benefit in keeping sets of anything together.

ANTIQUE SIGNS

Antique signs are amazing records of our past and powerful prompts to memories. Many of us remember eagerly awaiting the next Burma-Shave signs as we were crammed in the back of the station wagon on our family trips. Signs can also be beautiful works of art: Painted and gilded signs are technically identical to panel paintings, and neon signs are both sculpture and design.

Preserving painted and gilded wooden signs: These can best be preserved by following the rules and instructions for wood furniture found in Chapter 8, Preserving Your Furniture.

Preserving painted metal, enameled signs, and license plates: Painted metal signs are at risk primarily from corrosion and poor handling. Enameled (porcelain) metal signs are even more durable as long as they are not dropped or banged and are kept dry and clean. If you have a painted sign and the paint is intact, use mild liquid dishwashing soap and water to clean it. If the paint is not intact, wipe gently with a cloth dampened with distilled water.

Preserving neon signs: Neon signs are specialized electrical devices. Preservation of them involves following the rules and instructions for electrical devices listed previously in this chapter and keeping the tubes sealed and full of neon. This second item is best left to someone who actually knows how to make and maintain neon signs. One of the first clues that the neon has leaked is that the sign no longer works. As a general rule the leaks are microscopic and not visible.

BIOLOGICAL COLLECTIONS

In addition to collecting decorative or even functional manufactured items, many of you may collect bugs, snakes, flowers, or similar (or dissimilar) biological materials. One thing to consider when evaluating so-called natural history collections is to identify the kingdom that the sample comes from, plant or animal, because that has direct impact on what you do about it.

The second thing to consider is why you are collecting the stuff because it influences your choice of preservation strategies. There are many valid reasons: for later eating or planting; for cataloging your love of butterflies, flowers, or frogs; for creating the basis for scholarly work in the future; or for commemorating the gigantic trout you caught or the black bear you shot in the backyard.

Botanical Specimens

Preserving plant materials is pretty much dependent on two main things: getting the moisture out and protecting them from bugs. Here is how it's done in museums and universities.

Seeds

You will need the following supplies:

DON'S TIP:
It's Still Food

Just because you have prepared your collection of specimens properly does not mean they are in the clear preservation-wise. Since plants and dead animals are prime food for insects, rodents, and fungi, keeping your specimens protected from the ravages of pests has to be preservation priority number one!

Paper envelopes or cloth pouches

Dried silica gel

Desiccation (drying) chamber—a glass or PET jar with a lid or
    similar sealable container

Sealed container for the preserved seeds (polyethylene zippered
    bags are fine)

1. Place the seeds in a paper envelope or cloth pouch.

2. Put about 1 inch of dried silica gel in the bottom of the desiccating chamber.

3. Place the seed packet on top of the silica gel.

4. Add additional silica gel to cover the seed packet.

5. Seal the desiccating chamber and leave it for a week. Longer is fine.

6. Open the desiccating chamber and remove the seed packet.

7. Transfer the seeds to a clean enclosed container for long-term storage (double polyethylene zippered bags work fine) to protect them from pests.

8. Be sure to include in the sealed container a penciled note with information about the seeds.

9. Store the seeds in a cool, dark place.

Note: Dried seeds cannot be cleaned or displayed in any practical way. If you need to, brush off the dust, but once they are enclosed, dust is not a problem. If you must display them, take them out only on occasion, for any light will damage them fairly quickly. Plus, if you are interested in preserving the seeds for eating later or in having heritage seeds for planting at some future date, this method of preserving seeds is not for you. For advice and instruction on this type of preservation, check with your local extension agent from the state or county agriculture department.

Stems and Leaves

You will need the following supplies:

Acid-free blotter paper larger than the specimen

Heavy board larger than the blotter paper (large polyethylene
    cutting board works fine)

Weights as necessary

Dried silica gel

Needle and thread

Acid-free scrapbook or acid-free mounting board (usually archival foam core boards)

Pencil

Sealed container large enough for the scrapbook or mounting board

1. Place the blotter paper on a clean, flat surface.

2. Gently place the specimen on the blotter paper. Be sure to get the shape you want because after the specimen has been dried, it is very stiff and can be broken if bent trying to change the shape.

3. Gently place another sheet of blotter paper over the specimen.

4. Place the board over the blotter paper to serve as a press for drying the specimen flat.

5. Place weights on top if necessary.

6. Leave for a week in a sealed container with silica gel. Longer is fine.

7. It is okay to check the specimen to make sure it is progressing toward dry. You will know it is ready when it is stiff and dry.

8. Using the thread and needle, lash the specimen to the page of the scrapbook or the archival mounting board.

9. Use a pencil to write any important information about the specimen on the page or board next to the specimen.

10. Place the scrapbook or mounting board in a sealed container to protect the specimen from pests.

11. Store the specimen case in a cool, dark area.

Cleaning stems and leaves: The best you can do is gently blow the dust off them on a regular basis using a photographer's compressed air can. *Do not moisten.*

Displaying stems and leaves: Do not place in direct sunlight or other high ultraviolet exposure such as fluorescent light, and do not place in places with high humidity such as bathrooms. To keep them dust free place under glass or in a glass case.

Dried Flowers

You will need the following supplies:

Dried silica gel
Desiccation (drying) chamber—a glass or PET jar with a lid or
    similar sealable container
Sealed container for the preserved flower

1. Put 1 inch of dried silica gel in the bottom of the desiccating chamber.
2. Gently place or hold the flower so it barely touches the silica gel.
3. Gently pour in additional dried silica gel until the flower is completely covered. Be sure not to crush the petals.
4. Seal the chamber and leave it for a week. Longer is fine.
5. Open the chamber and gently pour out the silica gel into the container it came from. Remember, the dried flower is very stiff and fragile, so take care not to damage it.
6. Remove the dried flower from the jar and place it in a clean sealed container to protect it from pests.
7. Store the specimen and its new container in a cool, dark place. Be sure to label the specimen with any important information about it.

Cleaning dried flowers: The best you can do to clean dried flowers is to gently blow off the dust on a regular basis using a photographer's compressed air can.

DON'S TIP:
Reconditioning and Reusing Silica Gel

Dry silica gel is a critical element of the preservation of biological specimens because it serves to draw moisture out of the specimen and render it more resistant to decay. Since silica gel is somewhat expensive, you are probably going to want to reuse it as many times as you can, which in practical terms is forever. One simple way to get the moisture out of your used silica gel is to place it in a Crock-Pot set on high with a wooden board over the top. I have found that here in the mid-Atlantic region, after a week or so the gel is dried to the point where once it cools down, it is at about 5 percent relative humidity. It's not truly desiccated (0 percent relative humidity), but it is certainly low enough for my needs. If you live in the far north and do this in the dead of winter, you should be able to reach a moisture content of 3 to 5 percent relative humidity. Have a separate Crock-Pot for use in chemical preparation. Don't use the same one for your pot roast.

Displaying dried flowers: Dried flowers are delicate and brittle, and will likely crack and break if you try to handle or arrange them too vigorously. Before arranging dry flowers, mist them lightly with water from a spray bottle and place in a plastic bag for a few minutes until they are malleable and soft. *Do not soak them.* They will stiffen again as the moisture evaporates. Do not place in direct sunlight or other high ultraviolet exposure such as fluorescent light, and do not place in damp places with high humidity such as bathrooms. To keep them dust free place under glass or in a glass case.

Animal Specimens

To a certain extent the procedures for preserving animal specimens are similar to the ones for botanical specimens in principle. Protection from pests and prevention of water-driven decay are the main items on the list.

Insects

You will need the following supplies:

> Paper envelopes or cloth pouches
> Dried silica gel
> Desiccation (drying) chamber
> Stainless steel mounting pins
> Archival mounting board—usually acid-free foam core or
>   polyethylene foam sheet
> Pencil
> Sealed container large enough for the mounting board

1. Place the insect in a paper envelope or cloth pouch.
2. Put about 1 inch of dried silica gel in the bottom of the desiccating chamber.
3. Place the insect on top of the silica gel.
4. Add additional silica gel to cover the insect. Silica gel is like coarse sugar crystals and can be gently poured over the specimen. For winged insects do not submerge in silica gel because the wings are extremely fragile. Simply place the insect on top of the silica gel.
5. Seal the desiccating chamber and leave for a week. Longer is fine.
6. Once the insect body is fully dried, mount it on the archival mounting

board by pressing a stainless steel mounting pin through the torso of the body.

7. Use a pencil to write any important information about the specimen on the mounting board.

8. Place the mounting board in a sealed storage container to protect it from pests. Smithsonian collections are in containers akin to shadow boxes (see Chapter 5).

9. Store in a cool, dark place.

Cleaning dried insects: Follow the same instructions as given for dried flowers above.

Displaying dried insects: Follow the instructions as given for stems and leaves above. You can also display them in the archival plastic boxes described in "Time Capsule" in Chapter 5, Saving the Stuff Only a Parent Could Love.

Reptiles and Fish

When preserving marine specimens we are entering a whole new realm called wet storage. Historically, museums have put their snakes, fish, and lizards in a sealed jar of either formaldehyde or ethanol (grain alcohol). Recent research just down the hall from my lab at the Smithsonian suggests that ethanol is the preferred preservative for a number of reasons, not the least of which is that formaldehyde is really, really nasty stuff. It's very poisonous, will cross-link proteins, and with enough exposure it is a suspected carcinogen. Another option is freeze-drying, which is better from a scientific research point of view but is expensive and can distort or shrivel the specimen.

For most of your special specimens of snakes, frog, lizards, and fish, simply put them in a jar of grain alcohol and seal the lid tight. If you keep the jars in the dark, I'm thinking you could get a century out of this arrangement.

Cleaning preserved reptiles and fish: If your specimens are either freeze-dried or taxidermied, simply dust them with an artist's brush. If they are in a pickle jar, they will not need cleaning.

Displaying preserved reptiles and fish: For displaying specimens in a bottle of preservative, you simply have to keep the light levels as low as possible (dark is preferable when not being viewed) and safe from the danger of breaking the jar. For specimens that have undergone taxidermy, the dangers of display come primarily from light and infestation. Keep the light levels as low as possible (dark is best when not being viewed) and in a glass or plastic enclosure to protect them from wandering scavengers such as insects and rodents.

A Note on Taxidermy

Taxidermy is often considered one way to preserve animal specimens, but that's not really true. What taxidermy does is create a slipcover in the shape of the animal from the skin, which is fitted around a sculpted or stuffed core; it preserves the *shape* of the animal. Instead of getting the whole animal, all you are really getting are the external elements: skin or fur (highly modified with "tanning" chemicals to make them resistant to decay), horns and hooves, feathers, and glass eyes instead of the real ones. In the case of reptiles and fish you often aren't even getting that much. What you get instead is a painted resin casting made from a rubber mold of the original carcass.

Chapter 8

Preserving Your Furniture

Tables, chairs, beds, chests—furniture often serves as a testimonial to what we consider most important in our lives. Some houses are filled with pieces that no one can or should sit on. In other homes, comfort is the overriding factor in furniture selection. My home is a combination of antiques inherited from loved ones, recently purchased yard sale items, and stuff I made myself.

How can you take care of your furniture and still use it?

Preserving furniture while still enjoying it is a balancing act worthy of a circus tightrope performer. Paradise for furniture consists of dark, chilly, oxygen-free rooms. You can see how this setup plays havoc with the idea of home as a haven. Even the Smithsonian, where the most ardent furniture lovers congregate, provides air and some light for its visitors, though Smithsonian museums do remain a bit chilly. And another fundamental question arises with furniture: When preserving it, do you preserve as is or do you first remove all the dings and scratches?

Flash forward to the year 2045. As the committee from the Donald Williams Presidential Library rummages through my widow's cabin, they come across our old dining set. All the pieces seem to be in good condition except for one chair—mine—which looks as if it has taken a direct hit of buckshot on the back splat. When one of the committee members asks

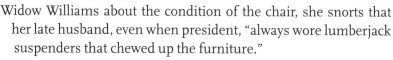

Widow Williams about the condition of the chair, she snorts that her late husband, even when president, "always wore lumberjack suspenders that chewed up the furniture."

On their drive back to the airport, the committee debates about displaying the chair. Should they first remove those horrific scratches or should they retain them as a reflection of the Great Man's ambivalence to fashion, not to mention his need for suspenders given his "mature" physique? My hope is that they leave my chair just the way it is because those marks and scratches are what makes it my chair.

The Smithsonian often preserves stuff "as is" because wear and tear often speak to the history of a piece. Still, this is a very personal question that only the owner of a piece can answer.

THINK "BALANCE"

The furniture decorating our homes is often historical as well as functional, which is a serious issue when considering how to best preserve this stuff. You would never think of writing a shopping list on top of a Picasso lithograph, but you wouldn't hesitate to pen that same list while resting your paper on a Chippendale table without a writing pad underneath. (I, though, cringe at the thought.) The answer, while not perfect, is think "Balance."

Don's Ten Truths for Wise Furniture Use

1. Plant your keister where it belongs: on the seat of the chair.
2. Don't stand on the chair or the sofa or the table or the piano.
3. Keep chair legs planted firmly on the ground.
4. Use coasters, writing pads, or protective covers to protect your furniture from scratches.
5. Don't eat on the sofa and don't store food in your collectible sideboard because crumbs invite bugs.
6. Watch out when it comes to candles, lanterns, fireplaces, and tobacco because wood and upholstered furniture make good kindling.
7. Treat light as the enemy. Draw the curtains or shades whenever you can and put ultraviolet filters on the windows.
8. Avoid extreme temperature and humidity changes.

9. Keep pets off the furniture.

10. Never, ever oil wood furniture.

THE CRITTERS THAT EAT YOUR COLLECTION

Insects, rodents, and fungi can destroy a collection of valued furniture in a short time. Most insects do not nibble on furniture as much as eat through it, creating tunnels in which they can live. Given enough time they can remove up to 90 percent of the mass of wood, leaving an outer shell and just enough internal "ribs" to keep it upright—well, upright for a while.

Rodents usually do not eat the wood for its own sake but instead gnaw through it to get to the food on the other side. The best way to deal with this is not to store any foodstuffs, including condiments, in your furniture. Since food also attracts insects, it is a good idea to keep food as far from your collectible furniture as possible.

Fungal damage, or rot, occurs in areas of extreme dampness at moderate temperatures. Unless your furniture gets wet and stays wet, this is not usually a severe problem. Mildew, the whitish fungi on the surface, is normally a housekeeping problem. Mold, which can be either light or dark, can etch finishes and stain the underlying wood. If the problem is severe enough, however, fungi can literally eat away and digest your furniture collection.

DON'S TIP:
Don't Crush the Pack Mule

Furniture was designed to carry a particular load. Don't exceed it. Allowing your newly grown six-foot-tall teenager to use his old childhood rocking chair invites disaster. And even if there is enough space, resist the temptation to fill the shelves of your antique cabinet with books.

DON'S TIP:
Monitor Your Collection Regularly

Piles of insect excrement and wood dust, called frass, under or on your object indicates an active infestation. Immediately quarantine the object, and if the infestation is confirmed, fumigate. Consult with a licensed fumigator and have him deal with it professionally. Fumigators have the ability and licenses to deal with the toxic materials necessary for pest eradication. Also increase the monitoring of all objects near the affected furniture because the likelihood of their being infested has now greatly increased.

WOOD FURNITURE

Listen very carefully: This section goes against almost everything you have ever read or been told about taking care of your wood furniture. *Do not polish with oil.* No debate. No "other people have differing opinions." No negotiation. Trust me. I deal with our nation's treasures, and furniture is my first, second, and third love—after my wife and kids, of course. The proper care is simple: clean and wax. Yes, no matter what your grandmother said, wax is the proper method of care.

This issue comes up every time I give a public lecture, and at least once a week I receive a phone call, letter, or e-mail similar to the following:

Dear Don Williams;

I need a general polish that will clean and protect wood furniture. What product is on the market that is a general cleaner and conditioner, that is not a paste wax, and that is easy for the consumer to use?

I would like the product to have the following benefits:

- It's easy to use—wipe on, wipe off.
- It cleans, polishes, and preserves.
- It removes mildew, water marks, and wax buildup.
- It reveals renewed depth and beauty.
- It is compatible with antique as well as new modern finishes.

- It produces instant rejuvenation or a polished look.
- It has some ultraviolet blockers.

Sincerely,
A Secret Admirer
(I may be making up this closing salutation.)

For most furniture owners an almost pathological need exists to *do something* to make the furniture, as we say in the trade, "brown and shiny." And, indeed, the regimen of waxing and cleaning furniture is an important part of the task of preserving it. Unfortunately, virtually all commercially available furniture care products other than good-quality paste waxes can be harmful to your collection. So, after careful cleaning, good paste wax is all you should ever put on your furniture.

Cleaning

This cleaning process is needed only when your furniture gets really dirty rather than just dusty. Under "normal" conditions your furniture will need

SMITHSONIAN STORIES:
A Well-Trained Eye Is Priceless

My favorite Smithsonian legend, mostly because I wish it had happened to me, involves a yard sale purchase. As the story goes, in the fall of 1968 one of the curators from the National Museum of American History was out for a weekend of antiquing in the nearby Shenandoah Valley. I can only imagine his thoughts and emotions as he spotted a red-painted chair, knowing instantly by the design that underneath the red paint was perhaps one of the rarest American antiques: a fancy gilt and paint chair by the innovative Boston maker Samuel Gragg. Its timeless beauty and Gragg's mastery of woodworking marks this chair as a truly important piece of Americana. Evidently, the Smithsonian Institution curator was the only one who recognized this treasure hidden beneath the red paint because the record indicates he bought it for less than $100 even though its value was much greater then and is today perhaps a thousand times higher. This story by itself keeps me stopping at yard sales to this very day.

a thorough cleaning perhaps only once a decade or so. The cleaning described here is for removing waxy, grimy buildup. Otherwise, simply dust your cleaned and waxed furniture with a soft, clean, lint-free cloth. Furniture made earlier than 1800 often had wax as its original coating, and cleaning as described here will remove that original finish—not a good idea. If you have some really old furniture and are uncertain about its finish, consult with a furniture conservator. Not all furniture conservators are members of the Wooden Artifacts Group of the American Institute for Conservation (*http://aic.stanford.edu*). I am not, for example, but it is a pretty good place to start looking.

You will need the following supplies:

Cleaning solution: mineral spirits* (very flammable) or distilled
    water with mild liquid dish soap

* CAUTION: Mineral spirits is also sometimes called paint thinner, *not* lacquer thinner. *Do not substitute a stronger cleaner* unless you want to strip off the aged varnish so prized on *Antiques Roadshow*.

Clean lint-free cleaning cloths or litho pads
Cotton swabs for those hard-to-reach places

1. Evaluate the surface and be sure it and the coating are stable and not apt to be damaged by the cleaning tools or solutions. In other words, is the finish intact and sound, or is it chipped, cracked, or even flaking off? If the former is true, proceed cautiously. If it's the latter, you need to consult a furniture conservator.

2. Find out what removes the dirt without affecting the surface underneath it. Dust can often be removed with the careful wipe of a damp cloth. Oily dirt or waxy residue can be removed with a solution of mild dish detergent and distilled water or with mineral spirits. However, make sure that the cleaning solution *does not* affect the underlying surface. Test a small, hidden area first before proceeding. If the cleaning solution does no damage, then proceed cautiously.

3. Dampen the cleaning cloth with the cleaning solution you have chosen and gently wipe the surface of the furniture until all the dirt is off. This often takes many wipes. Be sure to change the cloth to a clean spot every time you dampen and wipe. Otherwise, you may just be moving the dirt and grime around.

4. When the cloth comes away clean, you are ready to wax.

Waxing

Once you have cleaned off the waxy buildup or grime, you are ready to wax with a good-quality paste wax. Once you have waxed furniture the hard wax surface can be dusted more easily because it is smoother, and dust does not

DON'S TIP:
Penny Foolish and Pound Wise

When I clean furniture, my favorite wiping cloth is a small pad of lint-free cotton known as a lithographer's pad. You can find them at most paper and janitorial supply houses. The perfect size for cleaning, these pads are also fairly inexpensive, so I am not tempted to overuse them. I swipe off the dirt and throw the pad away.

embed in a smooth surface as easily. Waxing can occur infrequently (maybe once a year) because wax itself is not readily removed and does not degrade chemically. Waxing too frequently results in a clouded, built-up surface, so be sparing in your application.

You will need the following supplies:

Latex, nitrile, polyethylene, or vinyl protective gloves
Clean lint-free application rag, preferably worn flannel or T-shirt fabric
Good-quality paste wax (contains no silicones or exotic organic solvents such as toluene or xylene, which can act like varnish removers. Mineral spirits, also known as petroleum benzine, and hexane are fine.
Clean lint-free buffing cloth, preferably worn flannel or T-shirt fabric

1. Be sure the surface you are waxing is sound (not flaking) and clean. If it is flaking, you need to consult a professional before proceeding. Any force exerted on a table that is flaking will add to the damage that is already present.

2. Work in a well-ventilated space and put on your protective gloves.

3. Saturate the application rag with the paste wax, but do not use so much that there are clumps of wax on the rag.

4. Fold the application rag into a tight square or a tight wad so that there are no "loose ends" to snag on anything on the surface.

5. Gently rub the application rag on the surface until there is a very thin coating of the semi-solid paste wax over the entire surface.

DON'S TIP:
Silk Purse or Sow's Ear?

Waxing the furniture will not change the underlying character of the surface or finish. If the surface is craggy or rough and the coating is hazy, crazed, or just plain dull, waxing it, no matter how skillfully or conscientiously, will not turn it into a hand-rubbed piano finish.

6. Allow the wax to dry completely. Depending on the formulation, this could take from a few minutes to overnight.

7. When the wax is fully dry, vigorously rub the surface with the buffing cloth until it is uniformly shiny. If you prefer a higher sheen, repeat steps 5 to 7 to try to bring it up more.

WICKER, RATTAN, BAMBOO, RUSH, AND CANE FURNITURE

Since these materials are most like basketry, furniture made from them should be cared for just as you would baskets. Consult "Baskets and Gourds" in Chapter 7, Sorting and Preserving the Family Trash. The only thing I would add to that information is the reminder that furniture is to be sat in, not stood on. I say this because I have lost count of the rush and cane seat chairs I have seen with big foot holes in them.

COMPOSITE FURNITURE

Composite furniture is made from just about any engineered material, but the two major materials to consider are plastic laminates and manufactured wood fiber sheets.

Plastic laminates (such as Formica) are commonly on countertops. Essentially they are a stack of paper sheets impregnated with synthetic resins and a top layer of decorative plastic as the presentation surface. The main threats to plastic laminates are abrasion and heat. If you use nonabrasive cleaners to avoid scratching their surface and use hot pads or trivets to protect the laminates from scorching (and usually destroying the adhesive holding it down), your laminates will outlast you by centuries.

Wood fiber composites are called particleboard and fiberboard. While it is not true in every instance, manufactured wood boards tend to be less strong and more moisture sensitive than solid wood of the same dimension. If you have furniture made from manufactured boards, you have to be especially careful not to overload them with too much weight and make sure they do not get soaked with water. Too much weight will cause permanent warping, and too much water will swell the fibers, causing the material to expand and lose all dimensional or structural integrity. In other words, it will no longer look as it should and probably will not even stay together.

SMITHSONIAN STORIES:
Saving the Nightmare

Mixing wood and other materials to make furniture often results in trouble. Take, for example, a turn-of-the-century cabinet by Carlo Bugatti. Hand-painted ink drawings covered the sides and shelves, along with sheets of scarlet patinated copper punch work. The doors had panels of stained glass cased in wooden frames covered with pewter, brass, ebony, and ivory inlays, as did the cornice. The legs were wrapped in more red-patinated copper punch work. Gigantic hand-tied cream-colored silk tassels adorned the cabinet throughout. Bugatti created what I referred to as a preservation nightmare. Bugatti's designs are so bizarre that if you had a group of them in your bedroom and saw them on a moonlit night, you would swear you were having a nightmare.

Given how well wood, ivory, brass, pewter, ebony, and stained glass work together, is it any wonder we were yanking out our hair by the handful? Each one reacts to the environment differently and needs to be cared for in a different way. The most important part of this preservation process was to stabilize the environment around the piece as much as possible. The Smithsonian's Cooper-Hewitt Museum completely re-did its heating, ventilation, and air-conditioning system in order to guarantee stable temperature and humidity, and it exhibits this piece in very low light. Thanks to the hard work of a wide variety of specialists, the former glory of this fantastic cabinet has in large part been reclaimed, and it awaits your inspection at the Smithsonian's national museum of design in New York, the Cooper-Hewitt Museum.

CLEANING METAL HARDWARE

Brass

The knobs, bales, escutcheons, handles, and back plates all serve to make furniture more functional and beautiful. Keeping them clean is critical to their preservation. Fortunately, just one way exists to clean brass hardware safely, and that way is fairly simple. Brass hardware tarnishes with use and exposure to oxygen. However, sometimes even the simple task of cleaning can destroy the surface because of the commercial cleaner used. If you see green copper corrosion or the loss of detail, the odds are pretty good that you are seeing the result of such cleaning. To the rescue is Don's Polishing Slurry.

You will need the following supplies:

Paint-stripping gloves
Organic solvent filtering respirator (mask)
Soft bristle brush such as a toothbrush or an artist's oil painting
    brush
Three lint-free cloths (flannel or similar fabric)
Overhead projector film or Mylar (for use with nonremovable
    hardware) (see Don's Tip, page 130)
Spray gloss acrylic or cellulose nitrate lacquer (such as Krylon or a
    similar product)

Don's Cleaning Solution:

- One cup of acetone
- One cup of alcohol
- Shallow glass pan (large enough to hold one piece of the hardware)

Don's Polishing Slurry:

- One teaspoon of fine polishing abrasive (jeweler's tripoli, pulverized limestone from the garden supply or hardware store, ultrafine auto polishing compound, or even cigarette ashes)
- One tablespoon of alcohol or mineral spirits
- Small bowl

1. Put on the gloves. This will not only protect the hardware from the oils and acids on your skin but will also protect your skin from the solution, which is a mixture of organic solvents.

2. Carefully remove the hardware from the object. If you use tools such as pliers or screwdrivers, wrap Teflon tape around the tips to protect the hardware from being scratched.

3. Put on the mask.

4. Prepare the cleaning solution. Mix the acetone and alcohol together and pour the mixture into the glass pan.

5. Place the hardware in the cleaning solution.

6. With a soft brush, scrub the surfaces to remove any dirt and residue. Be sure to clean the back side of the hardware. You won't be polishing the

back side (after all no one sees it), but it does need to be cleaned. The back side is where much of the corrosion occurs.

7. Remove the hardware from the solution and dry it with a lint-free cloth.

8. Prepare the polishing slurry: Mix the polishing abrasive and alcohol or mineral spirits together in the bowl. You will have to make several batches depending on the amount of hardware to be cleaned because the polishing slurry is made with solvents that evaporate rapidly. *(Remember that Don's Polishing Slurry is best for your hardware. Commercial polishing agents often contribute to the deterioration of the hardware because they frequently contain harsh chemicals, such as ammonia or similar caustics, that corrode the metal, or coarse abrasives that leave the surface badly scratched. Anything with ammonia or salt eats the metal.)*

9. Dip a clean lint-free cloth in the slurry and begin polishing the hardware. You only need to rub gently with the cloth in order for the abrasive to remove the tarnish. Continue until the hardware is as shiny as you want.

Gold-Plated Hardware (Also Known as Gilt)

Never polish gold-plated hardware. You will rub the gold off. Clean with Don's Cleaning Solution only. Do not try commercial products because they often contain harsh polishing abrasives that will rub the gilt right off and

DON'S TIP:
Coating Hardware

If you want to prolong the polishing effect and add further protection to the metal, the hardware can be coated with acrylic or cellulose nitrate lacquer spray that you can buy from the hardware store. In a dust-free, well-ventilated space, spray the hardware with the protective spray finish. *Important:* Spray all the hardware evenly. First spray the back side. When the back side is dry, spray the front side. Be sure it is completely dry before replacing the hardware on the furniture. Obviously this isn't a permanent solution because this coating will need replacing. But done properly it can last for several years.

cleaning chemicals that will attack the underlying brass or bronze. Follow the instructions above up through step 7.

Silver-Plated Hardware

Follow the instructions for brass hardware, making sure to use the pulverized limestone as your abrasive. Silver requires the mildest abrasive possible.

Steel Hardware

Follow the instructions for cast iron artifacts in Chapter 7, Sorting and Preserving the Family Trash.

Nonremovable Metal Hardware

If the hardware cannot be safely removed from the furniture and still needs to be cleaned, polished, and coated, this can be done on the furniture provided the following precautions are scrupulously followed.

DON'S TIP:
How to Coat Gold Plate or Gilt

Gilt or gold plate can be lightly waxed with a hard uncolored paste wax such as Renaissance Wax (which is not as good for furniture because it is so hard and difficult to use on a textured surface). The wax serves as a protective coating that allows you to dust without rubbing off the gold.

1. Protect the surface of the furniture with two sheets of plastic film. Slide the sheets under the hardware from both sides to form an overlapping barrier. See illustration 8-1.

2. Dab the surface of the hardware with cotton swabs dampened in the acetone-alcohol mixture. Then scrub the metal surface with the swab. With-

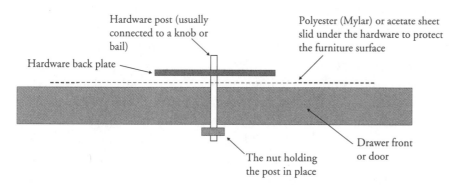

Hardware post (usually connected to a knob or bail)

Polyester (Mylar) or acetate sheet slid under the hardware to protect the furniture surface

Hardware back plate

The nut holding the post in place

Drawer front or door

Illus. 8-1. A detailed cross-sectional diagram of a typical setup for cleaning and polishing nonremovable furniture hardware.

out this precaution, attempts to polish the hardware will eventually end in disaster, as Louisa can attest: When she put too much solvent on the hardware, the solvent dripped past the plastic onto the surface of the furniture and acted like paint stripper.

3. Carefully polish the hardware, making sure none of the abrasive touches the surface of the furniture. Use particular care in applying any coating so that no protective varnish for the hardware gets on the object itself.

UPHOLSTERY

Historical upholstery determines the value and importance of seating furniture. Reupholstering fundamentally changes the character of the object.

Don's Rules for Preserving New and Old Upholstery

1. Expose upholstery to as little light as possible. You know my motto: "Where there is light, there is light damage." Period. Light is the enemy of textiles. Keep them in the dark whenever possible. If you can't keep them in a dark place, cover them with cloth slipcovers when company leaves.

2. Keep it clean by regular and careful vacuuming. (See illustration 8.2.) Dusting upholstery can be accomplished by a vacuum cleaner as long as you don't vacuum directly on the fabric. Instead, vacuum through a vinyl window screen or loose-woven linen. How? Tape the edges of a square foot of vinyl window screen or sew the edges of a square foot of coarse linen. Set the screen or linen on the surface, hold it firmly in place, and run the vacuum attachment across it. The dust is sucked through the openings of the vinyl screen and allows you to vacuum without the risk of abrading or snagging the linen. When you are finished with one area, pick up the vacuum nozzle, move the screen to a new location, and repeat until the entire surface has been vacuumed. Keeping upholstery clean helps reduce the risk of upholstery's number two enemy: bugs. Bugs actually view your upholstery as potential dinner as well as home.

3. If it's really, really old, treat it like Grandma. Upholstery weakens with age (just like Grandma). If you wouldn't sit on Grandma, don't sit on your really old upholstery. That creaking sound you hear in either case is a sign of bad things happening. Just show it off in a special place in the corner (again, just like Grandma).

Illus. 8-2. When vacuuming a textile, whether upholstery, tapestry, quilt, or carpet, be sure to vacuum through a screen with taped edges. Hold the screen flat against the textile and gently move the brush attachment back and forth across the surface of the fabric until clean.

The Perils of Pets

Real animal lovers accept that sharing their home with pets means always having to say they are sorry to the upholstery. They do, however, have a few choices in minimizing damage to the upholstery. They can place all the really good stuff in one or two rooms and, if there are doors closing off those rooms, they can simply shut the doors. If there are no doors, as in Louisa's living room and dining room, they can invest in an indoor electric fence. These fences do a wonderful job of ensuring that pets never enter those rooms without harm to people, pets, or furniture if installed and used properly. If those two suggestions fail, cotton slipcovers remain the only protection left. I guarantee you, though, that they are not urine proof.

HANDLING AND MOVING FURNITURE

In addition to using furniture wisely, it is important to handle it carefully. The moving project becomes increasingly difficult with furniture that is large and complex. Furniture that comes apart in many pieces or is unwieldy requires extra care and preparation.

To move your furniture, you should be equipped with the following: an appropriate number of lifters (one for small chairs, two for sofas, and up to four for really heavy, clunky objects; furniture pads or blankets; a dolly; cloth tape or soft string; and tissue paper).

The steps to take are so commonsensical that I'm almost embarrassed to write them down, but here they are:

1. Take off anything that can scratch or damage the furniture, such as jewelry, watches, pens and pencils, belts with big buckles, or the lumberjack suspenders I normally wear.

2. Wrap furniture hardware with tissue padding. This protects the handles, the furniture surface (if the handles have swinging bails or drops), the movers, and the surroundings in case you bump up against anything. Have you ever seen what Chippendale-style handles can do to expensive wallpaper? Not a pretty sight.

3. Create a clear path for the object you are moving. Make sure the dolly wheels and the movers' feet can travel smoothly on this path.

4. Measure all openings you have to travel through. This includes doors, windows, stairs, and so forth.

Lifting Furniture

It is critical to determine how the piece is constructed and what parts of it are removable or detachable. Without doing so, furniture can be seriously damaged through ill-advised handling. Here are tips on lifting furniture properly.

Chairs: Lift chairs by their seat frame, one hand near the front and one hand near the rear.

Sofas: Lift from both ends of the bottom frame of the sofa. Do not pick up from the arms or the back. This prevents damage to the sofa. Use two hands at each end of the sofa and lift with your legs, or you will need a book on back therapy.

Dining room tables: Lift by the frame that the top sits on. Do not lift by the legs or the top itself.

Drop-leaf tables: First determine which support members move. Is it simply a bracket or a swing leg? Fold the leaves down, cover with padding, and hold leaves down firmly by tying a band of cloth tape or soft string around them so that they cannot move. If the support is provided by a swing or gate leg, tie it in place as well. Grab the table underneath the end frame, called the apron.

DON'S TIP:
No Kid Gloves

In general, furniture should be handled *without* cloth or leather gloves. A good, firm grip is really important. If you make sure your hands are clean, you should be okay. For especially sensitive surfaces such as antique upholstery, unpowdered surgical-type gloves are fine.

LOUISA'S TALES:
Measure! Measure! Measure! Especially Stairways

At an estate sale I fell in love with and bought an antique wrought-iron, four-poster bed. The moment I got home, I measured my bedroom. The bed fit perfectly. Somehow, though, I forgot about the twisty, turny stairs that lead to my bedroom. Guess what? Halfway up the bed frame became stuck in the stairwell—and I mean stuck. I couldn't move it up or down, and the harder I tried, the more wedged in the bed became. My stairs became an instant obstacle course, as I had to climb through the bed frame to go from one floor to the other. Unfortunately, in order to dislodge the bed, I finally had to have someone cut off one of the posts. I've learned to always measure stairways as well as door frames.

Grabbing by the legs, especially swing legs, will increase the chance of damage to them. Grabbing by the side leaves will often result in fracturing the long rule joint that allows the leaves to drop. Picking up the table by lifting on the top rather than the apron may break the glue blocks that hold the top to the frame or strip out the screws that hold the top on.

Case pieces (cabinets, hutches, armoires, sideboards, dressers): While case pieces, especially large ones, may appear very different from tables and chairs, the same rules apply. Again, determine how it was put together and how it can come apart. Remove any drawers to lighten the load and carry them separately to the destination. If the drawers help keep the piece from wobbling too much, however, they should stay where they are. Be sure to empty them first. While the case piece can be moved similarly to tables and chairs—that is, by holding on to the bottom structure—it is better to move the piece on a dolly. This is safer for both the movers and the object.

Tall-case clocks: These puppies are among the most difficult pieces to

SMITHSONIAN STORIES:
Hidden Beauty

In the mid-80s one of my favorite curators in the Smithsonian, Carlene Stephens, called me to take a look at a black tall-case clock that was being donated to the Smithsonian. My friend and colleague David Todd, clock conservator at the National Museum of American History, and I drove four hours to the donor's home. We went into the dark basement to view this masterpiece that had been built in London during the reign of Bonnie Prince Charles. The provenance of the clock was perfect—it had been in the donor's family since its creation in the 1760s—and it was completely intact except for the three decorative finials that were supposed to be residing on the top. I could barely contain my excitement as David opened up the clock case.

Hmmm, I thought as I saw the flaking surface, this thing is in real danger of losing its paint. After we carefully carried the clock out into the light, I saw bright blue paint peeking out from the edges of what I had originally thought was black paint. The only reason it appeared black was that the family had "rejuvenated" the clock case by coating it with varnish about thirty-five times. The varnish had degraded over time, turning dark and totally obscuring the brilliant blue and gold-leaf details underneath. An account of how my colleague Mel Wachowiak and I removed these layers and revealed the clock's true beauty can be found at *www.alan.net/prgfeat/japanned.html*.

move because they are so ungainly and have big, heavy weights and delicate mechanisms inside them, as shown in the illustration below. You must remove the clockworks and weights from the case before moving the case itself, or catastrophe will be the likely result. When these elements are removed, lay them on a clean cloth in an out-of-the-way location until you are ready to reinstall them after the case is in its new location.

For especially old, delicate, or valuable clocks you may feel more comfortable having a professional horologist come and remove the works and reinstall them after the relocation is complete. You can find them under "Clock Repair" in the phone book.

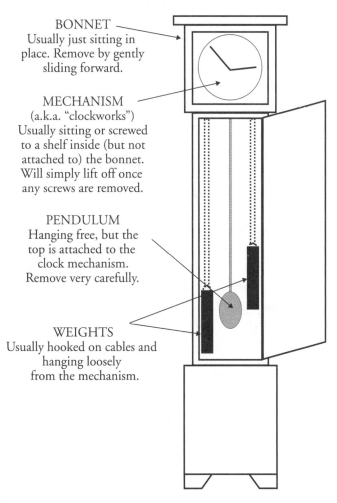

BONNET
Usually just sitting in place. Remove by gently sliding forward.

MECHANISM
(a.k.a. "clockworks")
Usually sitting or screwed to a shelf inside (but not attached to) the bonnet. Will simply lift off once any screws are removed.

PENDULUM
Hanging free, but the top is attached to the clock mechanism. Remove very carefully.

WEIGHTS
Usually hooked on cables and hanging loosely from the mechanism.

Illus. 8-3. Tall case clock, front view.

To do the task yourself, follow these steps:

1. Take out the weights. You don't want things as heavy as bowling balls bouncing around inside the case while you are trying to move it. The weights may smash the case and seriously hurt you if left in place. They are easy to remove because they are simply hanging from a cable on hooks.

2. Remove the pendulum. Failure to do this will result in severe damage to the clock mechanism from which the pendulum hangs. While this is also easy, it must be done very carefully because the pendulum attachment to the clock mechanism is very delicate.

3. Take off the bonnet (the top case) and move this separately.

4. Take out the clock mechanism and move this separately. Be very careful.

5. Gently lean the case over and lift with at least two people, preferably three or four.

6. When the clock is in its new location, reverse steps 5 through 1 to put it back together.

Moving Furniture

If you have figured out which path to take to safely move your furniture and how to best lift the furniture, you are halfway home. Now you must be sure to use the necessary number of hands for moving the furniture. In addition, have one person there who just watches for the hands moving the furniture as well as for the furniture. Move the furniture carefully. Don't rush. You'll be glad you did.

PART THREE

Pop Culture

Chapter 9

Preserving Your Sports and Political Memorabilia

Mickey Mantle. Ted Williams. Hank Aaron. Lou Gehrig. Roy Campanella. This collection of to-die-for baseball cards covers the bed in a charming picture my mother took of my younger brother and me playing. These were not the small bubble gum cards of our present day. These were the super-cool, oversized, 4-by-6 cards that came in boxes of tobacco products. Of course, the cards belonged to my *older* brother, who thankfully was at school, guaranteeing a certain safety for us little ones as we wreaked havoc on his stuff.

Two obvious facts jump out at me as I look at this particular photograph: First, an absolute treasure trove lies faceup on the bed. Second, I wore wild suspenders even at the age of three. While some of these cards later bit the dust between the spokes of our tricycles in our attempts to replicate the throaty sound of a Harley-Davidson, those that survived untouched were discarded in the family's 1958 move. How I wish we had known as kids what we know now. Had we expended even a modicum of care, much less a full preservation strategy, my niece's college tuition and perhaps that of all the nieces and nephews would have been covered. Perhaps one of the reasons I am so interested in keeping your stuff out of the dustbin is that so much of our stuff went into it.

THINK "HODGEPODGE"

Sports and political memorabilia cover the full gamut of materials and forms. Think about it. Baseball cards, posters, bumper stickers, pins, uniforms, equipment, flags, bobble-head dolls, buttons—each requires completely different care. So, accepting fate, I cover the breadth of these materials and artifacts with the graceful élan of Michael Jordan. Well, probably without his grace. After all, I am a man of considerably more "substance." My goal as a kid was to become a six-foot-nine, 235-pound power forward in the NBA. One out of two isn't bad.

There are so many materials and so many processes of deterioration for sports and political memorabilia that there are no universal truths that cover this entire chapter.

SAVING COLLECTIBLES FROM YOUR FAVORITE TEAMS

Whether hats, jerseys, sports cards, or equipment, these collectibles are a passion for millions of sports lovers.

Sports Cards

Like my brother before me and countless millions of fans throughout time, the basic entree into collecting sports memorabilia is through sports cards. They are readily available for a modest price, they capture our eyes and our hearts as we recount the exploits of our favorite athletes, and they provide a vehicle for transmitting traditions from one generation to another. Of course, trading cards of all shapes, sizes, and types are widely available and should be cared for exactly the same way as you would care for sports cards.

Don's Rules for Preserving Sports Cards

1. Get them out of the light.
2. Keep them dry.
3. Keep them cool.
4. Keep them out of the attic or basement.
5. Don't fold them.
6. Don't eat or drink around them.

7. Don't tape or glue them.
8. Don't staple or paperclip them.
9. Don't write on them.
10. Don't laminate them.

Storing Sports Cards

Many companies now cater to the needs of people serious about preserving sports card collections. They manufacture and supply the specialized sizes of archival materials required for the job. You can easily find sports-card-sized polyester envelopes to protect the cards from handling. All you have to do is carefully slip them in.

You will need the following supplies:

Clean white cotton gloves
Fitted polyester envelopes
Fitted archival boxes

1. Put on your clean gloves.

2. Pick up the cards by the edges and gently slide them into a polyester envelope. Place only one card in each envelope.

3. Place the protected card vertically into an archival box. Fill the box with the cards. Be sure you do not overpack the box so that you can remove the cards without having to jerk or damage them.

4. Store the archival boxes in a dark, cool, dry environment—below 75 degrees and 40 percent relative humidity.

Sports Posters

Glossy posters are usually more sensitive to moisture than other papers because they are typically clay coated and can glue themselves together when damp. This malady is called blocking, and it is practically incurable.

Don's Rules for Preserving Sports Posters
(or Any Posters for That Matter)

1. To prevent staining or other damage from oils and salts on your hands, it is advisable to wear white cotton gloves.

2. When lifting your posters, slide a stiff acid-free paper or mat board beneath them for support before moving them.

3. Avoid eating, drinking, or smoking near the paper and keep pens and markers away.

4. Posters can be stored in acid-free paper folders.

5. Get help if more than one person is required to move oversized or heavy posters.

6. Keep the area around the poster clean to avoid attracting insects and rodents.

7. Keep the light levels down. Control light intensity, proximity, and duration. The darker the better.

8. Don't handle posters more than necessary.

9. Don't slide posters around on top of each other.

10. Don't glue fragile posters on fabric, since fabric expands and contracts differently from paper.

11. Never use any pressure-sensitive tape to repair tears.

12. Don't laminate with plastic, since the heat or solvent used can cause damage and as a practical matter cannot be "undone."

To preserve and store the posters you will need the following supplies:

Soft artist's brush
Oversized acid-free folder
Insect trap

1. Dust off any food or other debris with a soft artist's brush and remove staples, paper clips, or Post-it notes from the paper.

2. Working on a large, flat, clean worktable, place the poster inside an oversized acid-free folder.

3. Identify a good storage place for your collection. It should be dark, cool, dry (but not parched), and pest free. Remember that the space has to be large enough to allow for flat storage of the poster.

4. Place an insect trap in the same general space as your poster.

5. Monitor the storage space for pests about once a month. Actually, the more often you monitor for pests, the better.

Preserving and Storing Extremely Large Posters

Extremely large posters present special storage problems because of their size. For this reason they are typically not stored flat but instead rolled up in a tube.

You will need the following supplies:

Acid-free cardboard tube at least 6 inches in diameter, and 6 inches
   longer than the short side of the poster
Acid-free tissue paper
Cloth string

1. Dust off any food or other debris and remove staples, paper clips, or Post-it notes from the poster.

2. Center the poster on the acid-free tube and gently roll the poster around it. Rolling on a large tube reduces the amount of stress that would result from a tight rolling around a small tube or no tube at all.

Note: The reason a poster is not stored inside a round tube is that the simple act of pushing the poster into the tube often damages the edges of the poster.

3. When the poster is completely rolled around the tube, wrap with acid-free tissue paper. Be sure to cover the poster completely with at least two or three layers of tissue.

4. Tie string around the outside at 6-inch intervals to hold the rolled poster and tissue paper covering in place.

5. Store the rolled, covered poster in a stable, dry, pest-free environment. Change pest traps as necessary.

Displaying Your Sports Posters

Sports posters are a specific form of art on paper. For display advice please refer to "Unframed Artwork on Paper" in Chapter 13, Taking Care of Fine Art.

Preserving Sports Clothing

For jerseys, hats, and uniforms that you no longer wear but want to preserve, follow the rules and instructions in "Vintage Clothing" in Chapter 14, Taking Care of Textiles.

Displaying Jerseys and Uniforms

One option for exhibiting jerseys and uniforms is to put them in a modified glass-front shadow box. For instructions on building shadow boxes see "Shadow Boxes" in Chapter 5, Saving the Stuff Only a Parent Could Love. Tailoring the shadow box for exhibiting your jersey or uniform is explained in the instructions and illustrations 9-1 through 9-4.

You will need the following supplies:

Polyester batting
Clean, firm, flat work surface larger than the dimensions of the
    object
Clean bedsheet or kraft paper to cover the clean surface
Tapestry needles, size 24 or 26 or as appropriate
Heavyweight 100 percent cotton thread
One-inch-wide hook-and-loop (Velcro)
Measuring tape
Scissors
Synthetic velour
Heavy-duty stapler

1. Wash your hands.

2. Carefully place the polyester batting on the work surface that has been covered with a clean bedsheet or kraft paper and cut it to fit inside the uniform.

3. Gently stuff the batting inside the uniform, making sure to smooth out any crinkles. This will prevent creases from forming along the front-to-back folds.

4. With a fine needle and thread sew the pieces of the hook half of a hook-and-loop system to the back edges of the uniform (about $\frac{1}{2}$ inch from the edge). See illustration 9-4.

5. Measure and cut the velour to fit on the backing board of the shadow box.

6. Wrap the velour around the edges of the backing board and staple in place.

7. Gently press the uniform against the velour backing so that the hook element can stick to it.

8. Close the shadow box.

Illus. 9-1. A typical display case for a sports jersey.

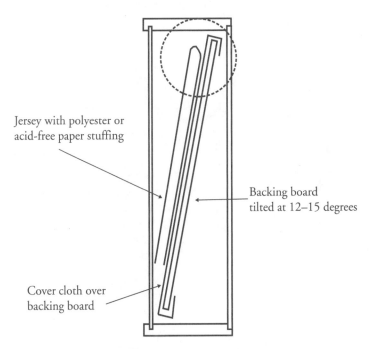

Jersey with polyester or
acid-free paper stuffing

Backing board
tilted at 12–15 degrees

Cover cloth over
backing board

*Illus. 9-2. Side cross section view of Illus. 9-1. Note the slight backward tilt of the
display panel, usually 12 to 15 degrees. This allows for full support of the artifact;
nothing is "hanging."*

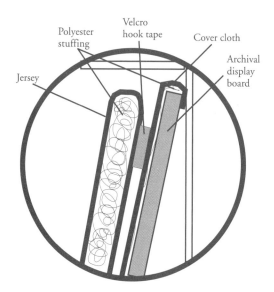

Illus. 9-3. Detail of the construction and assembly of the tilted display shadow box for a jersey. The cover cloth for the display board has to be stable and have enough "tooth" to allow the Velcro hook to grab it. It is stapled on the rear of the display board.

Illus. 9-4. The pattern for sewing Velcro hook tape on the rear of the jersey.

Displaying Sports Hats

Stuff the crown of the hat with polyester batting to the correct shape, then support the hat with an oval polyethylene foam block cut to fit the rim of the hat underneath the batting. Be sure to display the hat in a low-light, dust-free environment. See illustration 9-5 below.

Baseballs, Gloves, Footballs, Basketballs, Saddles, and Cleats

What do all these things have in common? I can hear the *Jeopardy!* tune winding down; the buzzer is about to go off, and you bet everything because it's Final Jeopardy! Well, Alex, the question is "What is a bunch of things made from leather?"

In virtually all instances of leather sporting goods, the leather is cattle, horse, or pig skin that has been chemically modified (tanned) to prevent it from rotting or decaying immediately.

Some leathers are durable; others are not. Why the difference? It all depends on the quality of the original hide and the tanning process and chemicals used. Early tanning, say the five thousand years before the mid-

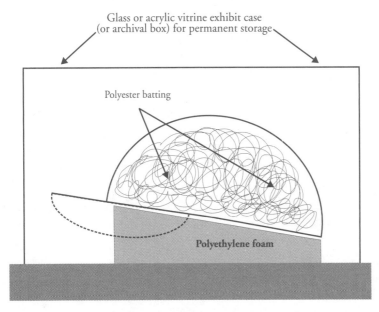

Illus. 9-5. A cross-sectional view of the method for exhibiting or storing a ball cap. (It is appropriate for displaying any hat.)

nineteenth century, was accomplished by vegetable tanning in which the necessary ingredients were obtained from soaking bark and other plant material together. Vegetable tanning results in a supple leather but one that is unstable and bound for degradation much faster than mineral-tanned leathers. Vegetable tanning was succeeded by mineral tanning, mostly with alum or chrome, which resulted in leather that was extremely durable and water-resistant and much longer lasting.

Cleaning Leather

First, inspect the leather to make sure that it is in good condition, that it has no widespread cracking or flaking or powdering red granules (usually evidence of the vegetable-tanned leather ailment called red rot). If the leather is in good shape, you may proceed. If the leather is in poor shape, consult a professional conservator before cleaning because cleaning damaged leather requires an expert's touch.

You will need the following supplies:

Soft artist's brush
Cotton swabs or litho pads
Distilled water
Triton 100 or nonconditioning liquid dish detergent

1. Dust off the surface using the artist's brush.

2. Wipe the surface with a swab or litho pad lightly moistened with distilled water.

3. If more aggressive cleaning is needed, make a solution of 1 percent detergent and 99 percent distilled water and repeat step 2.

4. If the surface of the leather is in good condition and has little surface texture, you can actually scrub a little with the swab or litho pad.

5. Rinse immediately with swabs or litho pads dampened with distilled water.

6. Dry by blotting immediately with clean litho pads.

Displaying and Storing Leather

For the most part leather should be displayed and stored similar to textiles, as described in Chapter 14, Taking Care of Textiles. If you follow the set of rules below, your leather objects should last for centuries.

1. Keep light levels low, preferably below 15 foot-candles. This is especially true for autographed baseballs, which you may want to keep as low as 5 foot-candles because the ink autograph will inevitably fade with exposure to light.

2. Leather objects on exhibit should be protected from dust and dirt; preferably they should be under glass in a closed display case or in a Lucite or acrylic case.

3. Leather is particularly sensitive to atmospheric contaminants and pollutants, so make sure any space containing them is clean. Keeping activated charcoal in the same space is also a good idea.

4. Stored objects should be wrapped in acid-free paper and stuffed in such a manner that they do not crease.

5. Leather cleats or sneakers should be stuffed lightly with acid-free tissue to maintain their shape.

6. Leather objects such as saddles and bridles should be supported with sculpted polyethylene blocks to maintain their shape.

7. Keep leather at about 50 percent relative humidity and at 60 to 70 degrees Fahrenheit.

DON'S TIP: Treating Leather with Leather Dressings

Leather dressings, such as Vaseline, Neatsfoot oil, and lanolin, are applied to leather objects that need to remain flexible and water resistant, such as saddles. For leather collectibles not in current use, leather dressings do little other than make the object greasy and sticky, and they attract dust and insects.

In virtually every instance autographs on memorabilia are extremely sensitive to light. They might be written with archival India ink and thus be fairly light stable, but don't count on it. More often they are written with whatever is at hand, usually a ballpoint pen or felt-tip marker. Be sure to keep autographs in the dark as much as possible. If you want to display your autographed memorabilia, the best compromise is to place them in an acrylic display case that can be covered whenever company is not around.

Short Takes: Sticks, Bats, Helmets, and Other Equipment

Sports equipment, whether used or stored, requires care so that it remains in stable condition. Follow the directions below for the various types of equipment and related care.

Sticks and bats: Preserve in the same manner described in "Wood Furniture" in Chapter 8, Preserving Your Furniture.

Helmets, shin guards, and shoulder pads: These are plastic, so preserve them as described in "Vintage Plastic and Rubber Stuff" in Chapter 7, Sorting and Preserving the Family Trash.

Hockey skates: Because of their construction (about half leather and half metal) and purpose (sliding across the ice on a sharp steel edge), vintage hockey skates present unique storage demands. Treat the top half as a leather shoe (see "Preserving Vintage Hats, Gloves, Shoes, and Purses" in Chapter 14, Taking Care of Textiles) and the bottom half as a piece of steel hardware (see "Cast Iron" in Chapter 7, Sorting and Preserving the Family Trash). If the blade is still sharp, wrap in fine polyethylene foam. Newer hockey skates are actually a plastic boot over a steel blade, so preserve the plastic part by following the instructions in "Vintage Plastic and Rubber Stuff" in Chapter 7, Sorting and Preserving the Family Trash.

Roller skates: Preserve the top half of a leather boot by following the instructions in "Preserving Vintage Hats, Gloves, Shoes, and Purses" in Chapter 14, Taking Care of Textiles. Preserve the bottom half (the metal part) by lubricating the wheel bearings with light machine oil: Place a drop of oil directly into the ball bearings around the axle of the wheel.

PRESERVING POLITICAL MEMORABILIA

Writing a section on preserving political memorabilia is a double-barreled joy for me. I am a political junkie who does not keep memorabilia other than my Calvin Coolidge button (Coolidge being the greatest president since Madison).

From a preservation perspective there is nothing unusual about political stuff. It's all made from materials and in forms covered elsewhere in this book, which makes it a pretty easy section to write. In literally every instance in this section I point you to some other place where the subject is covered in detail. Think of this section as your "links page" for preserving political memorabilia.

Buttons

Political and celebratory buttons tend to be made for the moment from the cheapest materials and by the fastest means possible. This means the cheap, unstable materials fade or even disintegrate quickly. Some buttons may last for centuries (silk-screened painted metal buttons, for example), but more often the button falls into the category of "here today, gone tomorrow" in keeping with what they are celebrating. This is especially true of those buttons where the design is printed on a plastic sheet that is then laminated onto a metal base. The images and designs, created with dye-based inks, are not lightfast, so they can disappear in a matter of weeks when exposed to high light levels.

Metal Buttons

Follow the cleaning, storing, and displaying instructions given in "Metal and Painted Metal Toys" in Chapter 4, Archiving Toys for Young and Old.

Plastic Campaign Buttons

Follow the cleaning, storing, and displaying instructions given in "Vintage Plastic and Rubber Stuff" in Chapter 7, Sorting and Preserving the Family Trash. The cautions about light sensitivity are even more applicable here because much of the printing on plastic buttons, or even plastic-laminated metal buttons, is not lightfast and can be faded by bright lights in a matter of weeks or months.

Posters

Preserve as you would sports posters as described earlier in this chapter.

Bumper Stickers

If paper, preserve as you would a gigantic stamp, following the general instructions in "Deterioration and Preservation of Stamps" in Chapter 12, Preserving Your Coins and Stamps. If vinyl, which is much shinier than paper (it is a thin sheet of plastic, after all), preserve by combining the principles of stamp storage with those contained in "Vintage Plastic and Rubber Stuff" in Chapter 7, Sorting and Preserving the Family Trash.

Flags and Banners

If they are textiles, preserve as described in "Historic Flags" in Chapter 14, Taking Care of Textiles. If paper, preserve by following the instructions in "Preserving and Storing Extremely Large Posters" in this chapter.

Cards, Letters, and Pamphlets

Preserve as you would letters by following the rules and instructions given for various types of letters in Chapter 11, Saving Your Books, Comic Books, Newspapers, Magazines, and Letters.

Photographs

Preserve as you would prints. See Chapter 3, Preserving Your Photographs.

Chapter 10

Preserving Entertainment Memorabilia and Media

Watching antique silent movies with my siblings remains one of my most enduring childhood memories. On the original projector (literally held together with rubber bands), we viewed Steamboat Willie, Felix the Cat, the Little Rascals, Charlie Chaplin, and dozens of others in silent classics as part of our nighttime calm-down routine. Only later did we learn that Steamboat Willie was the first "talkie"; we had thought Willie was silent because our projector produced no sound.

These evenings of unfettered revelry were usually interrupted at least a couple of times by breaking film. Our repair tool of choice was cellophane tape, which we stuck on the brittle, bent, brown film as quickly as possible so the mood would not be lost. I can only imagine what we were doing to these classics, playing them over and over again and sticking unstable adhesive tape on them whenever they broke. By the end they were definitely more tape than film.

On the morning of March 2, 1967, we had finished loading up the moving truck and found there was no room for the large box of films and projector. We left them behind, hoping to return for them later. Why we thought we might be returning is beyond me: We were moving eighteen hundred miles from the Great White North of Minnesota to the Great Hot South of Florida. When my older brother finally did get back to our old house years later, he discovered that the movies had been completely destroyed. How I wish we had saved them and, even more, how I wish we had saved the originals in a vault somewhere so they could serve as the cornerstone of my retirement portfolio. Those memories are still priceless. Almost fifty years later my siblings and I still chuckle at the Western where the good guy turns to the bad guys and says, "Git!" I have tried that line myself with an unqualified lack of success.

THINK "SUBSTANCE OVER STYLE"

Since the only unique thing about movie and entertainment collectibles is the subject matter, most of the care of event memorabilia is based on what the collectible is made of, not what famous figure is depicted on or by it. In other words, a movie poster of Marilyn Monroe is treated as a poster. The fact that Marilyn is featured does not change how the poster is preserved. When trying to decide how to save entertainment memorabilia, think "Substance Over Style."

Commemorative plates, mugs, and glasses: Follow the instructions for china as described in "Dinner China and Crystal: Cleaning, Storing, and Displaying" in Chapter 6, Saving Your Family Treasures.

Commemorative Christmas ornaments: Whether *Star Trek* or *Little Mermaid* decorations, follow the instructions in "Holiday Ornaments: Cleaning, Storing, and Displaying" in Chapter 6, Saving Your Family Treasures.

DON'S CAUTION:
Do Not Line Movie and Concert Posters with Fabric

One of the common mistakes made in caring for oversized movie posters and concert handbills is to glue fabric to the back side in an attempt to make the poster or handbill sturdier and help it last longer. This does not work. When the relative humidity changes, paper and textiles react in an opposite manner. When the humidity goes up, paper expands and fabric shrinks. When humidity goes down, paper shrinks and fabric expands. To protect your oversized posters, mat and frame them as described in Chapter 13.

Movie and concert posters, tickets, and similar memorabilia: Follow the instructions for preserving paper-based materials as described throughout Chapter 11, Saving Your Books, Comic Books, Newspapers, Magazines, and Letters.

Concert T-shirts: Follow the instructions in "Vintage Clothing" in Chapter 14, Taking Care of Textiles.

Plastic figurines, bobble-head dolls, and knickknacks: Follow the guidelines and instructions in "Vintage Plastic and Rubber Stuff" in Chapter 7, Sorting and Preserving the Family Trash.

Autographed photographs, such as my younger daughter's photo of heartthrob Orlando Bloom: Follow the instructions for prints in Chapter 3, Preserving Your Photographs.

Don's Rules for Keeping Recording Artifacts Clean

1. Never touch the surface of a recording.
2. Use clean white cotton gloves and handle the artifacts by the edges.
3. Recordings should not be left exposed to open air unnecessarily. Return the items to their containers when not in use and never leave storage containers open.
4. Do not place recordings near sources of dust, including paper or cardboard dust.
5. Keep the surrounding area clean.
6. Do not consume food or beverages in the area that recordings are handled.
7. Keep storage facilities as clean and dust free as possible.
8. The air-conditioning system should be equipped with dust-filtering equipment.
9. Keep equipment clean and in good working condition.

PRESERVING SOUND RECORDINGS

The most vexing problem in the media world is that the technology changes at a breathtaking rate. The formats for recorded sound have changed dramatically over the years, and I expect the changes will continue. For example, in an era where eight-track tapes are available at every flea market, eight-track tape players have virtually disappeared. If you cannot play a recording, whether an eight-track tape or a record or a cylinder recording, it is rendered completely worthless. In order for your efforts toward preserving recordings to be meaningful, they must be accompanied by equal energy toward preserving the playback device or mechanism. Otherwise, your collection will have little future usefulness.

That problem aside, the preservation of sound recordings is for the most part a study in the preservation of plastics, since, except for a few rare examples, recordings are plastic or composites containing plastic.

The overview of preserving plastic artifacts can be found in "Vintage Plastic and Rubber Stuff" in Chapter 7, Sorting and Preserving the Family Trash.

Preserving sound recordings, regardless of specific format, depends on following these principles:

Recordings must be kept contaminant free. Contaminants are either a deposit on the surface, such as dirt, skin, pollen, fungal spores, grease, smoke, lint, salts, or other chemicals, deterioration of the artifact material such as oozed-out plasticizers, depolymerized plastics, oxidized resins, and corrosion. When it comes to plastics, especially recording artifacts, contaminants are held to the surface by static. Simply wiping the surface does little to remove the contaminant, so a carefully designed, safe process is required to make sure the surface is clean. Such processes are generally water-based because water breaks static charges that hold the dust in place. Since water alone can do little for oily contaminants, cleaning systems include mild detergents to penetrate, break down, and remove them.

Recordings must be kept in a moderate, stable environment. Environmental stability is crucial to preserving recording artifacts. Temperature is directly related to the speed at which anything deteriorates, and when combined with its evil partner, moisture, doom is not far away. Wildly fluctuating environmental conditions make the problems worse. There is no single best temperature or humidity for all sound media. Each format, whether cylinders or records or magnetic tape, requires its own specific environment that is not appropriate for the others.

Recordings must be kept free from physical forces that would distort them. Distortion, even in the mildest form, can render sound recording artifacts nonfunctional. Out-of-round cylinders, warped disks, and stretched tape are no longer able to transmit fully or accurately the sound information they contain. As a general rule, distortion can be reduced or eliminated by controlling temperature (see Chapter 1) and placement (whether you place artifacts flat or upright when storing).

Don's Rules for Keeping Recording Artifacts from Distorting

1. Never leave recordings near sources of heat or light (especially ultraviolet light) because both adversely affect plastics.

2. Do not place heavy objects on top of recordings and do not place recordings directly on top of each other.

3. Shelve cylinders upright, records and tapes vertically, and CDs and DVDs horizontally.

4. Do not file recordings of different sizes next to each other if possible because smaller items may get lost or damaged while larger items may be subjected to uneven pressure.

EARLY FORMS OF RECORDINGS

Cylinders and records possess actual physical representations of sound. Both are a series of tiny undulating grooves from which sound is generated by a stylus (the needle) riding in the grooves and transmitting the undulations through an amplification system, resulting in audible sound. Not too surprising, the contamination of these grooves by dust and other accretions is a huge problem in the use of these artifacts, and cleaning cylinders and records, and keeping them free from distortion, is a critical component of their preservation.

With the exception of the earliest cylinders and master disks created in the recording studio, which were wax, all other cylinders and records are made from some type of plastic. The plastics section in Chapter 7, Sorting and Preserving the Family Trash, gives an overview of plastic that can help you better understand the reasons behind many of the instructions for taking care of your records.

You will find identifying features for each type of record. If you are having any trouble differentiating between the types of records, please consult an expert.

Wax Cylinders

The earliest form of recording artifacts was the wax cylinder in which was pressed the sound signals created for later playback. Not too surprising, wax cylinders and wax master disks are extremely sensitive to a range of deterioration and damage, such as distortion, melting, breaking, mold, and, since they are soft, dust and dirt contamination. Identifying wax cylinders is fairly easy: Gently press on the inside edge of the cylinder. If your fingernail leaves a distinct impression, it is probably made of wax. If it does not leave an impression, it is probably shellac.

Cleaning

Cleaning wax cylinder recordings is imperative for preservation. You must rid the cylinder (and flat wax disk recordings as well) of mold and mildew and any dirt in the grooves. If left uncleaned, the mold may continue to degrade the surface of the wax, and the dirt will scour the grooves as the stylus runs through them should it ever be played again.

You will need the following supplies:

Nitrile or vinyl gloves
Distilled water
Mild detergent (such as Triton 100 or Labtone)
Widemouthed glass jar
Flat soft artist's brush (¾ or 1 inch)
Polyethylene squirt bottle
Clean lint-free cloth or litho pads

1. Put on the gloves.
2. Prepare a cleaning solution of distilled water and 1 percent detergent in the glass jar.
3. By gently spreading two fingers inside the cylinder, lift and place an individual cylinder into the jar until the cylinder is completely submerged.
4. Remove the cylinder from the jar of cleaning solution.
5. Still holding the cylinder as described, take the artist's brush and apply it gently to the cylinder to dislodge any particulate matter.
6. Still holding the cylinder, douse it with distilled water from the squirt bottle to rinse it.
7. Set the wax cylinder on a clean, dry, absorbent pad to absorb the runoff.
8. Any remaining water that is beaded on the wax cylinder should be patted off with the cloth or litho pads.

Environment and Storage

Once the wax cylinder recording is clean, it should be housed and stored in an archival environment. Remember that once it is in storage, the two main enemies of wax cylinders and flat disk recordings are mold, which can etch the surface of the wax, and heat, which can distort the cylinder.

You will need the following supplies:

Glassine paper
Polypropylene foam sheeting (⅛ inch thick)
Adhesive tape
Archival boxes

1. Wrap the cleaned cylinder in clean glassine paper so that the entire cylinder is enveloped. *Do not* wrap the cylinder in fabric or cotton wadding because this may result in moisture being absorbed from the environment and held directly against the delicate wax surface. Surface mold will damage the wax.

2. Write any identifying information on one end of the glassine paper with a permanent marker.

3. Gently fold the ends of the glassine paper into the inner void of the cylinder.

4. Cut some of the polypropylene foam or synthetic (polyester or nylon) felt to make a single-layer sleeve around the cylinder. Tape the foam sheet into a cylinder to fit closely over the wax cylinder.

5. Slide the protective sleeve around the glassine-wrapped cylinder. Do not force it. Be sure it slides smoothly and snugly.

6. Place the cylinder in an archival box so that the cylinder stands on end. Several cylinders may be stored in the same box. There should be a tiny bit of wiggle room so that the cylinders do not distort each other.

7. Close the box and store it in a dust-free, cool room—about 60 to 70 degrees Fahrenheit and 40 percent relative humidity. Slightly cooler temps and slightly drier humidity are okay.

Acetate Records

Made in the first half of the twentieth century, these served as masters and are extremely collectible. They are recognizable because they look like a layered pancake. The outside is plastic, and the inside is metal or cardboard. These early recordings could be played on turntable amplifier systems, like the recording and playing of "Man of Constant Sorrows" in the popular film *O Brother, Where Art Thou?* Acetate disks were actually sandwiches of grooved acetate applied to either side of a thin aluminum core. Rarer examples include those made using a glass or cardboard core. This composite was then coated with nitrocellulose lacquer plasticized with castor oil.

The lacquer shrinks due to the loss over time of the castor oil, but the metal inner core does not shrink as the outside coating does. It is a sandwich run amuck. The outside "bread" shrinks as it begins to dry out, but its attached inner fixin's refuse to go along, resulting in internal stress. This stress leads to the record's outside coating (which contains the grooved recording) cracking and peeling, rendering the disk unstable. Other than cold storage (less than 40 degrees), there is virtually nothing that can be done to preserve acetate disk records.

Environment and Storage

1. Store in a cold, dry, stable environment. As with most chemical reactions, acetate degradation is accelerated with elevated temperature and humidity levels. Ideally, these artifacts are kept near freezing (less than 40 degrees) with very low humidity, less than 30 percent.

2. Distortions resulting from the degradation of the pyroxyline coating are the primary destructive force of these disks. Excess moisture will accelerate this degradation.

3. Acetate disks are susceptible to fungus growth, so keep them dry.

Shellac Records

Records made between 1900 and 1940 were made of shellac. They are typically black or red, heavier than vinyl records, twice as thick, and completely inflexible. "Shellac disks" is somewhat of a misnomer because the shellac is simply the glue binding the record together. The actual content of the record can be as little as 15 percent shellac; the remainder can be an almost limitless range of bulking agents and fillers including wood flour (finely ground sawdust), charcoal, minerals, and ground-up waste plastics. As one of three living aficionados of shellac, believe me when I tell you that the range of properties for shellac is immense. Since the characteristics of the record are as much a function of these fillers as the shellac binder, it is nearly impossible to predict the longevity of any particular shellac recording artifact.

In general, shellac records are relatively stable. Deterioration of the shellac binder is directly related to storage temperature and humidity. Over time the shellac record will inevitably become increasingly brittle due to ongoing chemical reactions within the material. The evidence of this is often a fine powder in the grooves of the record after playing.

Shellac also dissolves in alcohols such as methanol (wood alcohol), ethanol (grain and grape alcohol), and propanol (rubbing alcohol).

Cleaning and Keeping Clean

At some point in the deterioration process shellac becomes slightly water sensitive, which complicates the cleaning process immensely. A water/detergent cleaning solution is a problem because the detergent makes water penetrate more quickly. I have found the best means of cleaning shellac records is to give them a facial exfoliation treatment. I am not kidding.

You will need the following supplies:

Photographer's compressed air can
Face peel
Fan
Distilled water
Litho pads

1. Gently blow any loose dust off the surface with the compressed air.
2. Gently dab the face peel on the surface of the record, avoiding the label.
3. Place the record in front of the fan to dry it as quickly as possible.
4. When the cleansing film is stiff, peel it off.
5. Gently rinse the record surface with the distilled water, again avoiding the label. Dry it immediately by blotting it with litho pads and placing it in front of the fan.

This procedure works extremely well for all types of records that need cleaning, acetate records excepted. It removes dirt and grime gently and with minimal force.

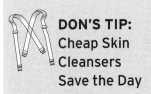
Environment and Storage

Where and how you store records determines how long they will last. Follow the instructions below to ensure the longevity of your records for centuries.

1. Store all records, shellac included, in archival glassine paper sleeves especially made for the purpose.

2. Place the record/sleeve inside the jacket, being sure not to force and distort the record. If you have an original sleeve, you may slide it inside the jacket if there is enough room. Otherwise, store it separately in a Mylar L fold as described in "Saving Comic Books" in Chapter 11, Saving Your Books, Comic Books, Newspapers, Magazines, and Letters.

3. Store records upright and snugly against each other to reduce distortion risks. Do not cram them together.

4. Store in a dark, clean, cool, dry space. "Vintage Plastic and Rubber Stuff" in Chapter 7, Sorting and Preserving the Family Trash, provides more detailed instructions. A good rule of thumb for records is 60 degrees Fahrenheit and 20 to 40 percent relative humidity.

Vinyl Records

The vinyl records of my youth are the most stable recording medium ever devised. Recognizing them is easy: They are thin, shiny, black, and slightly flexible. Records that are thick, shiny, black, and rigid are most likely shellac. If you keep them out of direct sunlight, avoid scratching them, and do not expose them to caustic chemicals, vinyl records can easily last several hundred years. These records are here forever, thank goodness. Losing my three thousand records would be traumatic.

Cleaning

Follow these instructions and your records and their players will thank you. Because vinyl records are plastic and thus susceptible to static buildup, you must be sure to address both the contaminant issue and the static issue.

You will need the following supplies:

Two plastic squirt bottles
Distilled water
Triton 100 detergent (a mild liquid conditioner-free dishwashing
    detergent will do in a pinch)
Measuring teaspoon
Synthetic velvet record-cleaning pad or bar (available from
    electronics stores)
Graphite antistatic brush or gun
Archival record sleeves
Photographer's compressed air can
Artist's brush
Hypoallergenic conditioner-free face peel

Routine cleaning should be done every time before and after playing a record. Do this:

1. Wash your hands thoroughly.

2. In one of the squirt bottles prepare a cleaning solution of distilled water and 1 percent detergent: To a 16-ounce bottle of distilled water add one teaspoon of detergent. In the other squirt bottle, put *only* distilled water. (You will use this bottle to rinse.)

3. Place the record on the turntable.

4. Place a few drops of cleaning solution on the velvet cleaning pad.

5. With one hand slowly rotate the turntable. With the other softly place the velvet pad against the surface of the record and wipe it.

6. Continue to rotate and wipe, moving the cleaning pad to expose a clean surface to the record, until the surface is visually clean.

7. Rinse the record by repeating steps 4 to 6 using only distilled water that has been put in the other squirt bottle.

8. Once the record is clean and dry, rotate the turntable and either brush the surface with the graphite antistatic brush or zap it with the antistatic gun.

9. Pick up the record by the edges only and flip it over on the turntable.

10. Repeat steps 4 to 8 on this side of the record.

11. Pick up the record by the edges only and transfer it to one hand. Place your middle finger in the center hole and your thumb on the edge.

12. Gently slide the record into the archival record sleeve.

13. Replace the record sleeve in the record jacket so that the opening of the sleeve is pointed up.

Extreme grittiness cleaning is for the times when you find the original 1953 Elvis recording at a yard sale and it is too dirty for routine cleaning. Try this:

1. Use the compressed air can to blow off any loose debris.

2. With the artist's brush gently apply the face peel to the plastic surface of the record. (Be sure to avoid getting anything on the label.) Do not scrub the surface but simply dab on as little face peel as possible while not agitating the dirt on the surface any more than absolutely necessary.

3. Place the record in front of a fan to dry the face peel as quickly as possible.

4. When the face peel has dried enough so that it has formed a soft but intact film, gently remove it from the surface. All the loose dirt in the grooves should come off with the film.

5. If necessary, repeat steps 2 to 4.

6. Once the particulate debris is off the record, continue with the routine cleaning instructions on page 165.

Environment and Storage

1. Vinyl discs are adversely affected by direct ultraviolet light and temperature fluctuations. Temperature variations eventually induce distortions on the record.

2. Remove shrink-wrap on records, as it will continue to shrink and warp the disc.

3. Store them as you would shellac records (above).

Laminated Shellac Records

Also known as Columbia disks, after the record company, these are an early form of flat records. You can recognize them by their paper core and rigid resin outer coatings. They have an oven-fused shellac powder surface that carries the grooves containing the audio signal. Preserve them as you would shellac records,

DON'S TIP: Cleaning Records

If you have a lot of records in need of cleaning, you might want to consider a sophisticated record-cleaning machine. It is like a miniature version of the floor washing and vacuuming machine I saw recently at the supermarket. It wets and brushes the surface of a rotating record and then vacuums off all the cleaning solution and gunk it carries. The only drawback is that these machines are several thousand dollars, so you really have to be serious about your record collection to purchase one.

but be aware that the cores are paper so you must be even more careful in cleaning.

Edison Diamond Records

The first fully synthetic recording artifacts were the Edison Diamond disks made from phenol (the first permanent synthetic plastic) cores with thin synthetic varnishes on the surface to carry the grooves. They are similar to acetate and Columbia records except that the core is made from a dark, rigid resin rather than aluminum or paper. In general, phenol presents no unusual degradation problems. Never use water to clean them because the filler used to make these records absorbs water, causing the record to expand. Preserve them as you would shellac records (above), but clean the face peel residue with an alcohol-moistened litho pad instead of water.

Vulcanite Records

Hard rubber, or Vulcanite, was one of the early materials used for making flat phonograph records. They differed visually from early black shellac in that they were not nearly so shiny, and if they were exposed to a lot of light, their surface would show a web of tiny cracks and appear dusty. For an

DON'S TIP:
Preserving Record Covers

In some cases, the record cover itself is important, either to you or as a collectible on the marketplace, and you need to take the following steps to ensure its continued good health. First, remove the record disk from the record cover sleeve and store each separately. The presence of the record inside the cover places a lot of stress on the cover, and often cuts through the bottom of the cover. Place the record cover in a polyester L fold or in a polyester envelope. Store or display it as you would a magazine, described on page 195 of Chapter 11.

overview of preserving rubber artifacts see "Vintage Plastic and Rubber Stuff" in Chapter 7, Sorting and Preserving the Family Trash.

PRESERVING MAGNETIC MEDIA: AUDIOTAPES, CASSETTES, EIGHT-TRACKS, AND VIDEOTAPES

Audiotapes and videotapes are really a long strip of plastic (the base) on which a layer of tiny magnetically sensitive particles has been glued. You therefore have a series of opportunities for deterioration: the plastic strip can degrade and the binder holding the ferromagnetic particles can degrade, disrupting the magnetic alignment or causing physical distortions in the particle layer that prevent the audio or video information from being used.

Audiotapes were manufactured on cellulose acetate films from about 1935 until the advent of polyester tapes in the 1960s. In almost every respect the polyester tape is superior: It is more stable chemically, it is stronger, and it is less sensitive to environmental fluctuations. High-density polyester (Mylar) is very stable, especially in comparison to polyurethane, the binder for the ferromagnetic layer. The only downside of polyester is that because it is much stronger and more elastic than acetate tape, it stretches rather than breaks. Stretching irreparably damages the ferromagnetic layer while breaking destroys much less of the electromagnetic information on the tape.

Don's Rules for Preserving Magnetic Media

1. Wear clean white cotton gloves and handle carefully.

2. Don't eat or drink around tapes.

3. Keep tapes in protective cases when not in use.

4. Keep tapes out of the sun. Not only will the heat cause the cases or reels to distort, but ultraviolet light will also make the binder go kablooey.

5. Store vertically so that the tape is not "on edge."

6. Make sure the playback machine is working properly.

7. Clean tapes before playback if they show any evidence of dirt or contamination.

8. Ensure that the tape is properly seated in the machine before use.

9. Don't "fast forward" or "fast rewind" because this adds a lot of tension to the tape. Let the tape run to the finish at normal speed.

10. Leave magnetic tapes on the take-up reel after use (run all the way to the end, or "tails out"). There are two reels; one is the playout reel (it is full when you start), and the other is the take-up reel (which is empty when you start).

11. If you have open reel tapes, make sure the ends of the tape are not flopping around. Either tape them to the reel or feed them through an opening in the reel to hold them securely.

12. Periodically make a duplicate copy of older tapes onto new tapes.

13. Be sure you do not record over older tapes and lose their contents.

14. Don't drop the tape reels or cases.

15. Do not crease the tape.

16. Keep tapes and tape players clean.

17. Store tapes in a cool (or cold for deep storage), dry, stable environment.

18. Bring tapes to room temperature before using if they are hot or cold.

19. *Avoid magnets.* They erase whatever information is on the tape if they are strong and close enough.

DON'S TIP: What to Do If Your Tape Smells Like Vinegar

Remember the problem with "safety film" back in Chapter 3? Vinegar syndrome is accelerated by moisture and iron (ferromagnetic) particles in the tapes. Once the process of disintegration has begun, it cannot be stopped by any means yet devised. It can be slowed by reducing the temperature, but the best thing to do for tapes that smell like coleslaw is to get them copied pronto.

Videotapes and Audiotapes: Cleaning and Equipment Maintenance

Dirt and magnetic tape do not get along. Dirt can and does scratch, gouge, and abrade a tape and its magnetic media to total destruction. Even more problematic is that dirty tape and tape players are inexorably linked. Each damages the other, so keeping one clean is pretty much useless unless the other is also kept clean.

You will need the following supplies:

Vacuum cleaner
Photographer's compressed air can

1. Gently vacuum reel-to-reel tape or cassette cases if dusty. Use a vacuum with a hose and brush attachment, and keep the motor away from the tape in order to reduce the risk of magnetizing the tapes. This creates static or interference on the tape. Do not vacuum the tape strand itself.

2. Using the compressed air, blow dust off the tape as you transfer film from one reel to another. Constantly rewind on the uptake reel as you clean to prevent the tape from turning into a pile of spaghetti in your lap. (For contaminants other than dust, such as oils, fingernail polish, or transparent tape adhesive, a professional expert should be consulted.)

To clean the tape player you will need the following supplies:

Cotton swabs
Rubbing alcohol
Distilled water
Mild liquid dishwashing detergent
Fine artist's brush
Small vacuum with an attached ¼-inch plastic or rubber hose
Piece of heavyweight cardboard
Silicone caulk

1. Gently swab the magnetic heads with rubbing alcohol, or a mild mixture of distilled water and detergent. Do not scrub with the swab; simply roll it back and forth over the surface of the head.

2. If using a mixture of distilled water and detergent as a head cleaner, be sure to wipe off the head cleaner afterward with a swab of distilled water only.

3. Brush with a fine artist's brush to remove dust from the tape player.

4. Finish cleaning the tape player by vacuuming with the small vacuum. (A standard vacuum hose or any attachments are too large to get into the area you need to keep clean.) The easiest way to do this is to get a piece of heavyweight cardboard slightly larger than the end of the vacuum hose. Punch a hole through the cardboard large enough to fit the rubber tubing. Run a bead of silicone caulk around the opening through which the tube is pushed. When you turn on the vacuum and place the cardboard over the end of the vacuum hose, the suction will hold the cardboard in place and the rubber tube will serve to pick up dust and dirt.

5. Cleaning the inside mechanisms (gears, motors, etc.) intrudes on precise and delicate machinery. It should be done by someone familiar with the inner workings of the machine. An electronics repair shop that specializes in vintage audio equipment is the place to start when looking for an expert to help you.

Here are some suggestions for taking care of and storing tapes:

1. Do not drop tapes. The impact could partially rearrange the magnetic particles, damaging the sound.

2. Store tapes away from any magnetic fields.

3. Do not store tapes in a plastic bag. The plastic bag will trap moisture.

4. Handle reel-to-reel tapes by the center hole rather than the edges because the pressure on the edges will damage them and ultimately damage the tape.

5. Ten-inch reels should have supports in their boxes so that the center bears the weight of the tapes rather than the edges.

6. Store tapes with an "archival wind" by letting the tapes play to the end at normal speed rather than fast-forwarding or rewinding, which places unnecessary strain on the tape and does not wind it smoothly. (Compare the edges of a spool of tape run at normal speed and one at high speed, and you will see what I mean.)

7. Always store tapes upright so that the center spool and the tape are parallel to the floor. This prevents edge damage to the tape.

Compact Discs and Digital Video Discs:
Cleaning, Caring for, and Storing

The CD/DVD stores digital audio and video information on a metallic foil laminated between two plastic laminae. To play back a CD or DVD, a laser beam shines through the bottom plastic layer and "reads" the information on the metallic core. Preserving CDs and DVDs involves not only keeping the information-containing layer stable but also keeping the transparent hard outer coating transparent and hard so that the laser can actually penetrate the plastic layer twice without disruption.

Unlike records and tapes, digital media do not require direct physical contact to collect the signal. Dust may not damage the actual CD or DVD, but it does interfere with how well the CD/DVD plays. In other words, on a musical CD/DVD the music may skip if the disc is not clean. Dust and other contaminants can contribute or even cause damage to the surface of the plastic, rendering the disc unreadable.

You will need the following supplies:

Clean white cotton gloves
Photographer's compressed air can
Distilled water
Triton 100 detergent
Litho pads or clean soft lint-free cloths

1. Always handle collectible discs with clean white cotton gloves to prevent oils and acids on your skin from contaminating the surface of the disc.

2. For discs in use, always handle by the outer edge and center hole only.

3. Use the compressed air to blow off any light surface dust.

4. If contaminants such as grease need to be cleaned, prepare a cleaning solution of distilled water and 1 percent Triton 100 detergent.

5. Dampen a lint-free cloth or litho pad with the cleaning solution and carefully blot the dirty area. Do not wipe because wiping with even a clean soft cloth may scuff the surface of the disc.

6. Rinse the cleaned area with distilled water alone.

7. Blot-dry using a litho pad or clean soft lint-free cloth.

Here are some suggestions for taking care of and storing CDs and DVDs:

1. Keep discs out of direct sunlight or intense artificial light (more than 50 foot-candles).

2. Store discs individually in dust-free cases or envelopes especially made for storing discs. Paper envelopes should not be used because they are too abrasive.

3. Never stack bare discs on each other.

4. Store flat in a protective case to reduce any risks from warping or contact damage.

5. For long-term storage, keep discs in a stable environment of about 50 degrees if possible and 40 percent relative humidity.

Note on Movie Film: Information about saving movie film can be found in "Film: Slides, Negatives, and Movie Film" in Chapter 3, Preserving Your Photographs and Films.

PLAYBACK MACHINES

Media playback machines, just like any mechanical devices, need to be actively maintained to keep them working properly. This is especially critical because not only does the machine itself have to work, but it has to work in a manner that does not harm the medium being run on or through it. A "sorta working" tape deck or movie projector can turn a valued collection of recordings or movies into a pile of confetti.

DON'S TIP:
Duplicate, Duplicate, Duplicate

Any active media-based artifacts, such as movie film, records, tapes, CDs, and computer and digital photo files should be duplicated. This allows the duplicate to be played while providing safekeeping for the original in deep storage. In fact, periodic replication is the only real strategy for preserving magnetic media because the degradation is fairly rapid and catastrophic. Of course, this is not necessary for your everyday CDs that you can easily replace with a quick stop at the store. But duplication is essential for those CDs, tapes, records, and films that contain extremely valuable or irreplaceable sounds or images.

Record Players: Gramophones, Victrolas, and Turntables

A gramophone is a "wind-up," spring-driven, record-playing machine with an external rigid horn speaker. A Victrola is similar except it has a built-in horn that is hidden in the cabinet. The rules and instructions for preserving the outsides of these early phonograph machines are the same as those described in "Wood Furniture" in Chapter 8, Preserving Your Furniture.

Don's Rules for Preserving the Inner Mechanical Workings of a Hand-Cranked Record Player

1. Clean and keep clean: Vacuum off loose dirt with a brush attachment. Wipe off dirt with a lint-free cloth and distilled water. Brush away the dust with a soft artist's brush.

2. Lubricate moving parts as necessary. Use lightweight machine oil for metal parts by placing a drop of oil at the point where the axle of the turning part goes through a bearing or housing block. Use powdered graphite for everything else that moves; brush it on the points of contact with a oo artist's brush. If you do not know what these terms mean, leave it to someone who does.

3. Release any tension on the windup spring. This is accomplished by allowing the turntable to run until it stops all by itself.

4. Store in a stable, cool, clean, moderate environment, enclosed in a clean container such as a polyethylene bag.

Movie Cameras and Projectors

Film projectors are fairly simple machines. In essence, both a movie camera and a movie projector are metal structures with a pair of motor-powered axles (on which the film reels reside), a series of guides to direct the film from one to the other, and either a glass lens to expose the moving film or a bright light somewhere in between that shines through the film moving past it so that a "moving" picture can be projected.

Like all machines with moving parts, movie cameras and projectors need to be lubricated. Use lightweight machine oil for metal parts by placing a drop of oil at the point where the axle of the turning part goes through a bearing or housing block. Use powdered graphite for everything else that moves, brushing it on the points of contact with a oo artist's brush. If you do not know what these terms mean, leave it to someone who does.

For windup spring-driven cameras, be sure that the spring is relaxed by letting the camera run until it stops by itself. When the spring is fully relaxed, the camera will do nothing when the "play" button is pushed. For electrical cameras and projectors, be sure that the wires are not dangerously frayed or broken. Frayed wires will show little threads coming loose. Broken wires can be detected by spotting the fractures and breaks in the wire's outer coating or insulation. For ongoing maintenance of the device, look at the owner's manual or consult a collector's association specializing in that particular device. You might be amazed at how specific collecting and restoring clubs can be.

Environment and Storage

Store movie cameras and projectors in a clean, cool, dry place with as little oxygen as possible. A damp environment causes accelerated deterioration of metal and plastic parts.

You will need the following supplies:

Vacuum
Lint-free cloth

Distilled water
Soft artist's brush
Two zippered polyethylene bags large enough to hold the item
Six sugar-packet-sized silica gel envelopes
Six packets of Ageless oxygen scavenger

1. Vacuum off loose dirt with the brush attachment of the vacuum.

2. Wipe off dirt with the lint-free cloth and distilled water.

3. Brush away the dust with a soft artist's brush.

4. Place the movie camera or projector in a large heavyweight zippered polyethylene bag.

5. Place the sugar-packet-sized silica gel envelopes inside the bag. The goal is to prevent condensation.

6. Just before closing the zippered bag, slightly tear one corner of each packet of Ageless oxygen scavenger. Put them in the bag and seal the bag immediately.

7. Place a second bag over the first and seal it.

8. Store the package in a cool place.

Cameras

Cameras are composite objects made of metal, glass, plastic, fabric, wood (found in really old large-format plate cameras), and sometimes rubber. It is nearly impossible to devise a perfect preservation strategy because these materials have different preservation requirements.

Much of preserving cameras is simply using common sense and not damaging them in the first place. They are delicate precision devices, a reality that becomes all the more obvious as the price and sophistication of cameras increase. While not exactly robust, an old Brownie or Kodak 110 "point and shoot" is practically indestructible compared to high-end 35-millimeter SLR or large-format cameras.

To preserve a camera:

1. Avoid impact damage by not dropping or banging your camera. Impact damage is especially likely on zoom lenses. Smacking a zoom lens can knock it out of kilter and damage the ring mount and even the body of the camera. Remember levers and fulcrums? Keep your zoom lens retracted unless you are actually taking a picture through it.

2. Keep it clean.

3. Keep it dry. Water (especially salt water) will corrode the outside and destroy the inside.

4. To prevent the glass lens from getting scratched, keep the lens cap on unless you are taking a picture.

5. Keep it in a case. Having a camera bouncing around unprotected is a really bad idea.

6. Store it in a cool, dry environment.

Cleaning

It is important to keep your camera clean because contaminants can corrode and jam the outside metal parts and pretty much destroy the insides. Dirt particles can jam moving parts and cause the camera not to work.

1. Wipe dust and dirt off your camera with a clean lint-free cloth or litho pad.

2. Do not use compressed air except to blow dust off the lens.

3. If the camera gets dusty or dirty on the inside, gently vacuum out the inside with a tube as described above for cleaning a tape player. Trying to blow out the dirt will simply push it further into the crevices.

4. If the camera has been exposed to salt air, wipe the entire outside of the camera case and lens with a clean litho pad dampened with distilled water. Repeat this several times, each time with a clean pad. Clean the front of the lens with commercial lens cleaner available at the camera store.

5. Dry off with a clean, lint-free, soft, cloth or litho pad.

6. If your camera gets wet on the outside, blot it dry immediately with a clean, lint-free cloth or litho pad.

7. If your camera gets wet on the inside, open it up and blot it dry immediately with a clean, lint-free cloth rag or paper towel and then take it in for repairs because it's going to need them. If the insides get wet with salt water, the camera is pretty much dead.

Storing

Since a camera has so many different materials, the best overall compromise for preservation storage is to keep it in a clean, cool, dry place with as little oxygen as possible. A damp environment would cause accelerated deterioration of fabric shutters and bellows, and may seep into compound lenses and cause fungal growth inside the lens. For long-term storage follow the instructions below.

You will need the following supplies:

Acid-free tissue paper
Camera case
Two zippered polyethylene bags
Silica gel
Ageless oxygen scavenger

1. Clean the camera.
2. Remove the batteries and discard them properly.
3. Wrap the camera in the acid-free tissue paper.
4. Place the camera in a fitted box to prevent impact damage. If you do not have the camera case, make a replacement from polyethylene foam covered with nylon fabric, fitted to the camera and placed inside an acid-free archival box.
5. Place the closed box or camera case inside the zippered polyethylene bag.
6. Place a sugar-packet-sized silica gel envelope inside the bag. The goal is to prevent condensation.
7. Just before closing the zippered bag slightly tear one corner off an equal-sized packet of Ageless oxygen scavenger, put it inside the bag, and seal the bag immediately.
8. Place a second bag over the first and seal it.
9. Store the package in a cool place.

Preserving the Exterior of Old Radios and Televisions

If plastic, follow the guidelines and instructions in "Vintage Plastic and Rubber Stuff" in Chapter 7, Sorting and Preserving the Family Trash. For wood cases follow the instructions for cleaning and waxing in "Wood Furniture" in Chapter 8, Preserving Your Furniture.

DON'S TIP:
Schematics
"R" Us

If you have an adventurous spirit, you can try maintaining and restoring vintage radios and televisions. You will need schematic diagrams and access to all sorts of arcane parts such as tubes, condensers, and tuners. Thanks to the Web, they are all at your Googlin' fingertips.

Preserving the Internal Mechanism of Old Radios and Televisions

Contact an expert in maintaining and restoring old electronics. An electronics repair shop that specializes in vintage audio equipment would be the place to start to find an expert who can help you. Electrical devices are not harmless. In the right situation electricity can be a lifesaver and convenience maker; in the wrong situation it can be a killer. And antique electronics can be particularly dangerous. They contain paper capacitors, which if dried out may blow up or burst into flames if voltage arcs across them when you throw the power switch. This is why I strongly recommend that you take these to an expert.

Chapter 11

Saving Your Books, Comic Books, Newspapers, Magazines, and Letters

THE FIRST TIME *I walked into Don's office I almost fainted. Rows of books lined the walls from floor to ceiling. Since books are a weakness of mine, I thought I had stumbled into Nirvana. The look and smell of old books triggers some of my fondest memories. While reading, I have been cast away on a deserted island, discovered Tutankhamen's tomb, and climbed the Himalayas. Books to me are magical. As I glanced through the titles of Don's books, though, I failed to find a single Shakespeare, Proust, Faulkner, or even a Forsythe. Instead, I found over two hundred volumes on historical paints and varnishes; the other thirteen hundred books focused on everything from prehistoric woodworking to the manufacturing of aerospace materials.*

As I gazed around his office, I detected a definite pattern of care. It became evident that Don loves each of these books. While his office might strike a casual observer as chaotic, in truth each book has its own special niche within his office at the Smithsonian. The largest books are laid flat on the shelves while the smaller ones rest in small custom-made mat-board boxes. In addition, there are hundreds of spiral-bound notebooks. If a book is very old and very fragile but Don still needs to use it regularly, he photocopies the contents and places it in a spiral notebook. That way he can still get at the information while safely preserving the original book.

Don's office serves as a great demonstration of proper book preservation. I went straight home and started reorganizing my bookshelves. My giant atlas now lies flat on my bookshelf, and my early edition of Charles Dickens's Christmas Carol *is no longer displayed fully opened (because that hurts the binding). I have undoubtedly added hundreds of years to the life of my book collection in just a few easy steps—and it didn't cost me a cent!* —Louisa Jaggar

Irreplaceable, clearly loved, used, and well cared for, my old books represent a knowledge base that transcends time and space. In one book I learn about my craft from an eighteenth-century carver and gilder, and in another I take lessons from a professional art restorer now living and writing in Germany.

Books are not the only place the written word opens doors of understanding and enlightenment. The letters your great-granddad wrote from the front line during World War I open a window to a past that only comes alive again when you begin to read about his worries and his dreams. How about the creative imaginings in the comic books you bought as a kid? I will always remember Superman and the Green Hornet.

THINK "VEGGIES"

The fundamentals of preserving books, comic books, newspapers, magazines, and letters are the same because each one is paper-based. Think of paper as a dried vegetable. Dried vegetables do best when they are kept cool, dry, and out of the light. The same general idea holds true for paper products such as books, comic books, magazines, newspapers, and letters. Like all vegetables, paper can rot if you don't take care of it properly. Paper, especially wood pulp paper, will change color and become brittle over time. Preventing or at least slowing down this aging process is what I do as a museum conservator. So whenever you take care of paper-based products, think "Veggies!"

Don's Ten Commandments for Keeping Your Paper Fresh

1. Get it out of the light.
2. Keep it dry.
3. Keep it cool.
4. Keep it out of the attic or basement.
5. Don't fold it.

6. Don't eat or drink around the papers you want to save.
7. Don't tape or glue the papers.
8. Don't staple or paper-clip them.
9. Don't write on them.
10. Don't laminate them.

It is important to note that whenever I say find a storage space, this means a place that is neither the basement nor the attic. Basements are too prone to moisture and flooding problems, and attics tend to get too hot and dry.

A SPECIAL WARNING ABOUT BOOKS AND BUGS

There are six-legged creatures that seem to exist only for eating your books and papers. The two most commonly encountered are silverfish and cockroaches. Silverfish thrive in dark, warm, moist conditions and are attracted by natural fibers and starchy materials, both of which are plentiful in books. With a little imagination you can envision them dining on paper pages and cloth bindings. Reality is worse than your imagination. Cockroaches like to eat something else entirely: They go after the binding glues in the book spine. Between the two they can make a book or paper collection go away.

**DON'S TIP:
Show the
Copy, Save
the Original**

To preserve an old piece of paper but also display it, do what museums often do: Make a photocopy of the original on the highest-quality rag paper you can get (rag paper is discussed later in the chapter). Display the copy and store the original.

PRESERVING VINTAGE BOOKS

A quick glimpse at a book tells you a ton of information. Is it bound (sewn) or simply glued together? Is it rag paper, paperboard, or wood pulp paper? Is it cloth or leather covered? Is it even wood panel book boards? And what about the pages and the structure holding the pages together? You need to think about both the cover and the contents in order to preserve your books. The cover is connected to the binding, and the binding is connected to the pages.

When preserving books you need to deal with two simple concepts: (1) handling and storing them carefully, and (2) controlling the environment in which they live. And remember that even I do not attempt to preserve every book. Some are important and valuable to me, some are useful, and some are disposable.

The method you choose to preserve your books depends on a host of items such as how old they are, how you use them, and how long you want to keep them. A brief account of the three-tiered preservation system for books looks like this:

Quick 'n' Dirty Method: Remember the book covers from elementary school? If you can measure and fold, you are good to go.

The Middle Road: Making a fitted storage box is the path to follow for books that are somewhat fragile. It is not too resource intense, and, again, if you can measure and fold, you are good to go. For virtually all books this will be the highest level of preservation necessary.

Pharaoh's Tomb: In adopting a "keep it forever" posture for your books, you need to do what a good friend of mine did: dedicate a room as a climate-controlled vault. With a little instruction it is not too difficult or expensive, but it requires very careful planning and execution. And, yes, I do understand if you are not willing to go to this level.

If you have concerns about leather binding or book covers, please review the section on leather artifacts in "Saving Collectibles from Your Favorite Items" in Chapter 9, Preserving Your Sports and Political Memorabilia. For leather bindings in especially bad condition, contact a book conservator.

Quick 'n' Dirty Method

If you have books you want to care for but they are not yet fragile, you can usually get by with sturdy shelves and a dust jacket or a half-box called a book shoe. A closed bookcase is always preferred to help keep critters out. *Never tape any dust jacket or protective cover to the book itself.*

You will need the following supplies:

Vacuum and artist's brush (if necessary)
Archival polyester or acid-free paper book jacket
Sturdy shelves
Pest traps

1. Wash your hands.

2. Gently vacuum the book with a brush attachment if it is dusty, or use an artist's brush and very carefully brush the dust into the vacuum's nozzle.

3. Cover the book with an archival-quality, acid-free paper or polyester book jacket that can be purchased from several companies listed in the Resources section at the back of the book. Follow the directions, which are pretty much the same as when you made book jackets in elementary school. In fact, you can easily make your own by purchasing the raw materials (heavyweight acid-free paper or polyester film) and doing all the folding, cutting, and fitting yourself.

4. If possible, lay the closed book flat on the bookshelf. In fact, oversized books pretty much require flat storage. It is okay to stack books flat provided the stack doesn't get too tall and unsteady.

5. Keep light levels as low as possible where the books are stored and moderate the environment. This means not too cold or hot (especially hot) and not too wet or dry (especially wet).

6. For books you rarely use, a good additional step is to wrap them fully in folded acid-free paper followed by placing them in a sealable polyethylene bag.

7. Place insect traps around the area where the books are living and monitor the space regularly.

The Middle Road

For books that are particularly old or in poor condition, you need to house each one in its own fitted box. Some of the suppliers listed in the Resources section have inventories of various-sized book boxes. (For those books with odd sizes requiring boxes not available from commercial sources, you can make your own by following the detailed instructions at the website *www.nedcc.org*.) Why is this a step up from the book jacket? Book boxes provide structural support from stress as well as protect books from the environment.

You will need the following:

Vacuum and artist's brush (if necessary)
Archival book box in which your book fits snugly without being
    forced
Pest traps

1. Wash your hands and make sure food and drink are not nearby.

2. Gently vacuum the book with a brush attachment if it is dusty or use an artist's brush and very carefully brush the dust into the vacuum's nozzle.

3. Place the book in the archival box, close it, and store it on a shelf as described above.

Pharaoh's Tomb

Keeping books forever requires a fair bit of planning and commitment, but it is within reach of most serious collectors. All you need to keep your books pristine for as long as possible is a well-controlled, isolated environment that is free from pests, light, and wild temperature and humidity swings. If you line the walls, floors, and ceiling in a room with 8-millimeter polyethylene sheeting, cover the windows with shading, and invest in an integrated control system for a window air conditioner and a dehumidifier, you, too, can have a Pharaoh's tomb for your books. You can disguise the polyethylene vapor barrier by adding wallboard on top of it, finishing it like a regular wall, and laying carpet on top of the floor.

You will need all the supplies necessary for the Middle Road method plus:

Activated charcoal buffering paper
Polyethylene zippered bags
Ageless oxygen scavenger
Dedicated storage space
Integrated climate control system where the temperature is kept at
    50 degrees and the humidity is 40 percent.

1. Prepare as instructed for the Middle Road method above but place a sheet of activated charcoal buffering paper on either side of the book before closing the archival box.

2. Slip the box into the zippered bag.

3. Just before sealing the bag, slightly tear one corner of a small packet of Ageless oxygen scavenger and slip it in the bag outside the box. Seal the bag immediately.

4. Place the sealed package in another bag and seal it.

5. Place the sealed package in your controlled storage room.

DON'S TIP:
Pillows for Books

One of the practices most damaging to old books is opening them flat. As the bindings age they become less flexible. If you hear an old book creak or pop when you open it, odds are good you are damaging it. When you open an old book, get in the practice of using small pillows or clean foam wedges on either side to keep it from opening all the way. This reduces the strain on the binding and will go a long way toward keeping the book in one piece for the ages.

DUPLICATING FRAGILE VINTAGE BOOKS

Many vintage books with wood pulp paper and glued bindings are simply too fragile to use and handle regularly. If you have old, brittle books that you use on a regular basis, either for pleasure reading or to use the information they contain, consider duplication as a primary preservation strategy. Since many books become less amenable to handling as they age and deteriorate, you need to handle them less. With the appropriate photocopying machine (vintage books may need a special photocopier machine—see below) or digital scanner and high-quality linen or cotton rag paper, you can make an excellent long-lasting replacement copy of an at-risk book.

Not every fragile vintage book can be photocopied on every photocopier or scanned on every flatbed scanner. For example, if the binding is old enough that the book makes an audible cracking sound when opened fully, the odds are good that the binding is too brittle for the book to be placed safely on the photocopier plate with both pages flat. In such cases you will need to find a specialized book-photocopying machine or scanner with a split, angled platen. These copiers can typically be found in the rare book room of large museum and university libraries. If they do not have one, the people there generally can tell you where a photocopier of this type can be found. If you do not have a museum or university in your neighborhood, ask an antiquarian book dealer for assistance.

This specialized copier allows you to place the book on the outside corner of a glass surface with a bend in the middle, usually about 90 degrees, so the book has to be open only halfway for a copy to be made. If you insist on proceeding without finding this specialized photocopier or scanner, the odds are pretty good you will be turning your book into a loose-leaf folio.

Once the duplicating is complete, place the original in its own fitted box and store it flat in a stable, safe environment so that it can be used again in the future if absolutely necessary. Otherwise, use only the copy.

SAVING COMIC BOOKS

Whether you have one comic book or several, the first step in deciding how to preserve your comics is to think about how you'll use them. Do you want to hold an occasional Show and Tell for your fellow comic book lovers? Do you want to seal them away until it's time to auction them on eBay? Do you want to save them for your buddies or your grandchildren?

How you use your comic book determines how you save it.

Quick 'n' Dirty Method

If you want to keep your comic book collection but have very little in the way of dedicated resources for long-term storage, take heart. The following steps will allow you to get the most out of your collection with the least expense and trouble.

You will need the following supplies:

Dry closet or drawer
Pest trap

1. Gently remove any food debris, dirt, paper clips, or staples from the comic book. If any of these are present on your eventually priceless stuff, consider yourself scolded. Also, if you have dog-eared any of the page corners, flatten them.

2. Identify a good storage place for your collection. Ideally, this place is dark, cool, dry (but not parched), and pest free. You don't want critters wandering in for a quick munch on your comics. A nice desk drawer or closet will do.

3. Stack the comics tightly, one on top of the other. Stacking reduces the oxygen surrounding the comics, a very helpful way to slow down deterioration. Stacking neatly also makes the comics more fire resistant. They can still burn, but it takes longer. Tightly packed paper burns very, very slowly.

4. Place a pest trap in the same general space as your stack of stuff but not on or especially near it. The opposite corner of the drawer or closet is fine. Why would a mouse be interested in your comic books? To scrounge a bit of nesting material or just to get through to the other side.

5. Monitor your collection. Take a look every once in a while to see how your storage system is working. Check for mouse droppings, bug carcasses, and mold. If you have none of these, you're good to go for twenty years or so, depending on how frequently you handle the collection of comics. If you leave them alone and

DON'S TIP:
Keeping It
Neat

To help keep things really neat, stack your comics inside a cardboard box that is the right size for the job.

don't touch them, the Quick 'n' Dirty Method is good for maybe forty years. But if you often take your comic books out to peruse them, you're looking at perhaps five years without noticeable deterioration.

The Middle Road

This method is up a level from the Quick 'n' Dirty Method but not yet at the level of Pharaoh's Tomb. You have to make a little investment in storage and housing items, but not too much.

You will need the following supplies:

L fold polyester sleeve
Archival-grade storage box
Dry closet or drawer
Pest trap

1. Gently remove any food debris, dirt, paper clips, or staples from the comic book or magazine. No, you don't have to pull the staples out of the spine, but that's a good question.

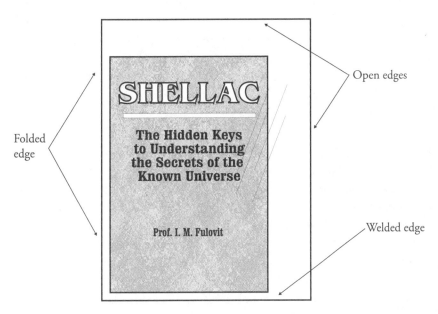

Illus. 11-1. An irreplaceable historical text being housed inside a transparent archival polyester L sleeve.

2. Place each comic inside an L fold polyester sleeve (see illustration 11.1). Sleeves are available in various sizes from archival storage suppliers such as those listed in the Resources at the end of the book. These folders reduce the damage from handling because you mainly touch the protective transparent sleeve, not the comic book itself.

3. Stack your sleeved comics flat inside an archival-grade storage box, available in a wide range of sizes from the same companies as the L fold polyester sleeves.

4. Store your treasures in the same good place you identified in the Quick 'n' Dirty Method—somewhere dark, cool, and dry. Watch out for critters. They're your biggest worry now.

5. Place a pest trap near but not on your prized stash.

6. Monitor your collection for pest and fire hazards such as wiring junctions. With a little luck you may get more than a century of safe storage from this storage option.

Pharaoh's Tomb

Okay, you have money to burn from your recent seven-figure inheritance, and you want to spend a bit of that fortune on caring for your priceless copy of Superman I, circa 1939. The critical keys to state-of-Egyptian-art for preserving your comics involves two separate ideas. The first is sealing the comic inside a "perfect" environment (a process called encapsulation), and the second is refrigerating your collection (not too surprisingly called cold storage).

You will need the following supplies:

Utility knife and straightedge ruler
Polyester encapsulation envelope
Polyester L fold sleeve
Buffered boards
Ageless oxygen scavenger
Heat welder or special tape to seal polyester envelopes
Storage box
Controlled cold storage

1. Gently remove any food debris, dirt, paper clips, or staples from the comic book or magazine.

2. Get a polyester envelope slightly larger than your comic. Cut buffered paper boards of the same size.

3. Place the comic in an L fold polyester sleeve and then place the sleeve between the buffered boards.

4. Slide this entire sandwich into the polyester envelope.

5. Slightly tear one corner of a small packet of Ageless oxygen scavenger and place it in the polyester envelope outside the buffered boards.

6. Seal the remaining edge of the polyester envelope immediately. Use either a heat weld or special tape supplied for this task to fuse the seam and get the envelope airtight as soon as possible. Work fast. Steps 5 and 6 must be done together in the space of a few seconds, or the oxygen scavenger will be wasted soaking up oxygen from the outside air and not from inside the sealed polyester envelope.

7. Place each comic in its own storage box. (You can't stack the envelopes because each one contains a tea-bag-sized packet of Ageless.) Since the comic is sealed inside the envelope, the box doesn't have to be anything special but just the right size, strength, and durability.

8. Put the entire assembly into controlled cold storage. Deterioration is in large part a chemical reaction, so you can basically double the life of the object for each 18 degrees Fahrenheit you cool it. In other words, if you store your comics at 52 degrees instead of 70, you have doubled their life. And if you store them at minus 20, you have extended the life thirty-two-fold! You

DON'S TIP:
Keeping Your Paper Crisp

You have to be very careful about pulling sealed paper artifacts out of the freezer for viewing. Strict rules apply—well, really only one rule, but it's very strict: Warming has to be a very slow process. Much the way a loaf of bread gets soggy if you take it directly from the freezer to the counter, your loaf of comic book will do the same. When you retrieve it from the freezer, you need to do so in stages. First, keep it in the refrigerator for at least twenty-four hours. Second, place it in an insulated cooler until it reaches the same temperature as the room. By slowing down the warming process you reduce (hopefully to zero) the moisture in the package as it warms, keeping your comic nice and crisp, not soggy.

do the math as to how long you can preserve your comics in Pharaoh's Tomb.

Alternative: Cold Storage with Occasional Viewing

Cold storage may be best for your object but pretty much assumes that you never need to see it or show it off again, especially if you follow the steps of the Pharaoh's Tomb plan. Here's a hybrid idea you may want to consider. Instead of putting buffered boards on the front and rear of the comic book you're saving, use a board only on the rear so that the front cover is still visible (and that's all you really want to show off to your buddies anyway, isn't it?) and then place it in a sealed polyester envelope.

Now place this package in a storage box, and then into long-term cold storage. This way you can retrieve it to examine or display.

TENDING TO NEWSPAPERS

When each of Louisa's two children was born, she went out and bought that day's newspaper. She still has them. And she is not the only person who saves newspapers. Most people save at least a newspaper clipping or two in

SMITHSONIAN STORY:
How Wonder Woman Keeps Her Cool

The Smithsonian Institution knows the value of comic books and how comics often reflect our national heritage. The original Wonder Woman comic was created during World War II to give young girls a heroine they could look up to as they faced the challenges of a nation at war.

It turns out that the same man who invented the polygraph (lie detector) created Wonder Woman. When his original drawings and papers were given to the Smithsonian for safekeeping, they included his complete set of Wonder Woman cartoons, already bound in book volumes. Now this role-model comic strip character lives in a cool, dry room in the Smithsonian Libraries. And she looks as good as new after more than a half century.

their lifetime. I have four complete newspapers myself, commemorating monumental moments of our time.

Newspapers can be preserved by using any of the three methods presented earlier in this chapter for comic books: Quick 'n' Dirty, The Middle Road, and Pharaoh's Tomb.

Quick 'n' Dirty Method

In general, the procedure for newspaper preservation is the same as for comic books (see earlier in this chapter), but there is one special note about stacking: Stack your newspapers folded the same way as they were delivered. And remember to monitor for pests once a month.

The Middle Road

The Middle Road steps for comic books apply in general to newspapers.

You will need the following supplies:

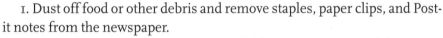

Buffered board or acid-free folder
Dry closet or drawer
Pest trap

1. Dust off food or other debris and remove staples, paper clips, and Post-it notes from the newspaper.

2. On a large, flat, clean worktable, unfold the newspaper so that you can see an entire page at once. Be sure to get any kinks out of the paper so that it lies perfectly flat.

3. Place a buffered board between the sections of the newspaper or place each section inside an oversized acid-free folder.

4. Identify a good storage place for your collection—that is, dark, cool, dry (but not parched), and pest free. You don't want critters wandering in for a quick munch on your stuff. A closet shelf, a hutch, or a dresser drawer should do the trick. Remember that the space has to be large enough to allow for flat storage of an unfolded newspaper. That's pretty big and, if the stack gets high enough, pretty heavy.

5. Place a pest trap in the same general space as your stack of newspapers.

**DON'S TIP:
The Ties That
Do Not Bind**

Don't bind newspapers by tying them with twine—the twine cuts into the edges of the paper. It's okay to bind your treasured newspapers like a book because book-style binding provides physical protection and keeps the papers compressed.

6. Monitor the storage space for pests about once a month. Actually, the more often you monitor for pests, the better.

Pharaoh's Tomb

Putting those treasured old newspapers away for the millennium requires the same general steps as saving Batman until the year 3000, so check out my Pharaoh's Tomb advice for comic books earlier in this chapter. The main difference is that you need physically larger preservation supplies and space, beginning with a large, flat, clean work surface.

You will need the following:

Map case—a large piece of office furniture specifically created to store oversized pieces of paper

Walk-in freezer or climate-controlled cold storage

1. Gently remove any food or other debris, staples, paper clips, and Post-it notes from the newspaper.

2. Unfold the newspaper completely on a clean, hard surface, making sure to get out any wrinkles.

3. Carefully place the unfolded newspaper flat in the drawer of the map case. You can stack them on top of each other until the drawer is full.

4. Place the map case in environmentally controlled cold storage. Since there should be no pest problem in such a space, there is no need to place a pest trap.

DON'S TIP:
Warm Slowly

If you want to remove your newspaper treasures from cold storage, let them warm up slowly between two blankets. Blankets serve to keep cold in just as well as they keep cold out. Since they are not encapsulated, there is less of a condensation problem, but still pay attention to this. If you follow this approach, you can probably get your newspapers to last for literally hundreds of years.

MINDING THE MESSAGE IN A THERMAL FAX

Thermal faxes are among the most self-destructive artifacts that can be found in our moment in history. If you have a thermal fax you want to preserve, forget it. It can't be done. The message will be lost in a short while no matter what you do even if the paper remains. Your best option is to make a photocopy of a thermal fax as soon as you know that you want to preserve it. Copy it on archival-grade paper (just about any uncolored high-quality rag paper will do) and put your preservation efforts into saving that. Treat the photocopy like an old letter. The ink on fused-process photocopies and laser prints is remarkably stable for long periods of time.

TAKING CARE OF MAGAZINES

Glossy magazines are more sensitive to moisture than newspaper because magazine paper is clay coated and can glue itself together when damp. This malady is called blocking, and it is practically incurable. Of all the paper-based products I deal with in this chapter, magazines are the most sensitive to water. Otherwise, the same Quick 'n' Dirty and Middle Road preservation steps for comic books mentioned earlier in this chapter also apply to magazines.

The rules for storing magazines using the Pharaoh's Tomb method are basically the same as those for comic books—minus the need for buffered boards. The clay sizing that makes the page glossy serves to neutralize any acidity in the wood pulp paper. But remember the additional warning about the moisture sensitivity of magazine paper stock. Because of the coating on the paper, magazines taken out of cold storage should be warmed up twice as slowly as other paper to absolutely reduce the risk of condensation. To accomplish this, wrap the magazine in heavy blankets when you take it out of the freezer to place in the refrigerator, then wrap it with a blanket when you place it in the insulated cooler forty-eight hours later.

OLD LETTERS

The letters that you properly save today can be read one hundred years or even one thousand years from now. By following the steps outlined in this chapter you can greatly retard the chemical degradation of wood pulp paper (by placing it between sheets of buffered mat board), protect rag paper from damage caused from handling (by placing it in polyester sleeves), and preserve the ink on all of them (by keeping letters in the dark). Combine these actions with fire, flood, and insect precautions, and you have a thousand-year collection.

Louisa's great-grandmother's accounts of her great-granddad's younger days live on because her great-grandma wrote them down. Who would have imagined her great-granddad was once a bootlegger? In these letters he is described as quite a character with a wicked sense of humor and a ready laugh. This same phrase could be used to describe Louisa's son, David. Truthfully, reading these old letters created a connection between generations that would not have happened otherwise.

Rag Paper and Pulp Paper

Your old letters are written on paper made from either cotton or linen—called rag paper—or on paper made from wood pulp. How do you tell the difference? Knowing how old the letter is helps. If it's two hundred years old, it's on rag paper. The wood-pulping process didn't come along until 1850. Even some modern stationery is on rag or linen paper. But letters from the Civil War era and later are probably on wood pulp paper unless they are on fine stationery. If your paper has turned brown and become

DON'S TIP:
Telling Rag Paper from Wood Pulp Paper

While it is not always possible to determine at first glance which paper you have unless you are an expert, one of the handiest tools at your command is an inexpensive, disposable pH strip that can tell how acidic or alkaline your paper is. Simply place a drop of distilled water in an out-of-the-way spot on the paper, and after a few seconds place the tip of a pH strip in the drop of water. Compare the color of the moistened strip to the color-coded key on the pH strip package, and you'll know the acidity of your paper. If it is very acidic, you have plain wood pulp paper. If it is neutral or even slightly alkaline, you have either rag paper or wood pulp paper that has been chemically stabilized.

crumbly, like old paperback novels or newspapers, it is almost certainly wood pulp paper. Fine stationery may be dusty, dirty, and even a little faded, but it is probably not too brittle no matter how old it is.

The main problem with old paper made of wood pulp is that it contains an acid that gradually turns the paper yellow and eventually causes it to disintegrate. Paper mills have long since figured out how to take the acid out of wood pulp paper. When professional preservationists need to stop the ravages of acid in old pulp paper, they use a process called deacidification. They bathe the paper in an alkali solution to neutralize the acid. This process stops some of the aging process, but it can also change the paper's color to gray and affect colored inks. Bright yellow ink can change to a soft pink. Because deacidification is tricky at best, I don't recommend that you try it.

Saving Letters on Wood Pulp Paper

For letters on paper made from wood pulp, follow the same procedure as for comic books described earlier in this chapter.

Saving Letters on Rag Paper

Rag paper is made from cotton or linen. In the old days it was made into pulp rags—such as worn-out clothing that was fermented and stomped like grape wine. Rag paper was therefore very expensive, but it's the most perfect artifact around. If it isn't eaten, burned, or destroyed by mold, rag paper will last forever. It can even survive a flood provided it isn't torn (water weakens paper, although it recovers its strength when it is dried out) or digested by insects and mold that move in as soon as the water subsides.

Quick 'n' Dirty Method

This method of saving old letters is generally the same as for other kinds of paper discussed in this chapter. But if you've popped to this page first, here's the whole process.

You will need the following supplies:

Dry closet or drawer
Pest trap

1. Gently remove any food debris, dirt, paper clips, or staples from the letter.

2. If the letter is folded, unfold it carefully so that it can be stored perfectly flat. Gentle handling is the key, and if the paper is a little stiff or creased, hold it over a steamer for a second or two to soften it. You can place the dampened letter between two sheets of acid-free paper and place a book on top of the damp paper to let it dry perfectly flat.

3. Identify a good storage place for your collection. Ideally, this place is dark, cool, dry (but not parched), and pest free. A nice closet shelf or a dresser drawer should do the trick.

4. Because letters are often individual sheets or of different-sized paper, they should be placed flat in a clean box so that they don't get scattered. Carefully stack the letters tightly one on top of another. This reduces the oxygen surrounding the letters, which is very helpful in slowing deterioration and actually makes them more fire resistant as well. They can still burn, but it takes longer.

5. Place a pest trap in the same general space as your letters but not on or especially near them. The opposite corner of the drawer or closet is fine.

6. Monitor your collection regularly. The best way to make your letters last is to keep track of how well your storage system is working. Check for mouse droppings, bug carcasses, and mold. If you have none of these and you do not handle the letters frequently, your letters should last for centuries.

The Middle Road

You will need the following:

> Polyester L weld folder
> Archival-grade storage boxes

The main difference between this and the Quick 'n' Dirty Method is that you place each individual letter—or, if the letter is particularly important, each individual sheet of each letter—in a polyester L weld folder. This eliminates most of the abrasion from handling. The second difference is that you store your letters in an archival-grade storage box.

With a little luck you may get five hundred years or more of successful storage from this housing option.

Pharaoh's Tomb

You will need the following:

Polyester encapsulation envelope
Polyester L fold sleeve
Heat welder or special tape to seal polyester envelopes
Storage box (not necessarily archival because the contents are
   sealed)
Controlled cold storage (refrigerator)

1. Gently remove any food debris, dirt, paper clips, or staples from the letter.

2. Get a polyester encapsulation envelope slightly larger than your letter and gently slide the letter into it. Rag paper does not really need any buffered board inside the storage envelope.

DON'S TIP:
Saving the Family Tree from an Inferno

Fire is one of the greatest threats to paper artifacts. While it can destroy a collection completely in a matter of minutes or seconds, there are some strategies for reducing the risks. Here's one example: One of my mother-in-law's passions is genealogy, and vacation trips are a mixture of visiting friends, family, courthouses, and historical archives. She spends hours on the road sorting through and cataloging all the documents she finds.

On one of these genealogy trips several years ago my in-laws' motor home burned to the ground. Fortunately, no one was hurt, but the contents of the vehicle were pretty much a total disaster. Amazingly, the genealogy documents, compiled lovingly over several years, survived nearly intact. Why? They were packed so tightly in their compartment that little oxygen was present. Without oxygen there could be no fire. The family records were scorched around the edges and soaked by the fire hoses, but in the end none of the collection was lost. After careful cleaning and drying, they are back at work, guiding further explorations into family history.

These days the family genealogy records traveling in the new motor home are photocopies. The originals are back home in a fireproof case.

3. Seal the remaining edge of the polyester envelope as demonstrated in the instructions on page 191. Use either a heat weld to fuse the seam or special tape supplied for just this task. When you seal the envelope it will be airtight.

4. These sealed letters should then be stored flat in a good sturdy storage box.

5. Put the box of sealed letters in controlled cold storage. Since this kind of storage cuts deterioration in half for every 18 degrees Fahrenheit it is colder, and since rag paper is among the most stable materials known, these letters should last well into the next millennium.

Chapter 12

Preserving Your Coins and Stamps

As a young girl I was given a piggy bank in the shape of a huge, droopy-eared plastic dog that I called Barney. I placed every spare coin I found inside that dog. I also saved buffalo nickels, many early 1900s pennies, and even some coins from the late 1800s. And whenever I moved to a new home, I lugged good old Barney with me. I never worried about anyone stealing my coin collection because who could even carry Barney out of the house? He actually required two people to lift him. My parents groaned whenever it came time to put him on the moving truck.

Later, I married, had two children, and still Barney traveled everywhere with me. I can absolutely state that the task of emptying Barney and going through all those coins was on my to-do list. (You know, the list of stuff you will get to the minute the children are away and you have scads of free time.) I just never got around to it.

Then one day I went looking for Barney. I am not sure why—Mother's intuition, I guess. It turns out that my daughter, Alex, then twelve, and her friends took Barney and emptied him out at Coin Star, one of those machines that changes all your coins into dollar bills. Alex got eighty one-dollar bills and knew she had hit pay dirt. I got zip and knew I had been robbed. May I add that Coin Star will not return coins? To be honest, the one person at Coin Star I spoke to could not stop laughing. The fact that I housed valuable coins in a huge plastic dog remains one of my larger mistakes in conservation. I certainly learned that housing is the number one issue in caring for coins. —Louisa Jaggar

Housing is the number one issue for stamps, too. In some ways coins and stamps are just about the perfect collectibles. It is relatively inexpensive to begin a collection, which makes both stamp and coin collecting a popular hobby for kids. Collecting can begin harmlessly with a single stamp chosen for its beauty or the exotic locale of origin, or with a fistful of coins gathered while traveling abroad. Over time it can escalate to the highest levels of sophistication and finance. My own daughters seem particularly entertained by the coins I've brought home from my many trips abroad.

No areas of collecting are as well established and cultivated as the assembling of coin collections (numismatism) and stamp collections (philately). Of course, this has both benefits and drawbacks: the rules about collecting, value, and preserving are fairly well established, but the arguments about those rules or the need for adaptation for unique circumstances sometimes become quite heated. And above all, maintaining the financial value of either coins or stamps remains a very important consideration.

THINK "HOUSING"

While stamps and coins are distinctly different in both their material character and preservation needs, one thread binds them together so strongly that it might as well be a steel cable: Do not touch! The best way to deal with the problem of handling and a whole host of additional deterioration issues is to place them in special containers that isolate them from their surroundings. This packaging, and thereby isolation of stamps and coins is called housing. Properly housing your coins and stamps reduces just about all the typical deterioration problems they face, so when planning how to safeguard stamps and coins think "Housing!"

Don's Rules for Preserving Coins and Stamps

1. Handle with care.
2. Handle with clean white cotton gloves.
3. Handle as little as possible.

4. To view them safely place them in the specific protective archival housings listed in the storage instructions below.

5. Keep stamps in the dark.

6. Make sure the moisture level in the environment is reasonably low.

7. Remove glue from the stamps to make them less attractive to bugs and fungi. (This is very controversial, so make sure you read that section carefully.)

8. Do not store them in the basement or attic.

DETERIORATION AND PRESERVATION OF COINS

The main problems for coins are corrosion and handling. Exactly how severe these are depends on the composition of the coins. For example, pure gold coins do not corrode at all—ever. That's one of the reasons gold (and platinum, although to my knowledge platinum is never used for currency coinage) is known as a "noble metal." However, gold is soft and susceptible to abrasion (being rubbed away) and distortions (nicks and dents). Gold is often alloyed or mixed with silver or copper to make it tougher and harder. Unfortunately, that makes gold coins susceptible to corrosion. Silver is less resistant to corrosion than gold, aluminum and nickel are even less so, and copper is fairly defenseless against corrosion over the long run.

Corrosion comes from components in the environment: moisture and pollutants. All by yourself you are a laboratory of corrosive agents, so perhaps what coins need to be protected from the most is you. Your breath, coughs, and sneezes contain quite a bit of moisture, and your skin is host to acids and even more moisture. Plus, your skin picks up and delivers a variety of contaminants: salt from the French fries you ate, chlorine from that dip in the hot tub or pool, and maybe acid from the tomatoes in the pizza sauce.

While it is a controversial topic, especially for coins with investment value, the process of safely cleaning coins to remove all possible corrosive contaminants is vital to their preservation. As I said earlier, if you consider your coins an investment, you should be aware that serious collectors sometimes consider the act of cleaning coins drastically reduces their monetary value. This is particularly true for archaeological coins. The dirt on these coins actually holds clues to their past (the layers of dirt can help explain where it came from and what the coin is), and particular types of light tarnishing, called toning, are considered part of a coin's value. In the case of archaeological coins, always consult an expert before proceeding. You can find one by contacting the American Numismatist Association at *www .money.org.*

Cleaning

When surface detailing is critical to their importance and appreciation, cleaning metal coins carefully is usually a two-step process. If you perform these steps in the sink, be sure to cover the drain. I use a Corning Ware pan.
    You will need the following supplies:

Polyethylene, polypropylene, or nitrile gloves
Distilled water
Anionic detergent (Triton 100)
Three clean polyethylene or polypropylene squirt bottles
Acetone
Alcohol
Clean, lint-free cotton flannel
Hair dryer

    1. Put on your polyethylene gloves. Although nitrile chemical-resistant surgical-style gloves are acceptable, do not use latex gloves while handling metal artifacts.
    2. Mix distilled water with a few drops of detergent in a squirt bottle.
    3. Fill a second squirt bottle with distilled water.
    4. Prepare a fifty-fifty mix of acetone and alcohol in a third squirt bottle.
    5. Wash the surface of the coin with the water-detergent solution. Hold the coin by the edges, rotate it, and squirt streams of the solution on both sides. Be sure you squirt it thoroughly enough to remove all surface dirt and water-soluble contaminants.
    6. Rinse the coin with the distilled water, making sure to flush all the detergent solution from the coin.
    7. Place the wet coin on the cotton flannel to soak up most of the water.
    8. Pick up the coin by the edges and dry it completely with warm air from the hair dryer. Be sure the air temperature isn't too hot for your hand since you will be holding the coin.
    9. Repeat steps 6 to 8, substituting the alcohol-acetone solution to re-

move any other surface contaminants. *Make sure you have adequate ventilation and have no sources of ignition nearby!* Do not perform these steps near a lit stove or even a lit candle. This cleaning solution is flammable!

10. Immediately place the coin in a coin sleeve as described below.

For coins, particularly ancient or even archaeological ones, the issue is corrosion. For any coin that has not been buried or subjected to other extreme environments, corrosion is manifest merely as surface tarnishing. On ancient or archaeological coinage (coins that have been buried for eons) corrosion can be present as a full-blown consuming event with spots of active, erupting degradation residing not only on the surface but also in the very structure of the coin. Fortunately, the solution is fairly simple. Recounting the sources of deterioration listed in Chapter 1 and earlier in this chapter, you know that metal corrosion needs two basic ingredients: moisture and oxygen. The preservation response to corrosion on coins is to keep them in containers that seal them, or at least protect them, from moisture and oxygen.

Housing and Storing

The processes of housing and storing coins for long-term preservation are well understood, fairly simple, and inexpensive for even the most inexperienced collectors. There are several layers of protection possible for coins, each one wrapped around the previous one.

The first level of housing is the archival folder or envelope. There are three main types of envelopes for housing coins in order to minimize deterioration. By simply placing your coins in these housings, you can preserve them almost indefinitely.

The first style of envelope is called a *flip,* which is really a tiny coin-sized envelope made from polyethylene, polypropylene, or polyester (Mylar). It often has two pockets, one for the coin and the other for a piece of paper on which to write any important information.

A *coin sleeve* is really a tiny polyester (Mylar) flat folder between two square cardboard pieces with a round cutout so the coin is fully visible. Simply stapling the edges carefully encloses the coin in an excellent protective housing.

The third type of envelope is a tiny *polyethylene zippered bag.* An

DON'S TIP: Cleaning Your Delicates

Do not use abrasive or chemical polishes when cleaning your coins because they can damage the delicate surface of the coins. Serious collectors prefer that the surface of a coin be untouched.

archival-grade zippered bag is usually made from virgin polyethylene and without excess plasticizers that can leach out and contaminate nearby materials. Simply place the coin inside, seal it, and you are done.

The second level of housing is a metal storage cabinet in which to place individually packaged coins. Wood is not a good choice for your coin collection because many woods contain chemicals that would be harmful to metal surfaces. Ideally, the metal storage cabinets or drawer units have either no paint on them or a type of paint known as fused-powder-coating or baked enamel to make sure no corrosive chemicals evaporate from the paint. If there is paint on the cabinet, be sure to ask about the type to help ensure that you are getting the best possible housing for your coins. In addition to providing additional physical protection for your coin collection and making organizing it easier, a metal storage cabinet filled with properly packaged coins has little room for environmental contaminants such as oxygen, pollutants, or moisture. As a practical matter, the drier the space coins are in, the better.

The third and highest preservation level of housing is a sealed storage cabinet specifically manufactured for storing fragile or chemically sensitive materials.

Short of a real-live sealed bank vault, this is the way to go if you are committed to preserving your coin collection. Be sure the cabinets have sulfur-free gaskets; otherwise, they are worse than storing your coins in nothing because you will be placing them in a sealed space with corrosive pollutants. The salesperson selling these items should be able to answer your questions. If he cannot, you need to shop somewhere else. To be sure, most folks won't go to this extreme, but if you are serious about your coin collection, this is where you are going to end up.

You can even improve the performance of sealed cabinets by taking two simple and inexpensive steps: (1) Put desiccated silica gel inside the case to absorb any moisture, and (2) place canisters of activated charcoal inside the cabinet to absorb any harmful pollutants. The simplest way to do this is to use filtering canisters from industrial respirators designed for removing organic solvents; these are available at most hardware and paint stores, especially auto paint stores. Place the canisters, which are about the size of an English muffin, in the cabinet and replace them every few months. You can even get canisters for acids or bases from laboratory supply houses listed in Resources at the back of this book.

DETERIORATION AND PRESERVATION OF STAMPS

Stamps are tiny artistic prints on paper. Their preservation needs are indistinguishable from other paper artifacts such as those covered in Chapters 11 and 13.

While stamps are about as different from coins as you could imagine from a materials point of view, the preservation concepts are nearly identical: They must be protected from the environment, and they must be protected from you. Obviously, the corrosion so dangerous to coins is not really an issue for stamps. As with all artwork on paper, the risks come from handling, light, biodeterioration, and inherent vice (bad paper or ink). While they can be abraded by careless handling and soiled by airborne contaminants, good handling and housekeeping habits reduce these risks to almost zero.

As with so many items cataloged in this book, one of the worst enemies that stamps encounter is your skin. Skin is damp and sticky and carries chemicals that are necessary for your health but are destructive to artifacts. The moisture on your skin can stain and encourage mold growth on stamps (the same is true for your breath as well, so wearing a mask when working with stamps is a good idea), and the acids from your skin can stain and in some cases change the color of the printing inks.

Stamps are almost a hothouse for biodeterioration. Think about it: They are made from paper (silverfish food), have a coat-

DON'S TIP: Tweezers Aren't Just for Splinters

A useful tool for handling stamps is a Teflon or Teflon-coated pair of tweezers with bulbous rounded tips. These tweezers won't scratch the stamp because of the bulbous Teflon tips. They are available from philatelic or laboratory suppliers.

ing (glue, which critters love to eat), and at some point many of them have been licked (and you know what the mouth is like).

Glue: To Remove or Not to Remove, That Is the Question

On the one hand, glue is part of the original fabric of the stamp, and any effort to preserve the collection by removing an integral component accom-

plishes exactly the opposite. It preserves the collectible but forever changes the nature of it.

On the other hand, from a strictly preservation point of view, the glue is a prime starting point for deterioration of stamps. Depending on when and where the stamp was made, the glue could be gum arabic (prior to 1900), dextrin (until 1970), or polyvinyl alcohol or other water-soluble polymer (to the present). These materials are not only moisture sensitive, which is what makes them good stamp adhesives, but the first two are a great source of rodent, insect, and fungi nutrients. For that reason stamp glue may be removed. If you are confident of your ability to keep your stamps protected from moisture, rodents, insects, and fungi, then removing the adhesive is not such an important issue.

Whether the glue from stamps should be removed is the kind of decision conservators and other preservation specialists must face daily when dealing with complicated collections.

To remove the glue from stamps (non-self-sticking), you will need the following supplies:

Acid-free blotter paper
Cotton swabs
Distilled water

1. Place the stamp facedown on a sheet of blotter paper.
2. Moisten a cotton swab with distilled water and gently roll it over the glue.
3. Gently roll another moistened swab across the back of the stamp to remove the glue. Do not scrub. Roll gently.
4. Repeat with new moistened swabs until the glue is completely gone.
5. Pat the stamp dry with a small square of blotter paper.
6. Place the stamp between two small squares of dry blotter paper and under gentle weight for two hours to make sure it is perfectly dry and flat.

To remove pressure-sensitive (self-sticking) glue from stamps, you will need the following supplies:

Acid-free blotter paper
Cotton swabs
Mineral spirits (use and dispose of carefully, along with the blotter paper, because it is flammable)

1. Place the stamp facedown on the blotter paper.
2. Moisten a cotton swab with mineral spirits and gently roll it over the glue.
3. Repeat with new moistened swabs until the adhesive is completely gone. Do not scrub. Roll gently.
4. Pat the stamp dry with a small square of blotter paper.
5. Place the stamp between two small squares of dry blotter paper and under gentle weight for two hours to make sure it is perfectly dry and flat.
6. Dispose of the swabs and solvent-laden blotter paper carefully because they are flammable. Either set outside to dry completely before putting in the trash or place them in an approved solvent disposal container.

Housing Your Stamp Collection

As with coins, the importance of housing and storing stamps for long-term preservation are well understood and fairly simple and inexpensive for even the most novice collectors. There are several levels of protection possible for stamps, each one building on the previous one.

The first level of housing is the archival folder or envelope. There are two main types of envelopes for housing stamps to minimize the deterioration. Both employ inert archival material in direct contact with the stamp and protect it from the surrounding environment—you included. By simply placing your stamps in these housings you can increase their life span immensely.

The first type of stamp container is simply an envelope, sleeve, or small folder made from acid-free archival paper. Inexpensive and easy to make and use, it is perfect from a strictly preservation perspective. Unfortunately, it is opaque, so the stamps have to be removed in order to view them.

The second type of envelope is a sleeve or tiny folder made from polyethylene, polypropylene, or polyester (Mylar). It has the advantage of being transparent, so you can examine the stamp while it is still in its protective housing.

The next level of housing is to place the individual packages of stamps in a fire-resistant folder and then in a box, preferably fireproof, or place them in an archival-grade stamp album.

For the highest level of housing for stamps, refer to the third and highest preservation level of housing for coins on page 206.

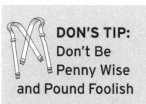

DON'S TIP:
Don't Be Penny Wise and Pound Foolish

As with coins, do not use housing made from polyvinyl chloride. These will damage the stamps. Polyester, also known as Mylar, costs only a bit more and is worth the extra few pennies.

Inherent Vice

Since some stamps are made from unstable materials, either in the paper, the ink, or the adhesive, there is only so much you can do to preserve them. If the paper is a poor-quality wood pulp paper, the discoloration and brittleness is pretty much inevitable. You can delay it with archival housing and by using buffers, but the bad stuff is going to happen sooner than if the stamp was on rag paper.

Stamps on envelopes: Many times stamps come into your possession with a fragment of an envelope still attached. In the case of rag paper stationery, this is not really a preservation issue as much as an aesthetic one. The stamp and envelope do not need to be separated for preservation purposes. However, if the envelope is made of wood pulp paper, it does become a serious preservation issue, and the envelope and the stamp will need to be separated. To determine the type of paper you are dealing with, try the pH test in Don's Tip on page 196. To separate the stamp from the envelope, follow the procedures described above in the section on removing glue. For preserving stamps and the envelope to which it is attached, refer to "Old Letters" in Chapter 11, Saving Your Books, Comic Books, Newspapers, Magazines, and Letters.

For stamps with light-sensitive ink, the only reasonable response is to treat them the way teenagers try to treat their parents: Keep them in the dark. Other inks "burn" or eat through the page due to the acidic or corrosive chemicals in the ink. In these instances you need to seek the advice of a stamp or paper conservator. You can obtain referrals for these specialists either at the American Institute for Conservation at *http://aic.stanford.edu* or the American Philatelic Society at *www.stamps.org*.

PART FOUR

Preserving Really
Valuable Stuff

Chapter 13

Taking Care of Fine Art

The huge Italian master oil painting rested safely upright against the wall while my boss and the auction house representative argued back and forth in English and French, growling at each other about where to hang it. The argument was almost as fierce as the battle scene depicted in the painting, with wild gesturing hands and loud passionate voices as each expressed his opinion about where to hang this masterpiece. As a budding conservator I felt lucky just to be in the same room as this magnificent canvas with its carved gilded frame, and I certainly knew better than to offer any comment. And, to be honest, at first I could not understand the point of the debate. The painting was six feet high and eight feet wide. It could be seen from the next county! So why all the arguing about location?

As my career progressed, I began to understand that location of artwork is everything. The painting had to hang in a place where it could not only be seen properly but also would not be damaged by excess light, careless housekeeping, direct air blowing on it from the HVAC (heating, ventilating, and air-conditioning) system, or other agents of deterioration. When together they agreed on the best place to hang the gigantic oil painting, a spirit of camaraderie emerged. This amazed me, but looking back almost thirty years, I realize that each respected the other's devotion to preserving great works of art, and a multimillion-dollar masterpiece is certainly worth an argument or two in order to ensure its longevity.

Whether the artwork is a sculpture fashioned out of wood, granite, marble, concrete, paper, steel, or bronze; an Old Master oil painting; a landscape, still-life, domestic scene, modern art, or historical panorama, concern for the location of the artwork on exhibit is almost always the top consideration. It's the first thing we think about at the Smithsonian, and it should be your first consideration, too.

THINK "LOCATION, LOCATION, LOCATION"

Fine art includes those objects whose primary purpose is to be looked at and enjoyed by the viewer. This could be the Picasso you won at auction for $3 million or the charming watercolor of Paris my younger daughter picked up while on vacation. As such, the location is critical for that enjoyment. However, the location is even more critical to its preservation because where it is displayed is the single greatest factor in accelerating or retarding its deterioration. So when deciding how to take care of your art think "Location, Location, Location."

Don's Rules for Location, Location, Location

1. *Never* hang artworks above a radiator or heat vent. You can assume both dirt and excessive heat will harm the artwork hung here. You might note that this space always shows streaky dirt marks on the wall sooner than any other space in a room and is usually warm to the touch. Heat speeds up deterioration. The dirt from the vent becomes deposited on the painting and frame, and requires frequent cleaning, which is also damaging.

2. *Never* hang artwork above the fireplace. Even the best fireplaces emit a certain amount of soot, and the chimney exudes warmth through the wall. Soot is dirt, and warmth dries the painting, which can lead to cracking. Where a painting is built into the wall, there is nothing to be done other than daily dusting. It should also be cleaned annually in situ by a professional painting conservator.

3. *Never* voluntarily place a painting in any space that becomes visibly dirty in a short period of time.

4. *Never* hang a painting directly in line with air vents. Even a painting across the room from a vent will receive a load of soot from the vent unless the vent is fitted with a filter to hold back the dirt. Place the painting where the air from the vent does not blow directly onto the painting.

5. *Never* hang paintings in any area that receives heavy traffic. Hallways that receive a great deal of traffic are potentially harmful spaces for paintings because people can bump into them. As mentioned earlier, humans are the greatest single source of damage to antiques. This includes their clothing, elbows, umbrellas, handbags, and any other items they may be carrying through the hallway such as potted plants, floral arrangements, and other stuff. Your precious art can be knocked off the wall, broken, scratched, smudged with messy fingers, and so forth.

6. *Never* hang paintings on any wall that receives direct sunlight. The photochemical damage done by sunlight is not to be underestimated. The good news is that the damage can be reduced or eliminated entirely by the use of curtains or shades on the windows to cut the sun's rays.

DON'S TIP:
Never Use Glass or Plastic Glazing for Paintings

In general, unless there are high security needs, glass, acrylic (Plexiglas), and polycarbonate (Lexan) covers are not recommended for use on paintings unless they were part of the original design by the artist. Glass is always potentially more harmful to the piece because of the possibility that it may crack, break, or shatter, especially in transit, and puncture the painting. While acrylic and polycarbonate do not break or shatter under normal circumstances (they "bulletproof" your bank, after all), they have the disadvantage of creating static electricity when rubbed. This means that when the surface is dusted with a rag or brush during cleaning, for example, static electricity is built up on the opposite side of the glazing (the side toward the painting). This static electricity can lift the design medium off its support and destroy the design. That's right: The static will actually yank the picture off the support (I have seen this even in museums). Plexiglas and polycarbonate also tend to scratch very easily and develop a very cloudy appearance over a period of time.

FRAMED ARTWORK

Framed artwork, which includes many different types of images, is divided into two broad groups: paintings and artwork on paper.

Paintings include oil on canvas, acrylic on canvas, and panels.

Artwork on paper includes watercolors, lithographs, drawings, engravings, etchings, gouaches (opaque watercolors), collages, and other composite creations.

Preserving Paintings

Preserving paintings requires you to pay attention to each of several causes of deterioration mentioned frequently in this book: Light, temperature, relative humidity, insects, humans, and atmospheric pollutants all have an impact on fine art. You also need to make sure they are hung properly on the wall and don't come crashing down.

Why do paintings require so much care? Paintings are multi-component pieces of art, unlike a bronze sculpture, tapestry, or piece of marble, all of which are usually made of one component or material. Paintings have a relatively delicate painted surface, which may be tender when new but becomes hard and brittle with age. The paint layer can rest on a paper, silk, wood, linen, cotton, glass, or metal base, which is usually coated with some sort of primer or "ground," traditionally a mix of powdered chalk and glue called gesso.

Illuminating paintings properly is critical to their preservation, regardless of whether it is oil on canvas, acrylic, or oil or tempera on panel.

Don's Rules for Lighting Paintings

1. The visible light level should not exceed 15 foot-candles. (See page 5 for more about measuring light.)

2. Ultraviolet light from the sun or unfiltered UV-emitting fluorescent lamps should never fall on the surface of a painting. This means never place your painting in direct sunlight, and, if possible, use UV-filtering glass for your windows.

3. Do not use picture lamps attached to the painting frame. Not only do they do a pretty bad job (the lighting is uneven; it is too dim at the edges and

too bright in the center) but they create unnecessary heat problems because they are too close to the painting surface.

4. Floodlights are preferred, provided they are not close enough to cause heat problems. If you can feel the heat of the lamp on the surface of the painting, it is too close.

5. Incandescent floodlights on ceiling tracks are also a good way to light paintings. The cooler, more diffused floodlights are always preferred to the use of picture lamps and spotlights. I particularly like 12-volt halogen floods because they can be placed several feet away from the artwork.

6. Fiber-optic lighting is the best because it provides excellent illumination while reducing the risk from heat almost to zero.

Your skin is damaged by the total exposure to sunlight, which is a function of the time spent in the sun and the intensity of the light (time of day, season, latitude). You understand the need to monitor both the intensity of the light on your skin and the length of time your skin is exposed to it. Too bright or too long an exposure, and your skin will burn. Like you, an artwork is damaged by the total exposure to light. Both the intensity and the length of exposure need to be monitored to safeguard the condition of the artwork.

Don's Rules for Handling Paintings

1. Avoid touching the painted surface of the painting at any time, especially when dealing with exposed, unprimed canvases used in modern painting. If the varnish on a painting is in poor condition, even gentle pressure will leave a mark that may require treatment of the entire painted surface.

2. Make sure that your hands are clean or, better yet, eliminate contact with the painting by wearing cotton gloves.

3. Remove watches or jewelry before handling paintings because they can damage the paint surface.

4. Handle only one painting at a time.

5. Move large panels and canvases with two or more persons.

6. Never stack paintings on top of one another.

7. If paintings have to rest on the floor, place them on thick carpet or pads. Never leave them standing directly on the floor because a hard floor can chip the edges of the painting.

8. It is always better for paintings to stand up rather than lie flat.

9. When paintings must be leaned against each other, make sure there is a layer of padding, such as acid-free mat board or bubble wrap, between items.

10. Never grab a painting by the top of the frame. Always carry a painting with one hand placed under the bottom of the frame and the other hand at the side, both at points where the frame is solid.

11. Handle only paintings that have an intact paint surface and a stable frame and stretcher.

12. If paint flakes or the frame parts become detached, save all the pieces in small plastic zippered bags. Repairs are much easier and less expensive if all the parts are available to the restorer.

Oil Painting or Acrylic Painting?

While oil paint is fundamentally different from acrylic paint, in the hands of an inspired artist they can be made to look the same. Distinguishing one from the other depends on (1) documentary evidence—in other words, what do you already know from records or conversations, such as was it painted in 1900 or 2000? If the answer is the former, you certainly do not have an acrylic. If the latter is the answer, you have no certainty one way or the other, and (2) analytical evidence through scientific testing. If we have to determine which material was used for a painting about which we know nothing, a series of chemical analyses are required. This often requires taking tiny samples from the painting and subjecting them to a variety of physical and chemical tests that are usually beyond your abilities as a collector unless you have a microscope with a digitally controlled high-temperature hot stage (which means you heat and control the melting of the sample), or instruments such as infrared spectrophotometers. That is the only way to make sure you have an oil painting or an acrylic.

OIL PAINTINGS

If you ask the ordinary person on the street, "What is art?" the answer will probably come back as a reference to some famous painting. For most people oil paintings on canvas are synonymous with art. With a tradition going back five centuries, the character and preservation of oil paintings are fairly well known, with the exception of those paintings created by "experimental" painters who step outside the boundaries of tried-and-true techniques and materials. Otherwise, the steps to preserving oil paintings are straightforward and simple if not always easy to accomplish: Maintain a stable, benign environment with moderate temperature and humidity. Keep them clean. Reduce the light exposure.

Temperature and Humidity

Generally, the best relative humidity for most oil paintings is between 45 and 55 percent and as much stability as you can get. Stability is usually more important than any specific number. Fluctuations should not be more than 3 to 5 percent per month. For some paintings humidity is the major concern; for others it is temperature. It is sometimes a difficult balancing act and should be guided by the types of paintings you have. Traditional oil over gesso on canvas paintings are more sensitive to humidity changes than temperature. For traditional oil paintings in poor environmental conditions, the sizing (like primer, glue that seals the canvas or wood panel), and paint layers of paintings can become extremely brittle. Paintings are likely to develop cracks and eventual paint loss due to flakes of paint falling off the surface of the canvas when the humidity is very low.

The support, if made of organic materials such as canvas, paper, or wood, may shrink or expand with changes in temperature and relative humidity in ways different from the paint layer or the ground. All of these problems relate to the problem of proper climate control.

Also, when humidity and temperature are high, mold growth is likely. It can stain the artwork and, if severe enough, break it down completely. Lowering relative humidity to at least 60 percent can halt fungal growth. If you have recurring problems with this, consult a painting conservator, who should be able to assess not only the environmental conditions but also the specific needs of the painting in relation to adjusting the moisture content of the environment.

Changes in humidity levels also change the properties of the ingredients from which the painting is made, especially the size and flexibility. While fungal activity is always a risk for most artifacts, including paintings, the greatest risks from uncontrolled temperature and humidity are structural.

Contamination

The buildup of dirt, grime, and pollutants on the surface of oil paintings is a serious issue and needs to be monitored and mitigated constantly. Paints often react with pollution in the atmosphere and change color. While it is not quite as serious as contaminants on acrylic paintings because oil paintings are generally tougher and harder, the presence of contaminants is deleterious and for the most part preventable.

Don's Rules for Minimizing the Dangers of Contamination with Oil Paintings

1. Keep the windows and exterior doors closed as much as possible. These are your primary barriers against outdoor pollution.

2. Do not allow cigarette smoking, if at all possible, where valuable artwork is exhibited or actively used. It causes a yellow film over the paints or inks used in many artworks.

3. Keep the filters clean on your HVAC system.

4. Keep away from food preparation areas.

Preservation

You will need the following supplies:

Clean white cotton gloves
Clean work area
Soft artist's brush
Photographer's compressed air can (see Caution 1 below)
Vacuum

Caution 1: Brush-dusting a painting that has a matte (non-shiny) surface (lean in binder or loaded with pigments) may burnish the painting and leave a permanent undesirable glossy imprint. In this case, don't brush. Instead, use a can of photographer's compressed air and gently blow off the surface.

Caution 2: Do not try to remove slight scratches, rubbed spots, or dirt marks.

Caution 3: If there is stuck-on grime, you will need to call in a professional to clean the painting. You can get a referral for a painting conservator in your area by contacting the American Institute for Conservation at *http://aic.stanford.edu* or by asking at your local art museum.

1. Put on your clean white cotton gloves.

2. Place the painting on a clean padded surface and hold it so that the painting is upright but leaning forward slightly.

3. Take the artist's brush and gently brush from top to bottom.

4. Repeat, this time brushing gently from bottom to top.

5. Brush gently from left to right.

6. Repeat, this time brushing gently from right to left.

7. If the rear of the painting and frame are in good condition, you may gently clean the back side with the brush attachment on your vacuum.

PANEL PAINTINGS

Not all paintings are executed on a canvas background. Many, including the *Mona Lisa,* are painted on a panel of solid wood. Panel paintings are usually painted with either oil paint or egg tempera, which is created by mixing dry pigments with egg yolks. Panel paintings have the same set of problems that paintings on canvas do, with the addition of new problems due to the interrelationship between wood and the surrounding environment. Since wood expands and contracts with changes of relative humidity, the concerns of stable environments are even more important here.

The "perfect" environment for paintings on wood panels is about 65 degrees Fahrenheit and any stable and sustainable relative humidity between about 35 and 60 percent. The exact numbers for temperature and humidity are much less important than their constancy. Extreme fluctuations in relative humidity will cause measurable change in the size of panels, which causes both warping of the panel and cracking and flaking of the painting itself. This results in eventual destruction of either the paint layer or the panel.

Fluctuations of humidity will first affect the bare wood surface and the rest of the rear, causing the painting to cup toward the rear.

If you have a panel painting, do not attempt to flatten it yourself because unless you are an expert in wood engineering, the results will likely be unsuccessful and will probably damage both the panel and the painting on it. Seek the expertise of a conservator experienced in preserving painted wood panels. You can get a referral for a painting conservator in your area by contacting the American Institute for Conservation at *http://aic.stanford.edu,* or asking at your local art museum.

ACRYLIC PAINTINGS

Artists' acrylic paints were introduced in the 1950s and have dominated the art and craft market ever since. The physical and chemical properties of acrylics are so different from oil paint that they warrant distinct guidelines for their care. Also, lesser-quality acrylic paints tend to have cheaper colorants, which fade easily under light, especially ultraviolet. Thus, fading may change the appearance of the painting due to the intrinsic nature of the materials, and this change cannot be reversed. Acrylic paintings usually develop fewer cracks than oil paintings when kept at room temperature because they are so much softer.

The relationship of an acrylic painting to temperature and relative humidity is generally the opposite of oil paintings: Acrylics are much more sensitive to temperature extremes than to humidity and moisture. Contemporary acrylic paintings become sticky at higher temperatures and brittle at colder temperatures. This is because the acrylic medium is a plastic that is sensitive to temperature changes; cold makes it brittle, and hot makes it soft. They are also more susceptible to mold and mildew than are oil paintings.

Don's Rules for Minimizing the Dangers of Temperature and Relative Humidity

1. Never let acrylics become too hot. Acrylic paint becomes extremely soft and puttylike around 140 degrees Fahrenheit or in the attic or car on a hot sunny day.

2. Never let acrylic paints become too cold. Cracks can form in acrylic paintings, especially those exposed to cool or cold temperatures. In extreme cold they can literally shatter like glass.

3. Don't keep acrylic paintings in a humid room. Mold growth on acrylic paintings can result if the temperature and humidity reach slightly elevated

levels. You must pay very close attention to this. Keep humidity between 40 and 55 percent.

4. In short, any acrylic painting exposed to extreme temperatures—in direct sunlight or freezing cold, for example—is at risk of immediate destruction.

5. The ideal temperature is between 60 and 70 degrees Fahrenheit.

Contamination

Unlike oil paintings, which harden to a firm surface even if they never actually chemically "dry," acrylic paintings are softer and will always remain slightly tacky. The upside to acrylics is that they allow for exuberant and immediate artistic expression. The downside is that they love dirt and dust. The paint surface holds on to dust and dirt and even absorbs them into the film.

To minimize the dangers of contamination, keep the environment cool, between 50 and 70 degrees Fahrenheit. If too warm, acrylics soften and can then trap dirt.

Preservation

You will need the following:

> Clean white cotton gloves
> Clean work area
> Photographer's compressed air can
> Vacuum

DON'S TIP:
Cold and Acrylics, a Bad Combination

The brittleness of acrylic paint at low temperatures is an important consideration when shipping paintings in the hold of an airplane or storing them in an unheated space where temperatures can get very, very cold. If by chance you leave an acrylic painting in your car overnight in January in my hometown in Minnesota, be prepared for the painting to turn into a pile of broken glassy shards if bumped or dropped.

Caution 1: Never touch or brush the painting's face because it may develop static electricity and attract even more contamination.

Caution 2: Never touch an acrylic painting because it may be soft enough to abrade or dent with just gentle contact.

Note: If the paintings acquire a gray veil on their surface or have developed yellow discoloration with aging, consult a conservator of modern art.

1. Put on your clean white cotton gloves.

2. Place the painting on a clean padded surface, holding it so that the painting is upright but leaning forward slightly.

3. Gently blow off the front of the painting with the compressed air.

4. If the rear of the painting and frame are in good condition, you may *gently* clean the back side with the brush attachment on your vacuum.

PRESERVING GILDED FRAMES

Gilded frames are also complicated objects made of different materials: wood, composition (a molding material for ornaments), gesso, clay, gold size (the glue that holds the gold leaf on the surface), and the gold leaf itself. As with paintings, this layered structure is sensitive to extreme environmental fluctuations. Make sure those do not happen.

Improper environments, storage, exhibition, or housekeeping can result in frames suffering from flaking gesso, cracking composition ornament, and worn gold leaf. Any frame that is in sound condition (nothing loose or flaking off) can be dusted with a soft artist's brush in the same manner as a painting.

UNFRAMED ARTWORK ON PAPER

Unframed artwork on paper includes pastels, engravings, etchings, charcoal and graphite drawings, watercolors, ink washes, and collages. These are most at risk from contact, abrasion, and loss of artwork.

Handling is probably the most common cause of damage for unframed art on paper. Paper is easily torn, creased, or stained, and artwork smudged or abraded and removed. *Handle paper as little as possible.* It is always preferable to handle the mat or frame holding the artwork rather than the artwork itself. In the absence of a frame or mat, handle a support sheet underneath the artwork. If you are not able to get your art matted and framed immediately, here are some guidelines for caring for them until you get that task completed.

Don's Rules for Preserving Unframed Artwork on Paper

1. To prevent staining or other damage from oils and salts on hands, it is advisable to wear white cotton gloves.

2. When lifting your artwork, slide a stiff acid-free paper or mat board below it for support before moving it.

3. Avoid eating, drinking, or smoking near the paper and keep pens and markers away.

4. Do not store Mylar or plastic folders, sleeves, or protective sheets on artwork with media that could be easily crumbled or rubbed off, such as charcoal, graphite, heavy gouache, or conte crayon. A static charge can build up that may lead to the charcoal or pastel being "pulled" from the surface.

5. Unframed artwork on paper can be stored in acid-free paper folders.

6. Get help if more than one person is required to move oversized, unwieldy, or heavy material. If you cannot carry the art comfortably with your two hands, get a helper.

7. Hold the artwork lightly by diagonal corners if the corners are strong, pinching the corners between pieces of folded acid-free paper. Move unsupported artwork by holding it catty-cornered.

8. Keep the area around the artwork clean to avoid attracting insects and rodents.

9. Keep the light levels down. Control light intensity, proximity, and duration. Dark is best.

10. If you have to handle the artwork with bare hands, wash your hands frequently and make sure they are dry before touching the paper or medium.

11. Keep any loose or broken pieces together.

12. Don't handle documents more than necessary.

13. Don't slide artworks around on top of each other.

14. Don't glue fragile paper on fabric, since fabric expands and contracts differently from paper.

15. Don't trim artwork or dispose of fragmented pieces.

16. Never use any pressure-sensitive tape to repair tears and missing pieces.

17. Don't laminate art on paper, since the heat or solvent used can cause damage.

FRAMED ARTWORK ON PAPER

"Would you like to come upstairs and see my etchings?"

The first time I read this pickup line in a novel, I was completely clueless about what it meant. As a lifelong craftsman I was familiar with the process of etching the surface of metal car and motorcycle parts in preparation for chrome plating. I never could figure out why a guy would invite a girl up to his apartment to see motorcycle parts.

Framed artwork on paper includes a wide range of techniques and formats: prints, drawings, collages, and watercolors. Prints include etchings, engravings, aquatints and mezzotints, lithographs, and woodcuts. Drawings are, uh, drawings using chalk, charcoal, graphite pencil, crayons, pastels, markers, or anything that can make a mark on a piece of paper. Collages are an assemblage of individual pieces, which can be anything from paper or textiles to plastics, composed in a desired expression and glued onto a paper sheet. Watercolors and ink drawings include washes (transparent watercolor), gouaches (opaque watercolor), and pen and ink or brush drawings.

Lighting

For many artworks on paper, most notably collages, watercolors, and ink drawings, lighting is the single most important issue concerning their preservation while they are on display.

Don's Rules for Lighting

1. Exposure to light (natural or artificial) causes fading, discoloration, and embrittlement of artwork on paper, especially watercolors, Japanese ink prints, and drawings of iron gall ink or felt-tip markers.

2. Light damage is permanent and cannot be undone.

3. Do not display your artwork where it may be exposed to sunlight.

4. Use curtains, blinds, or shutters in rooms where you hang your artwork.

5. Make sure any glazing over your artwork has ultraviolet filtering ability.

6. Follow the general strategies for lighting your art on paper as that for paintings, armed with the knowledge that the light level should be only one-tenth as bright.

7. Heat speeds up chemical reactions that lead to the degradation of paper. Avoid intense spotlights and hang prints and drawings away from radiators and heating ducts.

8. Keep the light low! Light levels for exhibiting art on paper should not exceed 5 foot-candles.

9. Don't expose documents to unnecessary light because this will result in fading and/or darkening.

10. Get in the habit of rotating your artworks on display. We do it in museums, and you should, too.

11. Don't allow lighting sources to come close enough to cause heat damage; it is especially severe when it can build up "greenhouse" style in an enclosed and glass-fronted frame.

Moisture

Avoid displaying or storing your artwork where temperatures and humidity (especially!) levels fluctuate wildly. High moisture causes paper to swell and expand as it absorbs water. If this happens and the paper has no room to expand (or even if it does), paper will appear rippled or, in extreme cases, wrinkled. Also, when paper is exposed to elevated moisture, it is at risk for accelerated chemical degradation (that is, foxing—spots that appear on the paper) and mold.

And that's just the paper. There are also the effects of moisture on the media. Many, if not most, artistic media for art on paper can be severely damaged by moisture. High, low, or fluctuating moisture can wreak havoc as media become softer (high humidity), harder or more brittle (low humidity), migratory, or respond physically different from the paper on which they reside.

Museum-quality matting and framing briefly protect paper from the potential damages of fluctuating relative humidity. Depending on how tightly the "package" is constructed, this protection from moisture and temperature variations can last for a few hours or even a few days.

Don's Rules for Moisture and Artwork on Paper

1. Keep the humidity stable and about 40 percent.

2. High humidity not only encourages mold and chemical deterioration, but it also swells the paper and can cause a type of warping called buckling where the paper gets bigger than the space allotted for it and starts to pucker like your skin after washing dishes.

3. Never have moisture around art on paper. Keep drinks away, keep plants away, and keep steaming food away.

4. Don't keep prints in high-humidity environments such as bathrooms, kitchens, and near hot tubs or exercise equipment—even framed artwork. (I say this, but even I have prints in the kitchen and bathroom, but they're not expensive ones.)

5. Be careful about the heat generated by light illuminating the artwork. Especially in enclosed glazed frames, localized heat can get very high, driving down the humidity to dangerous levels for the artwork by desiccating and embrittling it.

Bugs and Mold

Silverfish, book lice, and bookworms want to eat your paper artwork. In fact, they want to eat not just the paper but some of the artistic media as well, such as pastels and some watercolor binders. If your artwork looks worn away and you know it has not been abraded, you might have silverfish. Dead ones tend not to be much of a problem, but the live ones will keep chomping away. Since silverfish and other insects like a cool, dark, moist, undisturbed environment, you must turn your attention to these conditions if you suspect a problem. Identify and eliminate the moisture source and step up your housekeeping.

Don's Rules for Protecting Your Artworks on Paper from Critters

1. Check for evidence of critters on a regular basis.

2. Place insect traps near where you store your artwork on paper. Do not place insect traps on the actual art.

Matting and Framing Art on Paper

Archival matting and framing is the only real strategy for preserving art on paper that is going to be displayed. Proper matting and framing reduces almost completely the risks from handling and from brief moisture and humidity fluctuations. It can provide about as much light protection as possible while displaying the artwork.

The procedures and materials for doing this may seem daunting, and the description is very long. Even if you do not choose to mat and frame your own artwork, be sure that whoever does follows the procedure exactly. Consult the illustrations 13-1 and 13-2 to make sure you understand what is happening.

Matting and framing art requires three separate steps:
Step 1: Making the matting package
Step 2: Mounting the artwork to the back mat
Step 3: Assembling the mat in the frame

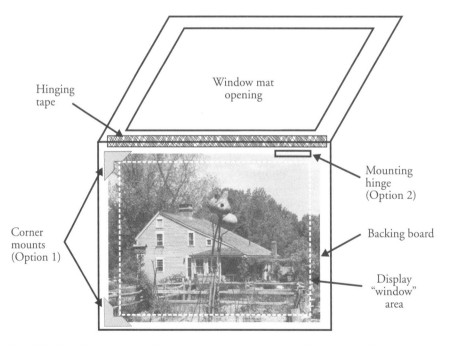

Illus. 13-1. This diagram shows two separate options for matting works of art on paper. The left end of the artwork is held to the backing board by corner mounts, while the right end is attached at the top only by paper hinges glued to the back of the artwork and the front of the backing board.

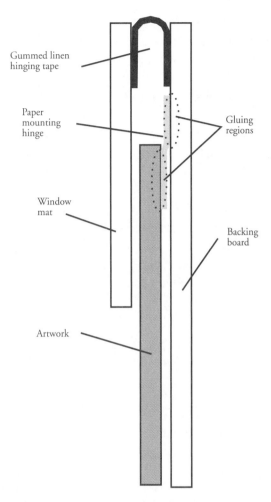

Gummed linen
hinging tape

Paper
mounting
hinge

Gluing
regions

Window
mat

Backing
board

Artwork

*Illus. 13-2. A cross-section diagram of the archival window mat system with the
artwork mounted to the backing board with acid-free paper hinges.*

Step 1: Making the Matting Package

You will need the following supplies:

4-ply acid-free archival mat board
Straightedge ruler
Razor knife or mat cutter
Moisture-activated linen tape or Japanese tissue strips and
    conservation-grade adhesive

1. Cut a back mat and matching window mat for your artwork out of the acid-free mat board using the mat cutting tools. The back mat should be at least 1 inch larger than the artwork on all sides. The outer edge of the window mat should be the same dimension as the back mat. The inner edge should be at the border of the graphical design.

2. Hinge together the back mat and window mat using the moisture-activated linen tape or a strip of Japanese tissue paper and adhesive. Linen tape is usually about 1 inch wide. If you are using Japanese tissue paper instead, use the ruler to tear a piece 1 inch wide as long as the edges to be glued together.

3. Place the artwork on the back mat and gently close the window mat over it. Maneuver the artwork into the exact location it needs to be in relation to the window mat.

4. Carefully open the window mat, making sure not to move the artwork.

5. Using a pencil, mark the back mat with the location of the corners and top edge of the artwork.

Step 2: Mounting the Artwork to the Back Mat

You will need the following:

> Japanese tissue paper
> Conservation-grade adhesive
> Ruler

1. Using the ruler as a straight edge, tear two paper strips from the Japanese tissue paper. These strips will be folded and glued to both the artwork and the back mat as hinges to hold the artwork in place and yet still allow a little flexibility in case the environment fluctuates. The hinges should total approximately one-fourth of the total top edge of the artwork. For very large artwork, multiple pairs of hinges may be necessary.

2. Use the adhesive to make each hinge adhere to the back side of the artwork along the top edge, with about one-tenth of the artwork sticking out past the hinge.

3. Place the artwork against the back mat, following the layout marks you made earlier.

4. Lift the hinges and apply the adhesive to make the hinges adhere to the back mat. *Never* glue the artwork itself to the back mat.

You have now created an archival window mat for your artwork. The back mat obviously supports the artwork and provides protection for physical damage coming from the rear. The window mat "frames" the image of the artwork and provides a valuable spacer for the front of the artwork, making sure it never comes into contact with any protective glazing in front of the artwork when in the frame.

Step 3: Assembling the Mat in the Frame

In this section I refer to the covering that is placed over art as glazing rather than as glass. That is because glass is not always the best choice, depending on the type of art.

You will need the following:

Frame
Appropriate glazing (glass) (UV-filtering acrylic or polycarbonate
     for watercolors, ink drawings, engravings, and etchings; glass
     panes for charcoal, pencil, conte crayon, or pastels)
Completed mat assembly, artwork included
Razor, utility knife, or scissors
Polyester sheet

DON'S TIP:
Adhesives for Preservation Matting

Traditionally, conservators used wheat starch or rice paste glue for adhering paper hinges. Once, while making some Japanese shoji screen doors for the large unit I built in our living room, I whipped up some rice paste for gluing the mulberry paper on the shoji grills. What a pain. If you cook your rice too little or too much, or don't knead it just right, it turns out to be a lumpy mess unsuitable for gluing anything together. My experience with preparing and using wheat starch paste is little better. Fortunately for you, a perfectly acceptable conservation-grade adhesive is as close as your local hardware or department store. Methyl cellulose wallpaper paste or clear gel glue work perfectly, and you don't have to fuss over them for hours getting them ready. In the case of wallpaper paste, simply add water and let it sit until it is liquid and lump free. Gel glue comes ready-to-use straight off the store shelf.

Ruler or straightedge
Acid-free 8-ply "backer board"
Glazing points or brads
Acid-free paper sheet almost as large as the frame's back side
Moisture-activated linen tape or conservation-grade adhesive

1. Place the frame, with the glazing (glass) in place, facedown on a clean surface.

2. Gently flip the window mat, artwork included, facedown in the frame.

3. Using a razor, knife, or scissors, cut the polyester sheet the same size as the back mat.

4. Place the polyester sheet (a moisture barrier) on the rear of the back mat.

5. Using the utility knife and straightedge ruler (or mat cutter), cut the 8-ply backer board the same size as the back mat.

6. Place this heavy backer board on top of the polyester sheet.

7. Using glazing points or brads driven into the frame rabbet tight against the backer board, fix the entire mat and backing package into the frame.

8. Using razor, scissors, or a knife, cut an acid-free paper "dust cover" to fit over the backer board, just slightly larger than the backer board itself.

9. Using the linen tape or the adhesive, glue the dust cover to the frame. Be sure to glue it along 100 percent of the perimeter.

Congratulations, you now have a genuine museum-quality housing for preserving and displaying your art!

DON'S TIP:
Covering Art with Glass: Bravo! Well, Sometimes . . .
If your artwork on paper is exhibited in a busy area or you are not certain how well you can control the environmental conditions, Plexiglas or glass fronts may be appropriate for framed art. But remember: If the media of the design is powdery or very fragile, such as pencil, pastel, or charcoal sketches, stay with glass. Acrylic or polycarbonate sheeting will develop a static charge when rubbed and can yank the media right off the paper!

Hanging Framed Artwork

These instructions are appropriate for any type of framed artwork, whether a painting, a watercolor, or even a gilt-framed mirror. Hanging framed art properly by following the instructions below provides the best chance for your art to survive intact and prevents many common problems: art falling off the wall, wires puncturing the painting, and so forth.

Hanging art on the wall is not a one-time experience. You must routinely check all the mechanical items that hold the painting on the wall to make sure the molding hangars, picture hooks, D rings, and screw eyes are not

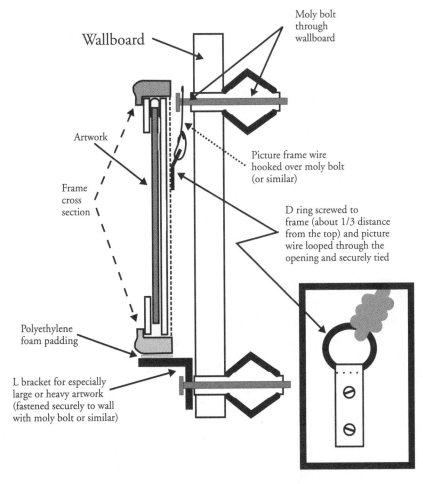

Wallboard

Moly bolt through wallboard

Artwork

Picture frame wire hooked over moly bolt (or similar)

Frame cross section

D ring screwed to frame (about 1/3 distance from the top) and picture wire looped through the opening and securely tied

Polyethylene foam padding

L bracket for especially large or heavy artwork (fastened securely to wall with moly bolt or similar)

Illus. 13-3. Hanging framed artwork.

loosening, and the cords and wires are not fraying, rotting, or corroding. Hooks can come out of plaster, screws can come out of wood, wires can wear through, and cords can rot. See illustration 13-3.

You will need the following supplies:

D rings
Stranded picture wire
Moly bolt wall anchors (if wall studs are not present or accessible)
Masking tape
L brackets as necessary

1. Find the average eye-level height of 5 feet 2 inches on the wall and draw an imaginary horizontal line there.

2. Many pictures have an arbitrary horizon line within their borders. Try to line up this horizon line with the imaginary line.

3. Hooks on the backs of the artwork can be attached to the wall with either nails or moly bolts (for heavier pictures—more than ten pounds).

4. Attach two D rings to the back of the artwork frame, an inch or two above the vertical midpoint. Always use at least two hooks for every picture no matter how small so that the piece will remain level and not tilt while on display.

5. Paintings may be suspended directly from the metal D rings secured to the frame or from appropriate-weight painting or picture wire. If the former, go to step 6. If the latter, go to step 10.

6. Precisely measure the distance between the two D rings and the height you wish to display the artwork.

7. Drill and insert moly bolts into the wall to line up exactly with the D rings.

8. With one person on each side of the painting, flip the D rings out a little from the rear of the painting so that they will snag on the moly bolts.

9. Gently lower the frame so that the D rings engage the moly bolts. Once they are engaged, gently release your grip while your hands are under the painting "just in case."

10. Painting or picture wire should be looped through D rings secured in the right and left sides of the frame so that the painting hangs from a double strand of wire (quadruple for heavy paintings). Place masking tape over the D rings to reduce abrasion on the wall.

11. If the wall is solid (such as brick, plaster, stone, or concrete), use moly bolts to secure metal picture hangers to the wall.

12. Picture hangers or wall hooks for hanging art on wood-framed walls should be driven into the wall studs for maximum stability.

13. With one person on each side of the painting, hold the frame at the bottom with one hand and hold out the wire from the frame with the other so that the wire will snag on the picture hooks.

14. Gently lower the frame so that the picture wire engages the picture hooks. Once engaged, gently release your grip while your hands are under the painting "just in case."

15. For heavier art or if there is doubt about the strength of the wall, also use L brackets mounted to the wall to support the bottom of the painting.

16. Check the hanging system regularly. Make sure the hangers, hooks, D rings, screw eyes, brackets, and wires are in good condition. All of them will degrade over time. Just because it hasn't fallen yet doesn't mean that your artwork is safe.

Drop Mounting

If the art is to be mounted on walls that should not be damaged by nails or screws—walls with valuable coverings, for example—a drop hanging method may be used.

You will need the same supplies as for framed artwork above.

1. If the room has a ceiling molding, nails or screws may be secured into the molding (and painted to match the color).

2. Wire with sufficient strength to hold the weight of the painting may then be dropped from the molding and attached to the back of the picture as follows: Hold the picture at the proper height and tie off the wire on one side. Hold the picture level and tie off the second side. Leave any extra wire or cable tucked into the back of the frame or taped into place in case the picture is moved to a different location.

SCULPTURE AND OBJETS D'ART

Everyone knows what sculpture is, but objets d'art? These are the small, three-dimensional artworks that are displayed indoors. If you have giant sculpture or sculptures that are outside in a garden, you need to seek professional help from a conservator.

Sculptures can be made from a variety of materials. In this book, we cover bronze, stone, brass, ivory, tortoiseshell, and ceramics, among others. If you have a wood sculpture, though, refer to the wood furniture section in Chapter 8, Preserving Your Furniture. For silver and gold figurines refer to the silver section in Chapter 6, Saving Your Family Treasures.

Bronze or brass sculptures, whether a diminutive figurine like the two ballerinas in my living room or the *Burghers of Calais,* Rodin's monumental masterpiece in the Smithsonian collection, are noted not only for their expressive detail but also for their patina. *Patina* is just a fancy word for on-purpose corrosion. As a metal caster myself I have come to recognize and respect the genius of patinators past and present. Through the skillful application of corrosive chemicals to the surface of metal sculpture, an unbelievable range of colors can be introduced to the sculptural expression. Yes, some corrosion is not only not harmful to bronze sculpture but is the whole point of the artwork! Fortunately for you, patinas on bronze and brass sculptures tend to be very stable. All you have to do is keep them clean and protected from other environmental corrosives, and don't rub them.

Stone sculptures are pretty much what you might think they are: hunks of stone chiseled into the desired shape and then polished or worked with tools to provide the desired surface texture and presentation. Caring for stone sculpture is pretty simple: Don't break it and keep it clean.

Don's Rules for Preserving Indoor Metal and Stone Sculptures

1. Patinas on bronzes are sometimes the point of the artwork. Do not use any cleaning agents that will destroy the surface. Simply dust them carefully with a soft artist's brush or soft lint-free flannel rag to get the dust off.

2. Handle carefully. Mishandling can damage or even break sculptures.

3. Moisture will cause corrosion on metal sculptures, especially when other contaminants are present such as salts and oils from bare skin.

4. A buildup of dust and grime will absorb moisture and serve to increase the risk of unwanted corrosion.

5. Chemicals in wood, paint, and plastics may cause corrosion.

6. Chlorine is an enemy. It actually eats away at metal. Keep your sculptures away from the pool or hot tub.

7. Chemicals from bare skin and cosmetics can etch into metal and stain stone and unglazed ceramic sculptures. They can cause permanent damage.

8. Wear clean white cotton, polyethylene, or nitrile gloves when handling sculptures. Do not wear latex or rubber gloves because they contain chemicals that can tarnish or corrode the metal surface.

9. When lifting or moving, hold the sculpture with both hands, preferably underneath.

10. Don't grab by spouts or arms when moving or handling. These are usually the weakest parts of the sculpture.

Displaying Indoor Metal and Stone Sculptures

These artworks can be displayed just about anyplace where they will not be exposed to harsh chemicals, such as near a pool or hot tub, or where they will not be bumped into and knocked over.

Preserving Bronze Sculptures

You will need the following supplies:

Nitrile or polyethylene gloves
Distilled water
Mild liquid dish detergent
Clean lint-free cloth rags
Hair dryer
Alcohol
Paste wax (see instructions for proper selection)
Used panty hose

1. Work in a well-ventilated area and wear nitrile or polyethylene gloves.

2. Remove jewelry or anything else that might scratch the surface as you work.

3. Gently clean with distilled water, mild liquid detergent, and a soft lint-free cloth.

4. Do not scrub hard or you might scratch or wear off the patina.

5. Rinse with distilled water and pat the surface dry with the lint-free cloth or by blowing on it with the hair dryer turned to low.

6. Grease and oil can be cleaned with a mixture of equal parts distilled water and alcohol as described in "Cleaning Removable Metal Hardware" in Chapter 8, Preserving Your Furniture.

7. Often, a coating of wax is applied to sculptures as routine maintenance to protect the surface from corrosive contaminants. Do not use automotive wax! You can wipe or brush paraffin, furniture, floor paste wax, or shoe polish wax evenly over the sculpture. (These waxes are all perfectly stable and easily removed with mineral spirits.) Shoe wax has the advantage that it comes in a rainbow of colors so you can actually use it to touch up areas of sculpture where the patina has been damaged or lost.

8. If the article does not contain ivory, plastic, bone, or other heat-sensitive material, a hair dryer can be used to warm the surface of the sculpture and let the wax penetrate the surface fully.

9. While the wax is still warm and soft, remove any excess from the surface with a panty hose or a clean, lint-free, soft cloth.

10. When cool, buff the surface with a clean, lint-free, soft cloth such as worn flannel or a T-shirt.

Displaying Bronze Sculptures

Display them in a secure corrosive-agent-free location (nowhere near the pool, sauna, hot tub, or bathroom) where they cannot be bumped into, scratched by passersby or housecleaners, or knocked down.

IVORY AND TORTOISESHELL

Ivory and tortoiseshell have been used to craft objects that run the gamut from everyday household items to intricate jewelry, carvings, and statues. The detailed ivory scrimshaw done by eighteenth-century sailors and tortoiseshell snuff boxes are just two beautiful examples. With proper care these objects can last and be enjoyed for many years.

Ivory is a specialized form of tooth. The most common source is elephant tusk, although other tusks (from walruses, sperm whales, and narwhals) have been used in making decorative objects. A synthetic ivory was produced from cellulose nitrate in the late 1800s and early 1900s. Called French or India ivory, it resembles the real thing but its structure breaks down over time. How can you tell the difference? With a magnifying glass: Synthetics have no grain pattern, while real ivory does.

Tortoiseshell is the outer plate of the shell of two species of giant sea turtles, and technically it resembles fingernails with freckles. Like ivory, it, too, has been imitated by numerous synthetic plastics.

Don's Rules for Preserving Ivory and Tortoiseshell

1. Wear clean, white cotton gloves when handling ivory. Touching with bare hands can result in staining with deposits from your skin or cosmetics. Environmental contaminants can also darken ivory (which can be considered a desirable patina).

2. Store these artifacts in closed cases that can mitigate the risks from moisture and temperature. Fluctuations in either can cause distortions or fractures.

3. Do not display ivory or tortoiseshell in direct sunlight or under bright lights because both light and heat damage can occur.

4. Do not display near sources of dirt, dust, and grime.

5. When storing ivory and tortoiseshell artifacts, wrap them in unbuffered, acid-free tissue paper or unbleached muslin and then place them in a sealed polyethylene zippered bag.

6. Do not use rubber, rubberlike latex, or polyurethane foam padding to cushion items made of ivory or tortoiseshell. If padding is required, use polyethylene or polypropylene foam.

7. Never oil ivory. It doesn't help to keep the ivory from drying out, and it makes it dirtier in the long run.

Cleaning Ivory and Tortoiseshell

You will need the following supplies:

Clean white cotton gloves
Soft artist's brush
Distilled water
Cotton swabs

1. Put on clean cotton gloves before handling.
2. Clean by dusting with a soft artist's brush.
3. Ivory and tortoiseshell that are in good condition (that is, they have a smooth, glossy surface) and have no applied decoration can be cleaned with

a little distilled water. Use a barely dampened cotton swab and dry the object immediately with another cotton swab or soft tissue.

4. Do not use water on any object that is cracked or otherwise damaged. Never soak objects.

The cleaning and repair of ivory, tortoiseshell, and similar materials is a delicate procedure. If an object is very dirty or damaged, and the above cleaning process does not work on the first try, consult a professional conservator because it is a very delicate procedure, and the chances are great that you will damage the object if you are not a professional.

Displaying Ivory and Tortoiseshell

Display ivory and tortoiseshell in a room that has a temperature around 70 (cooler is better) and 50 percent relative humidity. The most important issue is that the humidity does not fluctuate. Be sure the sculpture or artwork cannot be bumped into or knocked down and is out of direct sunlight.

CERAMICS, ART GLASS, AND STAINED GLASS

The general term *ceramics* is used for art objects made from clay (and other materials) and heated at high temperatures in a specialized oven called a kiln. Whether a ceramic is porcelain, pottery, raku, bisque, terra-cotta, or other type depends on how and from what it was made. While art glass and stained glass are not precisely the same stuff, their care is so similar that I have included them here as well.

The primary distinction in the care and preservation needs of ceramics, art glass, and stained glass is whether it is shiny or dull. The former suggests either high temperature firing, which renders a dense, glassy, and fairly hard surface, or the presence of a ceramic glaze, which is a hard, slick surface. The latter suggests low-temperature firing, yielding a softer, more porous, and rougher surface. That is a gross oversimplification from a technical standpoint, as any self-respecting ceramics scholar will tell you, but it is all I need to know as a conservator when it comes to keeping it around for a long time.

Don's Rules for Preserving All Ceramics

1. Handle carefully. The greatest risk is from breaking due to mishandling (such as dropping on the floor).

2. Never pick a ceramic object up only by a spout or handle. Grab by the body or major rim with one hand and keep the other hand underneath.

3. Special care needs to be taken for antique ceramics that have been previously restored. Adhesives used to put pots back together again can degrade and change appearance or properties over time. This degradation is usually accelerated by moisture, light, and heat.

4. Use two or more people when handling really large objects.

5. If an object has multiple parts (lids, etc.), handle them separately and keep track of them.

6. Don't display delicate or important ceramics out in the open. They are bait for pets and kids. Keep them in enclosed shelves or cases.

7. Ceramics that do not have a sturdy, broad base should be displayed or stored sitting in a fitted collar made of polyethylene foam covered with synthetic fabric. A custom polyethylene foam support should be fabricated (or carved) for each pot or ceramic, similar to making a fitted housing for

Christmas ornaments as described in "Holiday Ornaments: Cleaning, Storing, and Displaying" in Chapter 6, Saving Your Family Treasures.

8. Never wash collectible ceramics and glass with the dishes or put them in the dishwasher.

9. Never use newspapers to wrap or pad ceramics when storing and packing. Not only is newsprint very unstable, but ink can be transferred to the object if moisture is present. If it is a dull ceramic, that stain is usually permanent. At high temperatures, high humidity, or extended exposure this effect can even become true for shiny ceramics.

10. Contact a decorative objects conservator for advice if your ceramic or art glass gets stained, broken, or otherwise damaged. Don't try to fix it yourself. Never try to glue it back together yourself, especially with polyvinyl acetate glue, epoxy, rubber cement, caulk, cellulose nitrate or cellulose acetate adhesives, or super glue. When you finally get it to a conservator all that gunk will have to be removed anyway and it can be a real pain. An expert knows which adhesives and techniques to use for the best possible outcome in repairing damaged ceramics and related materials.

Don's Special Rules for Preserving and Displaying Shiny Pottery

1. Glossy ceramics can usually be handled safely with bare hands because shiny (glazed) ceramics are not particularly porous and absorbent. Fingerprints are not usually a problem, although with enough exposure to discoloring agents, even glazed ceramics can become stained.

2. Keep art glass and stained glass in cool, dry conditions to prevent migration of some of the ingredients in the glass. This can cause a dull, chalky appearance on the surface.

3. Shiny ceramics (usually porcelain) with metal mounts should not be wet with water. Remember, water and metals do not mix, and the water will remain behind the mounts for some time doing its nasty business.

4. Display them out of direct sunlight and in a secured location where they cannot be bumped into or knocked down.

Don's Special Rules for Preserving and Displaying Dull Pottery

1. Do not use bare hands when handling dull ceramics such as terra-cotta and raku. They are easily stained by skin oils and sweat because they are relatively porous and absorbent. Fingerprints can be permanently disfiguring.

2. The painted decorations on dull ceramics can be sensitive to strong light, which can cause some designs to fade and change.

3. Dull ceramics are usually sensitive to moisture and relative humidity changes.

4. Never stick tape or sticky labels on dull antique or collectible ceramics.

5. Don't use dull antique pots for food or flowers.

6. Keep dull ceramics and water far apart.

7. If you ignore the previous two rules, be sure to use an inner vessel inside the antique pot and a polypropylene foam inner lining between the two.

8. Display them out of direct sunlight and in a secured location where they cannot be bumped into or knocked down. Also, it is usually best to keep them in a dust-free case so that the textured surfaces do not become coated with loose dirt, something that can be difficult to remove given the nature of the surface.

Preserving and Displaying Shiny Art Ceramics and Glass

You will need the following supplies:

> Fine artist's brush
> Photographer's compressed air can
> Clean lint-free cloth
> Distilled water
> Cotton swabs
> Alcohol
> Hair dryer

1. Wash your hands thoroughly before starting.

2. Clean shiny ceramics by brushing off the dust with a fine artist's brush or compressed air.

3. Shiny ceramics not previously restored can usually be wiped with damp cloths or swabbed with alcohol for cleaning.

4. Air-dry immediately or use a hair dryer on low.

5. Display them out of direct sunlight and in a secure location where they cannot be bumped into or knocked down.

DON'S TIP:
Beware of
"Crizzled"
Veterans

Antique art glass and stained glass often become "crizzled"— a network of fine surface cracks resulting in a frosty appearance. Some ceramics that are very fragile develop crazed glazes. Do not handle these any more than is absolutely necessary because they are easily damaged.

Preserving and Displaying Dull Art Ceramics and Glass

You will need a can of photographer's compressed air.

1. Wash your hands.

2. Dust raku, terra-cotta, bisque, heavily colored art glass, and other soft, dull ceramics by blowing compressed air over the surface.

3. Don't dust dull ceramics with brushes or cloths if their surface texture is much coarser or the decoration is flaking because these are easily damaged.

4. Display them out of direct sunlight and in a secure location where they cannot be bumped into or knocked down. Also, it is usually best to keep them in a dust-free case so that the textured surfaces do not become coated with loose dirt, something that can be difficult to remove given the nature of the surface.

Chapter 14

Taking Care of Textiles

THREE YEARS AGO good friends of mine gave me an antique Mexican rug for my birthday. Deep reds, vivid oranges, and rich blues were woven throughout the rug, and beautiful fringe lined both ends. This legacy of Mexican culture and art obviously deserved to be displayed in a prominent place, and I set about trying to find one. I chose a hallway that the afternoon sun drenched in light because I wanted everyone to be able to see the beauty of my rug. I then needed to hang it. Being careful, I chose very slender finishing nails so as not to damage the delicate weavings. I nailed the rug onto the wall, and it truly was awe-inspiring. I say "was" because it "was" awe-inspiring—it is not anymore.

First, Chilli, my cat, decided the fringe made a nice toy. Next, the sun that helped display the rug so beautifully began to fade the colors. Then the weight of the rug pulled against the nails and created sizable holes. Since I was not checking the rug regularly, by the time I really looked at it, it resembled an old rag you would use to dry your car.

Textile conservators teach that textiles should be treated with the same care and respect that we lavish on our grandmas. It makes sense, since grandmas spread love in their wake wherever they go, and the textiles we treasure also impart warmth, color, and sometimes even a sense of our own history. The one important lesson I have learned is "Never do anything to a textile you wouldn't do to Grandma."

Well, I would never stick nails in Grandma, leave her in the sun's direct light, or let the cat use her as a play toy, and now I treat all my textiles with the same care.
—Louisa Jaggar

"Never do anything to a textile you wouldn't do to Grandma" is the single best advice I can give you in caring for your textiles. The irony in preserving textiles is that while they are among the most ordinary and ever-present materials surrounding us, they are also perhaps the most expensive items to purchase and repair, the most fragile to maintain, the most difficult to clean, and the most prone to degradation and a short life. For example, most textiles will not survive long when exposed to strong sunlight, yet that is exactly what we expect draperies to do. A living or dining room with several windows is often decorated with thousands of dollars' worth of draperies. Yet unlike other aspects of life, the aphorism "You get what you pay for" has virtually no application here. Expensive or cheap, elegant or crude, textiles enjoy sunlight as much as vampires do.

Make sure that your prized textiles—whether silk, wool, cotton, or synthetics—are not directly in front of a window or in a location that receives direct sunlight. If you can take a picture of your valued textile indoors without the assistance of a flash attachment, there is too much light. Light causes textile colors to change (fade) and degrades the fibers, so keep light low. Generally, it is not a good idea to leave textiles permanently on display. Light damage adds up over time and cannot be undone. Keep it low and use ultraviolet filters over windows and fluorescent tubes.

THINK "GRANDMA"

Think about how you should treat Grandma for a minute, and you'll be able to write the rules about preserving textiles yourself. The underlying rule is to treat textiles with tender loving care and gentleness. Mistreated textiles turn to powder, fade, and sag. They self-destruct before your very eyes. Remember, when caring for textiles, think "Grandma!"

Don's Rules for Preserving "Grandmas" and Textiles

1. Never hang Grandma from a nail.
2. Never leave Grandma out in the sun.

3. Never expose Grandma to too much light, inside or outside.
4. Never cram Grandma into a little box or into the trunk of your car.
5. Never stick pins or staples in Grandma.
6. Never fold Grandma or roll her up in a ball.
7. Never let bugs eat Grandma.
8. Never sit on Grandma if she is too old or creaky.
9. Never scrub Grandma with harsh cleaners.
10. Never drag Grandma around.
11. Never hug Grandma when you are dirty; a dirty grandma is an unhappy grandma.
12. Never put Grandma in the attic or basement. She doesn't like being baked or getting moldy.
13. Keep Grandma out of drafty spaces.
14. Never eat on Grandma.
15. Keep the pets off Grandma.
16. Never smoke or chew tobacco around Grandma.
17. Never splash water or drinks on Grandma.
18. Never let Grandma sit directly on wood, acidic paper, most plastic films, or adhesive tape.
19. Never snag Grandma with rings, watches, cuff links, belt buckles, and so forth.
20. If Grandma gets sick or hurt, take her to the doctor (in this case a textile conservator); don't try to fix her yourself.

BUGS, BUGS, BUGS

North America provides residency for a number of common textile-eating critters. These insects will eat natural fiber textiles, especially wool and silk, and feed off the dirty deposits on any fabric, natural or synthetic. The life cycle of these pests may be divided into four stages: the egg, the larva, the pupa, and the adult moth or beetle. The larval stage is the dangerous one because larvae feed on your valuables.

For the *clothes moth,* the larval stage will last between two months in a warm, humid climate and six months in a cool climate. The larvae of these moths are cream-colored caterpillars

**DON'S TIP:
The Itsy Bitsy Spider and Your Textiles**

Actually, spiders do not eat textiles but instead eat the insects that do eat your fabrics. So the presence of spiders may be a signal that some cloth-eating insects are at work in your home. If you see spiders in your prized folded quilt, you need to unfold it, inspect it carefully, and clean it.

with brown heads that will eat hair, horn, feathers, wool, mounted insects such as butterflies, mounted birds, mounted animals, furs, and the wool or horsehair stuffing in upholstery. Of course, not all moths are dangerous to your textile collection. An easy way to tell if a moth is a clothes-eating moth is whether or not it flies away from a lighted fixture. If a moth flies close to a light, you can assume it is not harmful.

For the *carpet beetle,* the larval period lasts at least three-quarters of a year. Beetle larvae have the shape of small red-brown beetles with numerous bristles; they molt several times before reaching maturity. Adult carpet beetles will try to go outdoors before or after laying their eggs. They are found near windows in the spring and feed on pet food, fruit, pollen, and flower nectar. If you bring flowers or cuttings in from the garden, spray these items with a pesticide before bringing them inside.

Dry cleaning will kill the larvae of clothes moths, and mothproofing will give some residual protection against moths and beetles. However, neither dry cleaning nor mothproofing will prevent a hungry group of insects from at least attempting to eat your valuables.

Two frequently used insect preventatives come in the form of moth balls and moth crystals, commonly available at grocery, drug, and hardware stores. When you buy moth crystals, be sure to read the label to see whether the active ingredient is naphthalene or paradichlorobenzene, or PDB. While naphthalene acts as a repellent against adult insects, PDB will kill the eggs the adults lay in your textile. I suggest using both types because they protect your textiles in different ways. To be on the safe side and make them easier to handle, place the crystals or mothballs in small fabric pouches as you might do for potpourri. Just take a square of cotton, place the crystals in the center, and tie the package into a pouch with cotton thread or string. (Do not use rubber bands because the chemicals in the crystals will soften or possibly dissolve the rubber.)

Examine textiles for pests as part of your regular housekeeping routine. Always separate infested textiles from the rest of the collection. Bug problems need to be dealt with immediately. Repeat after me: "Bugs are the enemy."

You will need the following supplies:

Sealable clean plastic bags
Household cleaning supplies: soap, water, sponges, towels, etc.

Fumigant (or, even better, the phone number of a competent fumigator)
Vacuum cleaner
Nylon window screen
Masking tape or cloth sewing tape (if the latter, you also need needle and thread)

1. Isolate infested items in sealed plastic bags until they can be treated.

2. Wear only synthetic fabrics while handling the infested item. (Bugs generally don't eat plastic.)

3. Remove clothing after handling infested items and wash clothing thoroughly without exposing other areas of the home or building. The same goes for you. Wash thoroughly.

4. All items that are infested, that show definite signs of insect damage, should be treated by the most effective measure possible. Have them professionally cleaned.

5. Once the infested items have been isolated and cleared of infestation, the area where they resided should be treated to rigorous housekeeping, including washing of walls and floors, and washing of all drawers and cabinets.

6. Fumigate to kill both the adults and the larvae. It should kill all eggs, but a second fumigation after a twenty to 30-day incubation period may be necessary for a severely infested textile. Please contact a professional when fumigating because many fumigants are poisonous.

7. Replace the textiles only after fumigating has been successfully completed. Vacuum to remove insect eggs (and mildew residues) from textiles. Be sure to wash and dry the nozzle of the vacuum between objects to prevent the spread of the infestation. (Hot water and dishwashing liquid are adequate for this purpose.) Vacuum through a protective screen as described in "Don's Rules for Preserving New and Old Upholstery" in Chapter 8, Preserving Your Furniture.

8. Prevent reinfestation through aggressive housekeeping of all areas. Vacuum carpets and carefully groom pets frequently.

9. Make inspection of your collections an integral part of housekeeping.

DON'S TIP: Clean All Textiles Before Storing Them

The clothes moth cannot survive on clean woolen items, only on soiled items. This is why it is necessary to dry clean one's clothing before putting them away for the summer rather than waiting until you need them again in the fall.

MOLD AND MILDEW

Mold and mildew are the enemy. Prevent them. While mold and mildew are problems for all kinds of organic material (wood, leather, paper, etc.), no material is damaged as quickly or as extensively as textiles. The rate and degree of damage may be different among fabrics, but the prevention and preservation of them are identical.

Mold and mildew are a temperature and moisture problem. A good rule of thumb is that if Grandma is comfortable, your textiles are comfortable. A temperature range of 65 to 70 degrees Fahrenheit and a relative humidity range of 45 to 55 percent are just right. Uncontrolled temperature and humidity variations from doorways, windows, chimney flues, vents, or ducts and condensation at exterior walls are all potentially damaging. Avoid placing textiles in these areas.

Mildew growth, fungi spores, and bacteria can exist everywhere there is air. High humidity, warm temperatures, and poor ventilation together provide the ideal conditions for mold growth. Generally, stagnant air above 70 percent relative humidity will support mold on cottons and linens, but silk and wool require nearly wet conditions of more than 90 percent relative humidity. Soiling, food residues, and the casual handling of textiles will increase the growth of mildew on fabrics.

Mildew problems require you to address the environmental conditions that caused the mildew in the first place. Reducing the humidity in the area and increasing air circulation are critical to reducing the risk from mold and mildew.

To deal with mold and mildew you will need the following supplies:

Fans
Dehumidifier
Air conditioner

1. Inspect the storage or display area to identify water sources. Whatever the problem is—inadequate insulation, leaking pipes, flooring, ceilings, or windows—fix it.

2. Install fans in the affected area and leave them running to make sure there is adequate air movement.

DON'S TIP: Textiles Are Early-Warning Indicators

Textiles are the "canary in the coal mine": the presence of mold and mildew is a sign that you have problems with your microclimate.

3. Install a dehumidifier in the area and make sure it drains out of the area.

4. Install air-conditioning in the area to lower the relative humidity and temperature.

5. Check your storage boxes or display areas bimonthly during warm months. Things that are in closed spaces without much ventilation are prone to developing mold growth.

If you are dealing with a moldy textile, you will need the following supplies:

Clean, washed cotton sheets
Vacuum
Protective nylon screen
Storage containers as appropriate

1. If your textiles are moldy or mildewy, immediately remove the textile from its present location.

2. Dry it out by spreading it carefully on a clean, dry, absorbent surface.

3. Fans can increase the air circulation in the vicinity of the objects, but don't point the fan directly at the textile itself.

4. Always clean any mold residues from textiles before putting them in storage.

5. Vacuum through a protective screen as described in "Don's Rules for Preserving New and Old Upholstery" in Chapter 8, Preserving Your Furniture. If necessary, use a soft brush to gently loosen the residue if the fabric beneath is sufficiently strong. Test a small area to make sure the textile is strong enough. This means the fabric does not fray or change in any way other than it is cleaner after being vacuumed. If you notice fraying or any changes, stop and consult a textile conservator.

6. Reinstall textile only after the space has been cured of mold and mildew problems. If not displaying, replace in storage according to the directions specific to the type of textile.

CAUTION: **Mildew weakens textile fibers and threads.** If the mildew growth has caused enough damage, removing that growth may harm the textile further. For this reason it is recommended that mold removal be done only by a qualified textile conservator on textiles badly damaged or of

DON'S TIP:
Be Careful When You Use Moth Balls

Moth crystals can be harmful to human health. They emit toxins that are poisonous. Thus, the containers in which these crystals are used should be sealed and should not be in an area where people typically work, sleep, or live. If you can smell the moth crystals, thymol, or eugenol when you enter a room, these substances are still present and active and are leaking from your storage container. Do not use this room on a regular basis.

great value. Contact the American Institute for Conservation, *http://aic .stanford.edu,* to locate a textiles conservator in your area.

STORING YOUR TEXTILES

Storing textiles properly is not complicated. They need to be placed carefully in an environment with low or no light, moderate humidity and temperature, no bugs and mold, and in containers with stable materials such as archival boxes and acid-free tissue and paper boards that do not contribute to further deterioration. The issue of providing a ventilated or sealed envelope for storing textiles is extremely important. It is vital to furnish an excellent barrier against moths and dust for textiles in storage; however, in some situations the interior of a sealed plastic bag may become so damp that

DON'S TIP:
Be Careful When Storing in Plastic

If you do store your textiles in plastic, make sure it is virgin polyethylene (not recycled) with minimal plasticizers or polypropylene. Research shows that in addition to the problems already mentioned, poor-quality plastic bags can cause more damage than they prevent, such as yellowing of the items stored inside, due to the chemicals given off by the bags themselves. You will need to ask before you buy to ensure you are getting the type of bag you need.

molds can grow. In climates that are too moist or too dry, cotton sheeting and acid-free tissue can be used to insulate textiles.

PRESERVING BEDROOM AND DINING ROOM LINENS

Storing flat textiles such as pillowcases, sheets, tablecloths, and napkins is fairly simple. The biggest factor to avoid is direct contact with raw wooden surfaces, which will cause these items to yellow. You can do one of a few things to prevent this, whichever is feasible in your situation.

You will need the following supplies:

Vinyl or latex work gloves
Shellac and oil/resin varnish
Fine-bristle paintbrushes
Alcohol and paint thinner for cleaning the brushes
Clean white cotton sheeting (alternative—see step 1)
Acid-free tissue
Acid-free cardboard tubing

1(a). Put on the gloves. Paint the interior of your storage shelves or drawers with several coats of shellac followed by a few coats of oil/resin varnish such as alkyd or polyurethane. Be sure this is absolutely dry before placing your linens inside.   *OR*

1(b). Line your shelves or drawers with clean, white cotton sheeting. This will provide a washable buffer between your valuables and the wooden storage surface. This sheeting will have to be laundered at least annually. Line the other wooden surfaces with acid-free tissue paper. This paper should be changed annually because it will absorb the acidic fumes from the wood.

2. Once you have created a barrier between the textiles and the wooden storage surfaces, you are ready to place the textiles. If the items are small enough, roll them onto an acid-free paper tube (remember, creases are the enemy) or a tube that has been covered with either acid-free tissue or clean cotton sheeting. Napkins and pillowcases can easily be stored this way.

3. Much larger items such as sheets and table covers can be folded gently—never with creases pressed into them—and laid inside the storage space. If space permits, their fold lines should be stuffed with acid-free tissue to prevent creases from forming along the folds.

PRESERVING VINTAGE UPHOLSTERY

Ideally, if antique upholstery is present on a chair, sofa, or similar item, it should not be sat on but should have a cord draped across the front edge to discourage visitors from sitting there. If this is not feasible, slipcovers are another alternative that might be considered during entertaining.

Never remove and discard original upholstery. If nothing else, it can serve as a valuable research document, adding to the history of decorative arts. In the case of original upholstery, once it is removed from a piece, the value of the piece decreases considerably, no matter the condition of the upholstery. If you must remove it, store it carefully like the valuable historical document it is.

Don's Rules for Preserving Valuable Upholstery

1. Do not place the upholstered item directly in front of a window. As has been stated previously, sunlight is one of the most damaging elements of the environment in which valuables must survive. Try to find another space in the room that receives much less light than directly in front of a window.

2. Keep food and drink tables far away from upholstered pieces. And use slipcovers whenever possible during parties.

3. As soon as possible blot up any drinks or food items that are spilled on the upholstery. Do not rub back and forth on the surface but instead tap up and down with a clean sponge or cotton cloth. It may be necessary to let the food item dry and then remove it by vacuuming the dried residue from the upholstery surface. If the upholstery becomes stained due to food or drink, have a professional dry cleaner who is familiar with cleaning antiques re-

move the stains or consult a textile conservator. To find a referral go to *http://aic.stanford.edu.*

4. If serious damage such as a cut or tear should occur during use, call a textile conservator. Even if you sew regularly, antique upholstery requires expert attention. Don't try to perform impromptu textile conservation yourself. Antique or valuable textiles may not be what you might think, and their properties may have changed dramatically with time and deterioration. For that reason any stains, rips, or tears should be brought to the attention of a textile conservator who can repair the damage while minimizing the loss of value that the textile suffers when repaired in any way.

Cleaning Antique Upholstery

The cleaning of upholstery (removing stains and other discolorations or deposits), as mentioned above, should be left to conservators or other specialists in the care and preservation of vintage textiles. But that does not mean there is not something vitally important that you can do: removing, through careful vacuuming, the dust and other matter that is simply sitting on or in the upholstery.

To vacuum antique upholstery, refer to the illustration on page 133, which shows you how to properly vacuum textiles. In addition, you will need the following supplies:

Protective nylon screening
Masking tape or cotton twill tape (if the latter, you also need needle and thread)
Vacuum cleaner with brush nozzle

1. Wrap the edges of the nylon screening with cotton twill or masking tape in advance so the harsh edges of the screen will not tear or cut the upholstery fibers.

2. Put the vacuum on the lowest suction available on your vacuum cleaner and attach the smallest brush your vacuum has.

3. Vacuum your upholstery through the screening. This protects the upholstery by holding down the upholstery fibers and yet it allows the soil to pass through and into the vacuum cleaner.

4. Vacuum only in the direction of the pile, if there is one, or simply be consistent in the direction you choose to go. Vacuum the surface of the up-

holstery very slowly, allowing the suction of the vacuum to pull the soil out of the fibers.

PRESERVING RUGS AND CARPETS

Carpets and rugs take a beating from feet. To preserve an important or valuable carpet avoid walking on it and do your best to prevent other people from walking on it, too. Of course this is not a reasonable option in most homes.

If you cannot prevent people from walking where the rug is located, perhaps you can provide some protection by placing a cover over the rug during periods of normal use. A heavy muslin or canvas cloth on top of the carpet reduces the wear dramatically and can easily be removed for those times you want to display the rug.

In addition, you can also reduce the amount of wear to the underside of the carpet by placing a good-quality pad underneath it to minimize the abrasion between the floor and the carpet. A good carpet pad used in conjunction with a canvas cover cloth will protect both the front and back sides of the rug.

Choosing the carpet pad is fairly important because it tends to fall into the category of "out of sight, out of mind." Once it is down it stays down unless you are the most conscientious housekeeper on the block.

Padding should be composed completely of synthetic fibers rather than rubberized padding or felt. Rubberized underlays very often have sulfur in their composition, which disintegrates. When it does, it crumbles, especially with a lot of traffic, and becomes embedded in the structure of the carpet. As for the felt type of pad, most often the exact composition is unknown. There could be woolen fibers present, which will attract many kinds of pests.

A carpet pad should be fitted to each individual carpet, cut to within an inch of the carpet's outer edges, and not be so thick ($1/4$ inch or less) that people will trip over the edge of the carpet.

Vacuuming Valuable Rugs

The objective in cleaning valuable carpets is slightly different from that of cleaning average carpeting. You want to preserve as much carpet fiber as possible while at the same time removing the dirt and soil from the surface of the rug. To do so you should follow these instructions:

1. Do not use the beater bar to vacuum the surface of the rug because it abrades and removes some of the textile fibers. Rely only on the suction mechanism of the vacuum.

2. Vacuum only in the direction of the pile of the rug. You can tell the direction of the rug by running your hand over it. If it feels smooth, it is with the pile. If it feels rough, it is against the pile. Vacuum in the direction of the smoothness of the pile.

3. Vacuum slowly in the direction of the pile once rather than run the vacuum back and forth over the same area many times. Take your time. Removing the soil is not instantaneous. It may take a few seconds for the soil to work its way up through the rug fabric to the nozzle.

Storing Carpets

You will need the following supplies to prepare your carpets for storage:

Vacuum
Rigid cardboard or aluminum tube (see step 2)
Clean cotton sheet large enough to wrap the rolled carpet
Cotton tape for tying the rolled carpet
Two or three really good friends with strong backs

1. The first step in preparing floor coverings for storage is to vacuum them as described above. Valuable floor coverings such as oriental carpets and custom-designed carpets are very often made of wool. This makes them especially attractive to pests, a problem exacerbated if they are placed in storage while dirty.

2. Prepare a sturdy tube, preferably 6 inches or more in diameter, on which you will roll the carpet. If the tube is acid-free cardboard, simply cut it approximately 12 inches longer than the rolled-up carpet will be. If the tube is not acid-free cardboard, wrap it first with acid-free tissue paper.

3. Roll the carpet *face out* around the storage tube.

4. Once the carpet is completely on the tube, wrap a clean cotton sheet around it. Tie cotton twill tape or cotton string around the roll, at the ends and at various spaces down the length of the roll.

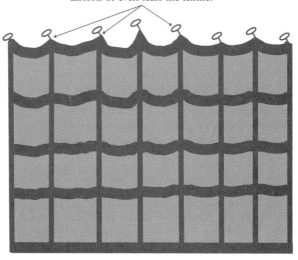

Hanging by pins causes localized damage because the weight of the textile pulls it down from the pins and distorts or even tears the textile.

Illus. 14-1. Illustrating the damage (exaggerated) caused by hanging a textile by numerous points rather than a continuous support system.

HANGING TAPESTRIES, QUILTS, AND RUGS FOR DISPLAY

Hanging textiles properly is an exacting task, so I have provided a lengthy description and diagrams to help you understand how it all goes together. Textiles should not be hung by simply supporting them from a few points. Museums use hook-and-loop tape (Velcro) attached across the full width of any rug, quilt, or tapestry being hung. The hook-and-loop complements attach directly to each other and provide full support over the width of the textile. This equal distribution of weight keeps the textile from being pulled more heavily in one area than another.

The Hook-and-Loop System

In this method you will be attaching one-half of a Velcro system to your tapestry, rug, or quilt and the other half to a board that is attached to the wall. When the two halves of the Velcro system are pressed together, your textile will be hanging exactly as museums exhibit theirs. It also allows the entire textile to be on display. Please read through the entire procedure before beginning.

There are four steps to this procedure:

Step 1: Attaching the loop to the textile
Step 2: Attaching the hook to the mounting board
Step 3: Attaching the mounting board to the wall
Step 4: Connecting the loop and the hook

You will need the following supplies:

Measuring tape
Cotton webbing tape (as long and wide as the hook-and-loop strip)
One-inch- or 2-inch-wide hook-and-loop strip at least 12 inches
    longer than the width of the object
Sewing machine
Clean, firm, flat surface larger than the dimensions of the object
    (if necessary, use floor area)
Clean bedsheet or kraft paper to cover clean surface
Masking tape
T square up to 72 inches long
Straight pins with ball heads
Heavyweight 100 percent cotton thread
Tapestry needles, size 24 or 26 or as appropriate

Step 1: Attaching the Loop to the Textile

1. Measure off $1/2$ inch from the top and bottom of cotton webbing. Using the zigzag stitch if possible, machine-stitch the soft loop component to the cotton webbing along the top. Return to the beginning of the webbing (do not simply turn the webbing around) and machine-stitch the lower edge. Check to make sure the tension of the machine stitching is proper and does not curl the tape as you are sewing.

2. Prepare a clean area and yourself for work. Assemble the equipment and supplies. Lay out the bedsheet or kraft paper, ensuring a taut, flat work surface by securing the edges only with masking tape.

3. Lay the object facedown. The object should lie flat on the flat surface.

4. Determine the effective horizontal line of the object by laying a T

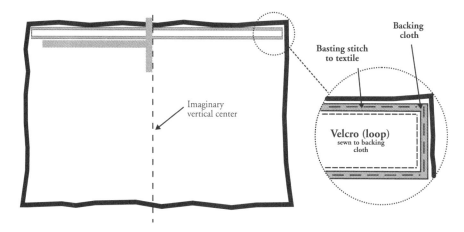

Illus. 14-2. You are looking at the back side of the textile. To hang your textile by the Velcro method, first find the center vertical line. Using a T square, lay out a straight line perpendicular to the imaginary vertical center ½ inch below the top. Then follow the instructions for attaching the Velcro and backing cloth to the rear of the textile. This will attach to the Velcro's mate on the wall.

square parallel to the vertical threads. Align the loop tape perpendicular to the vertical threads rather than parallel to the horizontal threads. Often the distortion of the textile will cause a somewhat wavy top and bottom when the perfectly straight horizontal line is established. This is okay. Trying to straighten out a warped historic textile will result in more damage through the stresses of yanking it straight or square. If it is distorted, leave it that way.

4. Align the webbing from step 1 along that horizontal line but at least ¼ inch below the top edge of the object. The top edge of the handwoven or hand-constructed textiles may not be consistently parallel to the webbing.

5. Pin the webbing in place starting at the center and working to the sides.

6. Count the number of pins used.

7. The webbing and hook-and-loop should extend a few inches beyond the width of the textile on either side.

8. Baste (loosely sew) the webbing with quilt thread through to the front surface of the textile. Start from the top center and work to the edge.

9. Use a fine hand stitch to attach the webbing from step 1 completely to the back side of the textile. Avoid sewing through the threads of the textile; instead, sew between them. For heavy textiles (rugs, tapestries) use 100 percent cotton buttonhole/carpet thread, doubled. For lighter textiles use ap-

propriately lighter thread. Use a blunt #24 or #26 tapestry needle if possible. Stitches must go through to the front of the object to secure the textile to the hook-and-loop mounting system and to prevent future damage to the yarns of the textile. Stop 1 inch before the outer edge of the object.

10. Remove all pins. Count them. You will really regret leaving one behind when it comes time to handle the textile for hanging.

11. Cut the webbing and hook-and-loop 1/4 inch to 1/2 inch short of the edge of the textile. Secure the end of the webbing and hook-and-loop to the textile by hemstitching the two with the remaining thread. Sew through the front of the textile. Remember to bind off the sewing thread to the webbing rather than to the textile.

12. Remove the original basting threads from the cotton webbing side.

Step 2: Attaching the Hook to the Mounting Board

After the hook-and-loop webbing has been completely stitched to the textile and the edges of the hook-and-loop webbing have been cut and hemmed, the complement can be prepared for the wall. You will need the following supplies:

Measuring tape
Wood board 1 inch by 4 inches by the length of the hook-and-loop
    webbing minus ¾ inch
Polyurethane varnish and brush
Washed unbleached cotton muslin or similar cloth
Aluminum tacks, stainless steel staples, or cadmium-coated flat-
    head nails
Hammer or staple gun

1. Measure the width (left to right) of the textile exactly.

2. Cut the hook-and-loop to the measurement of step 1.

3. Cut the mounting board $3/4$ inch less than the measurement from step 1.

4. Measure the height of the textile (top to bottom).

5. Put the textile away.

6. Brush 2 coats of polyurethane varnish on all sides, edges, and ends of the mounting board, allowing the varnish to cure and dry thoroughly.

7. Wrap the board with the cotton muslin and staple it to the back side of

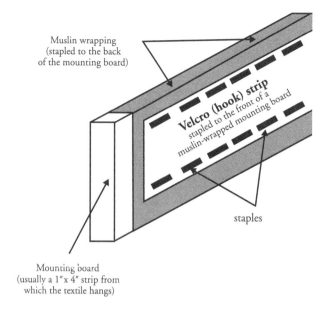

Muslin wrapping
(stapled to the back
of the mounting board)

Velcro (hook) strip
stapled to the front of a
muslin-wrapped mounting board

staples

Mounting board
(usually a 1″ x 4″ strip from
which the textile hangs)

Illus. 14-3. The Velcro (hook) strip attached to the mounting board.

the board. This ensures that nothing from the mounting system will con-taminate the back of the textile.

8. Secure the hook-side complement of the hook-and-loop 1 inch from the top edge of the board using a staple gun with stainless steel staples or a hammer with stainless steel tacks.

9. Once this edge is secure, turn the corner and secure the corner.

10. Stretch the hook-and-loop and secure it along the entire length.

11. Turn the corner and secure the side edge.

12. Put away the tools except those needed to secure the board to the wall.

Step 3: Attaching the Mounting Board to the Wall

You will need the following supplies:

Measuring tape
Carpenter's level
Safety glasses
Moly bolts, screws, or nails
Magnetic or acoustic stud finder
Power drill and bits

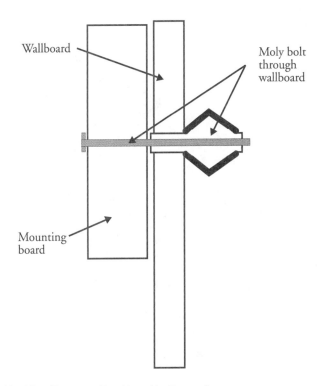

Wallboard

Moly bolt
through
wallboard

Mounting
board

Illus. 14-4. Attaching the mounting board to the wall.

1. Determine the location of the textile on the wall. With the measuring tape and carpenter's level mark the location of the mounting board on the wall. Museums generally display textiles at least 12 inches above the floor and use a 60-inch or 62-inch center line (the center line matches the center of the object to the average viewer's eye, the distance from the ground). Make a drawing of the wall space to check the figures or use a big piece of brown wrapping paper cut to the size of the textile. Do not use the textile itself. Think about the placement of any furniture. It is easier to put up a textile or take it down if the wall space does not have heavy furniture in front of it.

2. Consider the wall construction and attach the mounting board. Make sure your fasteners are appropriate for that wall. Always wear safety glasses when drilling or for similar activities.

For a framed wall that is drywall or plasterboard over wood: Drive nails or screws through the mounting board into the wood studs to hold the board to the wall.

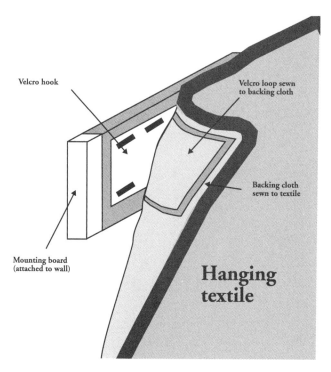

Velcro hook

Velcro loop sewn
to backing cloth

Backing cloth
sewn to textile

Mounting board
(attached to wall)

**Hanging
textile**

Illus. 14-5. One end of the textile peeled back, showing the structure of the complete Velcro hanging system.

For a framed wall that is drywall or plasterboard over metal studs: Drive screws through the mounting boards into the metal studs to hold the board to the wall.

For masonry or heavily plastered walls: Use expanding wall anchors or moly bolts of appropriate size and number. To do this, drill holes through the board with wood bits of the right size for the bolt, then drill holes in the masonry (with a masonry drill bit) large enough for the expanding anchors or moly bolts. Additional information about securing artwork to the wall is contained in the section "Hanging Framed Artwork" in Chapter 13, Taking Care of Fine Art.

Step 4: Connecting the Loop and the Hook

1. Hang the textile. Holding the textile in place against the wall, gently pat the loop portion on the textile against the hook portion of the mounting board, from the center out.

2. Adjust the hanging. It is almost impossible to get the textile to hang perfectly the first time. To adjust the textile and get it to hang as evenly as possible, peel off the loop at one side or the other to adjust the hook-and-loop complements to match exactly. The end of the textile should just barely catch the corner turn of the mounting board on each side. If the textile waves slightly at the bottom, adjust by raising the corners of the textile from the sides. The weight of the hanging may cause some distortion. It is not uncommon to have to raise a heavy textile at the sides up to $3/4$ inch above the hook-and-loop complement. Or try to lower the center $1/2$ inch.

3. Whatever the character of the textile, do not try to push or block it into a shape in which it does not want to hang.

Other Display Options

Textiles can be displayed by draping them on quilt racks with cross bars, provided the cross bars are padded with polyester batting and acid-free tissue or washed unbleached muslin. Also, an even safer method of display (for the textile) is to fabricate a padded panel tilted back at 15 degrees to

DON'S TIP:
Size Doesn't Matter . . . or Does It?

A textile is not necessarily stronger just because it is larger. In fact, the larger and heavier the textile, the more risk it faces from both handling difficulties and the forces of gravity (if it is a hanging textile such as draperies or tapestries). All sorts of goofy laws come and go, believe me. (We live near Washington, D.C., and know all about stupid laws.) But the Law of Unintended Consequences, Murphy's Law, and the Law of Gravity are here to stay. The fact that a textile is bigger does not mean it is tougher; in fact, it probably needs even more care than a small textile.

Textiles weighing more than twenty pounds or pile rugs longer than 72 inches may require a central strip of hook-and-loop across the center back of the object to reduce the amount of weight the top hook-and-loop webbing—and textile—must assume. However, most hanging textiles do not require such additional work if they are in good condition. If the textile is larger, more cumbersome, has tears or holes or other signs or damage, or if it is a lightweight and fragile object, a professional textile conservator should be engaged.

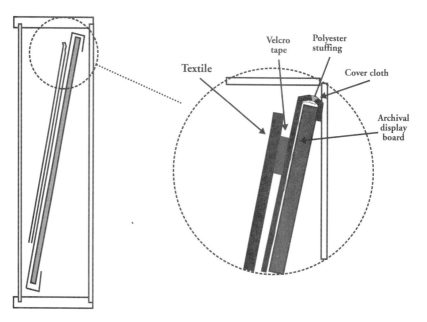

Illus. 14-6. Cross section of tilted shadow box display case for textiles.
Detail (at left) of the tilted display shadow box for a textile. The cover cloth for the
display board has to be both archivally stable and strong enough to hold the textile. It
is stapled on the rear of the display board. The 12 to 15 degree tilt allows the textile to
be fully supported while on display.

which the textile can be affixed as described above, with the tilted panel bearing the weight of the textile on the entire area.

Essentially you would be creating a large "foam core" board padded with polyester batting, which is then covered with washed unbleached muslin. Above is a diagram of such a system, which can be thought of as a shadow box or display case, with the textile inside being displayed on a board that tilts back slightly.

PRESERVING DRAPERIES AND CURTAINS

All the damage to textiles mentioned in this chapter are present and sometimes amplified with draperies: light, moisture, bugs, contaminants, pets, people, and so forth.

All fibers except glass are affected by sunlight, relative humidity, and air pollution while hanging at the window. Here is a list of things to think about when it comes to caring for your draperies.

1. Sacrificial linings and sheers are a great help in protecting the drapery fabric. Draperies with insulated backing that reflect the light last longer. The more opaque the lining or sheer, the better.

2. Synthetic fibers such as polyester, nylon, and acrylic, or a blend of these, have greater resistance to light exposure than any of the natural fibers (cotton, linen, and silk).

3. Cleaning draperies annually and rotating their location periodically adds measurably to their longevity. Because of the difficulty in laundering draperies dry cleaning is the usual approach.

4. Many fabrics and dyes are sensitive to dry cleaning solvents and methods. Be sure to deal with a dry cleaners who is experienced with draperies. Bring in all matching drapes, headers, and other matching pieces for cleaning at the same time in case the dyes have poor colorfastness.

5. Some dyes fade or change color from the effects of atmospheric pollutants. This is called fume fading. Acetate blend draperies show this more than others. The heat of deodorizing after dry cleaning can accelerate fume fading.

6. Draperies in direct contact with windows will often show large yellow rings, brown lines, or discolored areas. This develops slowly and is caused by moisture from rain or window condensation. Also, moisture may soften any sizing and any water-sensitive contaminants. As the moisture slowly dries out, sizing and contaminants migrate to the outer edge of the wet area, forming the ring. These stains also become more apparent after dry cleaning. Wet cleaning and bleaching are often needed to remove these stains, and not all drapery fabrics respond well to this.

7. Some fabrics, especially those made of natural fibers (cotton, linen, wool, silk, rayon), will both shrink and stretch due to humidity. In high-humidity conditions the yarns swell and become thicker, causing a shortening of the fabric. In dry weather the moisture content goes down, the yarn is no longer as thick, and the weight of the fabric from hanging may cause it to go back to its original length. Synthetics such as polyester, acrylic, and nylon are often blended with natural fibers to reduce the amount of stretch and shrinkage.

8. Some fabrics shrink even in the small amounts of water used in dry cleaning. The standard tolerances used in the dry cleaning industry are 4 percent shrinkage for washable fabrics and 2 percent shrinkage for dry cleanable items.

Storing Draperies and Large Hanging Textiles

You will need the following supplies:

Vacuum
White cotton gloves
Acid-free storage boxes the length of the drapery
Acid-free tissue

1. Because many valuable draperies and tapestries are made of wool and silk, they are especially attractive to pests as food sources. This means that the first step in preparing window and wall coverings for storage is a thorough front and back vacuuming of the draperies or wall coverings.

2. After vacuuming, remove the draperies or tapestries from their display spaces. This usually takes at least two people because these textiles tend to be quite large. Each person should be wearing white cotton gloves.

3. Remove all hooks from the tops of the draperies. This will avoid snags and rips that could occur when someone tries to unwrap or hang the draperies the next time. Sometimes the hooks slip out of place; other times they are stitched into the pleats and need to be cut out. If these are the original hooks and original stitching, do not cut out the hooks but leave them in position. They are historical documentation.

4. Find or construct a cardboard box, preferably acid free, made to the length of the draperies or curtains. This will help prevent the folding and creasing of the curtains to fit them into the box.

5. Lay the draperies out on a long table and place a layer of tissue paper or

DON'S TIP:
The Mythology of Cedar Chests

Using cedar chests to preserve your valued textiles is one of those myths that has little if any factual basis. They do not keep insects out, nor does the cedar aroma do anything in particular to the insects when they wander in. In addition, the reason cedar chests smell the way they do is the presence of aromatic oil in the wood itself. As the oil evaporates, it provides the familiar sachet. Unfortunately, as those very same oils evaporate they can deposit on your textiles and stain them.

cotton sheeting over their entire length. Roll the draperies from one side edge to the other, interleaving the tissue as you proceed. This will help pad the folds and avoid crushing the fabric.

6. Line the box with tissue paper, again preferably acid free. Lay the rolled drape inside the tissue and wrap the tissue around the draperies.

7. Close the box or place the lid on top.

8. Store the box in a constant climate, as discussed in Chapter 1. The worst place to store this box would be in a damp basement, where mold would likely form by the next time the draperies are needed.

VINTAGE CLOTHING

A few years back I forayed into the world of vintage clothing and bought a black zoot suit. The billowing cut of the outfit combined with my own physique made me look like an incoming cold front. This ended my excursion into the world of the fashionably dressed.

Fortunately, the needs of vintage clothing are little different from those of any other collectible textile. Keep them clean, out of the light as much as possible, and away from bugs, mold, spaghetti sauce, red wine, chocolate, and lit cigarettes. For long-term storage, treat them like any other textile. One textbook example of these preparations is given in the section below about preserving a wedding gown.

The critical area for preserving antique clothing items is in short-term storage. The most important consideration is how you hang them in the closet between wearings. Always hang vintage clothing on padded hangers,

LOUISA'S TALES:
Creating Vintage Clothing

Any piece of clothing that you greatly prize will benefit from the instructions included here. The clothing does not have to be an antique to deserve quality care. I have a coat I bought in Paris, a black strapless gown that I adore and hope to see at least one of my granddaughters wear (I am planning ahead for when I have grandkids), and several suits that I want to wear for years. I treat them as I do my vintage clothing because my hope is that they will grow to be antiques.

which help prevent the fiber from weakening. Fiber failure leads to rips, tears, unraveling, and just plain old holes. Using padded hangers prevents or minimizes this problem.

Making Padded Hangers

Padded hangers are commercially available through many sources, including better clothing and department stores. As long as the materials used are good (no polyurethane or latex foam, for example; you should use polyester batting to pad the hanger) and are covered with a soft, clean fabric they are fine. However, they tend to be rather small. For historic textiles the ideal is for the padding to be as thick as practically possible. The larger the curve, the less the damage. For that reason I have included simple instructions on how to make your own custom-fitted padded hangers. You will need the following supplies:

Scissors
Polyester batting
Wooden single-arm hangers (for shirts and jackets)
Wooden triangle hangers (for pants and skirts)
Sewing tape, needle and thread
Clean, washed muslin

1. Cut and fit the polyester batting to wrap around the particular hanger portion (hanger arms for shirts, dresses, and jackets; cross bars for pants and skirts) approximately 1 inch thick for a total thickness of at least 2 inches when you count both sides.
2. Gently tie the batting in place with thread or sewing tape.
3. Cut the muslin to fit over the batting as a cover.
4. Sew the muslin cover, in place if necessary, to complete the padded hanger.

Antique Wedding Dresses: Cleaning and Storing

Perhaps no individual garment is more important to personal and familial history as a woman's wedding dress. Often passed down through generations, taken in or let out depending on the sizes and fashions of the newest generation, a woman's wedding dress symbolizes her hopes and dreams as she begins a new phase of her life. My wife's wedding dress was made on

SMITHSONIAN STORIES:
First Ladies' Gowns

One of the most popular exhibits at the Smithsonian is the First Ladies' Gowns at the National Museum of American History. For several years, while the exhibit was closed, my colleague Polly Willman examined, cleaned, and conserved the entire collection. What she found when caring for these gowns reveals a great deal of information about not only how times have changed, but also how the role of First Lady has evolved.

Modern First Ladies' gowns are fashion artworks created solely for the Inauguration Ball, artwork specifically designed to set the tone of the First Lady's tenure within the White House. This was not always the case. In the old days, First Ladies wore the nicest attire they had, rather than have a gown created especially for the event. And then, the gown often went on to have a long and productive career clothing the First Lady and perhaps her friends and relatives, too.

Polly discovered that many of the gowns had been modified, sometimes extensively, over the years. This presented a vexing problem: Should these gowns be displayed as they were, with all the modifications intact? Or should they be restored to the way they were when worn to the Inauguration Ball or whatever special event the First Lady attended?

The decision was made that if the alteration is associated with the First Lady herself, the dress will remain unchanged. For example, Frances Cleveland's wedding dress as well as Caroline Harrison's inaugural gown were altered by the First Ladies themselves, so the gowns are displayed with all the alterations intact.

Mary Todd Lincoln's floral striped dress came to the Smithsonian after having been altered many times. Polly had excellent documentation of the original appearance of the dress from two Matthew Brady photographs. She and her colleagues were able to determine how the dress got from A to B to C to D by analyzing the construction marks in the gown. Unfortunately, there was only enough of the original fabric to return it to its B construction. Polly also knew Mary Todd Lincoln had given this dress to a cousin and theorized the 1860s (the B construction) alterations were the cousin's. So the dress was returned to its 1860s construction and exhibited in an "altered" state with an explanatory notation in the exhibit label.

four days' notice by her mother, an award-winning seamstress. By making the dress as an act of love, my mother-in-law started a family tradition. The good news is that both my daughters are slightly smaller than my wife, so the dress can be altered for either of them. The bad news is that they want an over-the-top double wedding. The *really* good news is that they are only fifteen and seventeen and I have informed them that they cannot start dating until they are twenty-eight.

Like my wife's wedding dress, other dresses have been or will be passed from generation to generation—threads binding the generations together.

Any historical or antique garment from another era requires attentive care because of the increased fragility from whatever deterioration has occurred over the years, whether from use and abuse at weddings or simply the effects of time. Antique clothing, even if only used once or twice, is more likely to rip than much newer similar items.

When thinking about antique wedding dresses, it is important to remember that aging fabric often discolors slightly—"white" is a relative color. Many old fibers, such as aged cotton or linen, are likely to appear beige when compared to brand-new synthetic fabrics. If an antique wedding dress has the same color throughout, even if it is not snow white, it is probably the appropriate color.

Spots and stains on a wedding dress are another matter, however, and should be dealt with immediately. If the dress is in good condition, without deep stains (stains that penetrate all the way through to the back side of the fabric), take the dress to a dry cleaner who specializes in antique clothing. For old, difficult stains such as food and drink, contact a textile conservator rather than a dry cleaner. Aged stains can be difficult to remove. For example, perspiration stains often can be removed from aged cotton clothing provided it is in good condition, but antique silk fabric is often too weak to survive an aggressive cleaning by you or anyone else.

If the dress has several separable components, such as a petticoat and veil, each should be prepared and stored individually within a larger case. Acid-free tissue can be inserted inside folds and to pad out sleeves to minimize creasing. Ideally, every textile, wedding dresses included, should be stored lying flat in archival packaging materials. This is not always practical. Some dresses must be hung because there is no space to store them flat (a boxed flat wedding dress can be larger than a bed); in those instances, hang them from padded hangers and then cover them in a zippered or sewn cotton or fine linen clothes bag. *Never use plastic bags!*

For horizontal storage the dress components should be padded with acid-free tissue, folded gently (be sure to pad the insides of the folds to prevent creasing) and carefully placed in a large acid-free storage box. These boxes are available at most formalwear or dry goods stores or archival suppliers.

If you are faced with really difficult problems in preserving an antique wedding dress, consult a textile or costume conservator.

Plastic pearls and rhinestones: Sewn-on plastic "pearls" create yet another level of headaches because they can impart stains as they degrade. If you can, isolate them from the cloth with acid-free tissue paper. Do this by placing the tissue paper between each of the plastic pearls and the fabric.

Real pearls: Real pearls present no problem. When you rub real pearls with your teeth, they feel rough. Fake pearls actually are smooth and slide right across your teeth.

Preserving New Wedding Dresses

If no antique wedding dress exists to wear on that special day, then the search is on for a new one. Frequently, outlandish amounts of time and money are expended in the pursuit of the perfect dress. I've even heard unbelievable tales of a wedding dress costing more than a brand-new precision sliding carriage table saw. That's just not right! But even more appalling would be not preserving this dress for your own future generations. What do you need to do? Simple: dry-clean, being careful to point out all stains to the dry cleaner and then checking before you store the dress to ensure the stains have been completely removed. Once it is returned from the cleaner,

DON'S TIP:
Weddings as Performance Art

To best protect and preserve a vintage gown you are using, consider treating it as a stage costume for a particular act of the wedding drama. Wear it for Act 1 (wedding ceremony and photography) and change into something more contemporary for Act 2, the festivities afterward. Louisa strongly disagrees, but then she is a woman, not a suspender-wearing guy.

remove the plastic cover, check to make sure the dress is cleaned properly and the stains removed, and store the dress as described above.

Preserving Vintage Hats, Gloves, Shoes, and Purses

Hats should be cleaned and their crowns padded with acid-free tissue paper. They should be placed in an acid-free box large enough to hold the hat without squeezing or crushing it at all. Ditto gloves with the fingers of the gloves gently stuffed with acid-free paper or polyester batting. They should be wrapped in acid-free tissue and placed in an acid-free box. Shoes should be gently stuffed with polyester batting or acid-free tissue before being wrapped in acid-free tissue and placed in an acid-free box. Store in a stable, cool (60 to 70 degrees Fahrenheit), fairly dry place (40 to 50 percent humidity), and keep an eagle eye out for bugs, mice, and especially mold when it comes to antique vegetable-tanned leather.

For more information on leather artifacts, read the sections "Cleaning

SMITHSONIAN STORIES:
You Found *What* in the Attic?

There are millions of objects in the Smithsonian, so it's impossible to display more than 1 percent at any given time. Even famous objects get moved into storage sometimes. When the selections were being made for the America's Smithsonian, an exhibition celebrating the Smithsonian's 150th anniversary, a cardboard hat covered with worn beaver fur was discovered on a shelf. To the untrained eye this might have looked like part of a cheap old Halloween costume. But this was no ordinary stovepipe hat. Abraham Lincoln wore it the night he was assassinated.

Lincoln's top hat was selected to go around America on tour. With great caution the exhibit designers fashioned a sealed exhibit box with an earthquake-proof platform. Not only did this platform protect the hat from any moving fiascoes, but it also provided protection in case an earthquake struck while the hat was on display in California. Noisy crowds of people came to see the Smithsonian's 150th exhibition as it traveled around the United States, but when they stood in front of Lincoln's hat, the crowds almost always fell silent. You never know what you will find in the "Nation's Attic."

Leather" and "Displaying and Storing Leather" in Chapter 9, Preserving Your Sports and Political Memorabilia. The information there will guide you in preserving vintage leather clothing and accessories, especially in understanding the differences between vegetable- and chrome-tanned leathers.

Purses should be cleaned before storing (especially if you have had food or anything else edible inside them). Vacuum the inside to remove any crumbs and wipe with a soft lint-free cloth dampened slightly with distilled water. Allow to dry completely and then gently stuff with polyester batting or acid-free tissue. Place in an acid-free box padded with the same archival materials.

Furs

Furs are among the most exquisite delicacies for critters and should be stored in refrigerated vaults for long-term preservation. Prepare them for storage as you would a wedding dress. For furs you wear regularly and want to keep in your closet, be sure to hang them on well-padded hangers and enclose them in a zippered cotton or silk garment bag. The weave of the fabric must be fine enough to keep out insects.

HISTORIC FLAGS

Nothing speaks to American pride more strongly than our flag. The Star Spangled Banner, the actual flag that flew over Fort McHenry and inspired

SMITHSONIAN STORIES:
NASA Scientists Work to Help Save the Stars and Stripes

Technology developed to help explore Mars was also used to explore the deterioration of the two-hundred-year-old flag. A special camera, called the Acousto-Optic Imaging Spectrometer, used infrared light to take images that provided a virtual map of all the stains on the Star Spangled Banner. The naked eye could not see many of these stains. The goal of the Smithsonian is not to restore the flag so that it looks brand-new but, rather, to stabilize it to ensure that it is still around for future generations. With a little help from NASA we are doing just that.

the anthem, represents the determination of Americans as well as the hopes of a new nation—all these dreams encapsulated in a piece of fabric. As such, the care this flag receives is enormous. NASA scientists, Smithsonian conservators, and many more have helped discover how to care for our flag. It is hoped that these instructions will help you save your family flag, whatever your flag's nationality.

Cleaning and Storing

Historically, flags have been made from whatever fabric was available at the time. You can find old flags made from cotton, linen, wool, and silk. Modern flags are made from synthetic fibers such as nylon, rayon, and polyester. Often the colors of the old flags fade easily or wash out. If you decide to clean your flag, take it to a textile conservator. You might want to consider the importance of the dirt or staining, though. I know this sounds peculiar—preserving dirt and stains? But the dirt and stains often tell a story of their own. Many collectors of military flags find them to be valuable sources of information because of gunpowder, blood, and other deposits.

To store flags, follow the rules and instructions in "Preserving Bedroom and Dining Room Linens" in this chapter.

Displaying

It is best to display flags lying flat on a clean muslin surface under glass to keep the dust off. Do not attach the flag to the muslin. If you must display a flag upright, follow the instructions in "Hanging Tapestries, Quilts, and Rugs for Display" in this chapter.

Never display a historic collectible flag outside. The risk of damage is simply too great from ultraviolet light, brisk winds tearing the fragile fabric, insect attacks, and kids with rocks, pellet guns, and water blasters.

Remember to treat your flags with the same respect you give your grandma!

Chapter 15

Preserving Musical Instruments

"I love it when it comes to life like this," my elder daughter said softly as she threw the switch to start the blower on the pipe organ. In the next few seconds the organ did seem to come alive, breathing and humming, patiently awaiting her instructions. As her fingers came to rest on the keys, I found myself anxiously waiting to hear the first magnificent notes boom out. My daughter had been a professional church organist since before she could drive.

She loves that organ. How do I know? Well, she asked if I could take her to the church *on a school vacation day* because technicians were going to be giving "her" organ its hundred-thousand-note tune-up. Pleased at her interest, I enthusiastically agreed. The entire day she listened to and questioned the specialists, poking her head in and out of the back of the instrument. I felt so proud. My daughter's curiosity and enthusiasm also affected the technicians, grizzled veterans though they were. They offered her a job on the spot to train with them.

One of the most memorable comments the technicians made was that organs, like most pneumatic/mechanical devices, need to be "worked out" to keep them flexible so they do not get stuck in a fixed position or configuration by remaining unmoved. The control mechanisms need to remain precise, which means that flexing them constantly is a good thing. And the airtight fabrics on the pneumatic valves also need to be "exercised" to keep the valves from getting permanent creases that would hasten their demise. If an organ simply sits there untouched, even in a perfect environment, it will soon be in a sad state. And so it is with virtually all musical instruments.

Without constant monitoring and, in some cases, intervention, maintenance, and upkeep, instruments cease to function as they should and, in many cases, cease to function at all. Putting most artifacts in a static environment and leaving them alone is the best course of action, but that is not necessarily true with musical instruments. Certainly they need optimal environments, but they also need to be played at least occasionally (because it is the fastest way to find out if anything is going wrong and is in need of immediate repair) and actively maintained in order to remain musical instruments for as long as possible. Here is the paradox: A use and maintenance regimen does indeed shorten the life of the artifact. Playing is not part of the preservation per se, but it does allow for immediate diagnosis of any preservation needs. Without use, a musical instrument can deteriorate without your knowledge to the point that it ceases to be a musical instrument and instead becomes something that merely looks like a musical instrument. That "something" may last indefinitely, but it is no longer a musical instrument.

And there end the similarities.

Musical instruments are made from wood, ivory, brass, leather, iron, steel, aluminum, bamboo, coconuts, plastics, electronics, paper, and just about anything else that can produce sound. They usually operate by one of two means: pneumatic or mechanical, and sometimes both. In the former, air is blown through or over the sound-generating part, such as a reed in a woodwind or a hollow space in a wood recorder or bamboo flute. In the latter, the sound is generated by striking, rubbing, or plucking the sound-generating part, such as a piano or any instrument with strings.

THINK "USE IT OR LOSE IT"

Since musical instruments are so idiosyncratic, I don't advise doing much *to* them. That is why this chapter has very few step-by-step "how-to" maintenance instructions. Instead, I suggest focusing on the environment surrounding the instrument. Combine a controlled environment with gentle periodic playing, and you will considerably extend the lives of these artifacts. So when preserving musical instruments, think "Use It or Lose It."

STRINGED WOODEN INSTRUMENTS

When the strings on an instrument, which are held under tension, are struck, they produce sound. A guitar's sound is generated when the string is plucked or strummed; a violin's strings vibrate when they are rubbed by horsehair bundles; and a piano plays when the heavy metal wires are struck with a device called a hammer and a wooden soundboard or electronic amplifier projects the sound.

The complicated nature of musical instruments leads to a lot of questions. Are the necks, soundboards, pin blocks, harps, and so forth, strong enough to withstand the tension of the tightened strings, without which the instrument is merely a sculpture? Is the instrument fitted with the right strings? Is it tuned properly or overtuned to the point of snapping the neck or soundboard? Do all the moving parts move as they are supposed to? Like the human eye, if any part of the instrument does not work properly, neither does the instrument.

From a materials point of view, guitars, violins, and most other wooden musical instruments are highly specialized fancy wooden boxes.

Wood, no matter how old or how it is fashioned, has an ongoing relationship with moisture. When the air is drier than wood, the wood gives off moisture and shrinks. When the air is more moist than wood, the wood absorbs moisture and swells. This cycle is endless: as long as wood is wood, this is what it does. Given the delicate structure and precision workmanship of musical instruments, it is clear that maintaining a stable environment is paramount to their care and preservation.

Rapid changes in temperature or humidity are bad news for complex wooden artifacts. This is because the wood does not respond to these changes equally in all directions, and the wood and the varnish also react differently from each other. In some cases these reactions are relatively benign, affecting the tone *and* the tune of the instrument as the dimensions and stiffness of both the instruments and the strings change. In extreme cases the temperature and humidity fluctuations can cause cracks in both the finish and the wood.

Most wooden stringed instruments are finished with a high-gloss varnish of one kind or another. Many of these finishes age gracefully and wear well while others do not. Traditionally, musical instruments were coated with natural resin spirit varnishes, oil/resin varnishes, or synthetic lacquers. These are often sensitive to alcohol, perfumes, and plastics such as imitation leather straps and urethane foam padding, frequently used in instrument cases.

Don's Rules for Caring for Your Stringed Wooden Instruments

1. The best environment for a wooden musical instrument is about 65 to 75 degrees and about 50 percent humidity.

2. Perspiration will eventually damage any varnish or metal hardware, so always wipe the instrument off with a clean, soft cotton cloth every time before putting it away.

3. Polish the wood finish with good paste wax as described in "Wood Furniture" in Chapter 8, Preserving Your Furniture. Since instruments are handled and rubbed much more than most furniture, you may have to polish more frequently than furniture.

4. Unless you know that the instrument's varnish is an epoxy or catalyzed polyester (1970s or later), assume it is sensitive to organic solvents and plastics. This means don't let plastic bags or similar materials touch the instrument.

5. Take off your jewelry before you handle or play the instrument.

6. If you use an instrument stand, cover the cushions with clean cotton flannel and replace the covering frequently.

7. Always relax the strings with a half-turn or two of the nuts if you are putting the instrument away for more than a couple of hours. This means you must retune when you next go to play.

8. Spilling alcohol, soda, or food on the instrument can take off some finishes. So can perfumes and other cosmetics, including lotions.

9. Notwithstanding the histrionics of rock stars, don't smash your instrument after a big set. It tends to shorten its productive life span.

10. Never ever use an oil-based polish on a musical instrument. These polishes can penetrate cracks and seams, contaminating the surface and making future repairs difficult.

11. Never use alcohol on the wood of an instrument. Alcohol will remove many types of violin varnish. The older the varnish, the more susceptible it is likely to be.

12. Musical instruments are not toys, so don't let children treat them like toys.

13. Instruments are delicate and must not be dropped, lifted improperly, or treated irresponsibly. Treat instruments gently and pick up carefully with clean white cotton gloves to avoid touching the varnish.

14. Hold the instrument by the neck (not the scroll) and the base when moving.

15. When not in use, place the instrument on a clean padded surface.

16. If you have a good, sound, well-fitting case for the instrument, keep it in the case with a clean cloth draped over the strings when not being used. Be sure the interior of the case is clean, the fabric is not fraying or powdering, and the padding has not deteriorated.

17. Keep the instrument out of the light as much as possible.

18. If there are wide variations in humidity where the instrument is stored, place the instrument in the case, close it, and place the case in a sealed polyethylene bag. This will buffer the instrument against sudden humidity changes. *Warning:* Do not put the plastic bag directly over the instrument because there is the likelihood of problems between the plastic and the varnish.

19. Be sure you have the right strings on the instrument. Strings that are too heavy or are tuned too high can literally break a bridge, crack the soundboard, or even snap an instrument in half. I'm not kidding.

20. Keep the instrument away from cold outside walls and off the drafty floor.

21. Never leave wooden musical instruments in unattended cars if the outside temperature is too high or too low or if the sun is shining.

22. Avoid leaving your instrument near a heating vent or radiator.

Preserving Guitars

In addition to the preceding rules for stringed wooden musical instruments, please add these considerations when caring for guitars:

1. Follow the same instructions as those for cleaning and waxing wood furniture in Chapter 8, Preserving Your Furniture.
2. Always remove the strap from the instrument when not in use.

Don's Rules for Preserving Viols (Violins, Violas, Cellos, and Bass)

Few musical instruments are the recipients of more lavish attention and care than those in the violin family. The result of such care is that many viols that are more than two hundred years old are still being played today. A violin's health and longevity are dependent on three things: care and maintenance, the mitigation of environmental changes, and use and abuse. Some routine maintenance such as routine cleaning can be done by you.

SMITHSONIAN STORY:
A Quartet of Quartets

Thanks to the generosity of benefactor Herbert Axelrod, the National Museum of American History collection contains four amazing viol quartets (two violins, a viola, and a cello) from four different golden ages of stringed instrument making. The oldest of these is from the mid-1600s, created by Nicolo Amati, mentor to Antonio Stradivari. This same Stradivari (Stradivarius violins ring a bell?) is the maker of the most famous of the Axelrod quartets, which dates back to the 1700s. The third quartet, by the French violin maker Jean-Baptiste Vuillaume, dates from the 1800s. Sergio Perreson, who made the quartet from the 1900s, rounds out the headliners. These remarkable instruments are played between twenty and forty times a year. These viols are made of the finest materials and with the greatest skill; their conservation needs are minimal, since they are handled (almost literally) with kid gloves. The most important preservation issues are making sure they get cleaned after every use, that they are always kept in a stable, clean environment, and that they are occasionally played. Following these practices, the collection will be around for centuries without a problem.

Other, more finicky repairs, adjustments, and maintenance should probably be left to a skilled violin maker or technician.

In addition to the preceding rules for stringed wooden instruments, please add these considerations for instruments in the violin family.

1. A skilled violin restorer or conservator should thoroughly clean a frequently used violin at least twice a year. In general, you are better off sticking to routine wiping off of rosin, dust, and fingerprints, and leaving the serious cleaning to an experienced specialist. Virtually all viols of any quality have delicate spirit varnish finishes that can be easily damaged by unskilled attempts to clean.

2. Remove the rosin dust with a soft brush or flannel cloth immediately after playing. It is very important to keep the surface of stringed instruments free of colophony (rosin), dirt, and dust. Rosin is your fiddle's enemy because it sticks to the strings, fingerboard, and varnish, where it deadens tone and eventually turns gummy and black. Rosin is slightly acidic and when left for long periods of time can attack the varnish. When the rosin and dirt have built up to a considerable extent, it can even dampen the freedom of vibration of the belly. The sound comes out muddy rather than crisp.

Cleaning Viols

Do not use any commercial cleaners or organic solvents, especially alcohol, to clean your instrument. Instrument varnishes are almost always natural resin spirit varnishes that can be easily removed with these materials.

You will need the following supplies to clean a violin:

Soft brush or flannel
Artist's brush
Vacuum cleaner (with nylon or gauze screen attached; see "Don's Rules for Preserving New and Old Upholstery" in Chapter 8, Preserving Your Furniture)
Nylon screen or gauze
Lint-free cotton cloth
Distilled water
Mild liquid dish detergent
Paste wax
Alcohol wipes
Waxed paper

1. Remove the rosin dust with a soft brush or flannel cloth.

2. Dust the wooden parts of string instruments with a soft artist's brush, brushing all the dirt toward the nozzle of a vacuum cleaner. (Make sure the nozzle is covered with gauze or nylon screen to prevent anything loose being sucked into the vacuum.)

3. If dusting fails to remove ingrained stains and dirt, damp dusting can be done provided the finish of the instrument is in good condition. Intact and smooth varnish can be gently rubbed with a soft cloth moistened in distilled water to which has been added a few drops of detergent.

4. Gently clean the neck and fingerboard with a rag dampened with distilled water to which a few drops of mild detergent have been added.

5. Polish the varnished surface with a high-quality paste wax, as described in Chapter 8.

6. Strings also need to be cleaned: Pinch each string individually with a clean, dry, lint-free cloth and rub the full length.

7. More resistant rosin/string dirt can be removed with alcohol hand wipes. First, slide a piece of waxed paper underneath the strings so that the entire wood and varnished surface is protected. Fold the wipe into stamp size, pinch each string in the fold of the wipe, and run it up and down until the string is clean.

Don's Rules for Bow Care

1. The bow hair can be wiped of excess rosin in the same manner as viol strings.

2. Rosin should be cleaned off the bow stick in the same manner as the viol body.

3. Loosen bow hair when not playing the instrument to prevent warping of the bow.

4. Warped bows need to be repaired by specialists.

5. Cut off broken bow hairs. Do not tear them out because this will likely lead to more damage.

6. Bow hair needs to be replaced periodically by specialists if one of the following problems is present:
   a. The bow hair is so dirty that the bow sounds rotten
   b. The bow hair is so saturated that it cannot be charged with rosin
   c. The bow hair tends to skip
   d. The bow hair has lost a large number of hairs (more than twenty)

Preserving bows: Long-term storage of bows is a bit problematic, because carpet beetles love horsehair. Wrap in fine cloth, seal in a polyethylene bag, and then store in a box with a nugget of camphor (white crystalline material that smells like moth balls).

Pianos and Harpsichords

I have a special place in my heart for pianos. When I was younger, I worked restoring the cases of pianos for a gifted piano technician who taught me an awful lot about them, most notably how complicated they were and how much the soundboard affected their tone. And not only do my daughters play beautifully, but Dave Brubeck and, presumably, Grieg, Chopin, and Beethoven did, too. How cool is that? Debussy still brings me to tears.

For pianos and harpsichords the exterior, whether ornate or plain, conceals a complex system of levers, fittings, and springs that must all work together to make the thing work well. An unassuming exterior often conceals very complex and delicate mechanisms that contain several hundred parts. Each time you press on one piano key, up to three dozen separate pieces work together to make one note, and on a full-sized keyboard there are eighty-eight notes. This complexity makes preserving keyboard instruments a real challenge.

The typical piano is about 75 percent wood. If you glance through the previous section and reread Chapters 2 and 8, you will suddenly have an idea about where I am going: The main trouble in preserving pianos has to do with the relationship of wood to metal, and both of them to moisture.

The most expansive components of pianos are the soundboard, the big flat, thin piece of wood underneath the strings; the pin block, which is the slab holding the devices that tighten and loosen the strings; and the iron plate that holds all the strings under tension. Because wood swells with extra moisture in the air and shrinks when the air gets drier, the soundboard is changing all the time. With enough change in the environment, the soundboard will swell and shrink to the point of cracking. In fact, I would venture to say that most pianos in temperate-climate homes have cracked soundboards.

Don's Special Rules for Caring for Pianos and Harpsichords

In addition to the preceding rules for wooden musical instruments, please add these considerations when caring for wooden keyboard instruments. In preserving pianos it is best to think of them as furniture containing a sophisticated and delicate mechanism of mostly wooden parts.

SMITHSONIAN STORY:
Two Hundred Pianos

The collection at the Smithsonian's National Museum of American History contains over two hundred pianos, harpsichords, and claviers. Pianos and other keyboard instruments have lots of moving parts, many of which are either tiny or made from delicate materials. Playing such fragile antiques frequently would eventually result in some catastrophic damage. For those keyboards that were most often used in concert (concert pianists are notorious for pounding on the keyboards), museum specialists replace the original inside mechanisms (moving parts inside the piano), known as "actions." The original "inners" of the piano are then placed in climate controlled storage, so the antique piano you view on display has all new stuff inside. One other interesting note is that the collection specialists at the museum use the sound of the pianos to gauge the performance of the environmental control system. If the piano is sharp, the humidity is too high. If the piano or harpsichord is flat, the humidity is too low.

1. Always wash your hands before playing.

2. The faces of keys are either ivory or plastic. Care for them accordingly. Plastics are covered in Chapter 7, Sorting and Preserving the Family Trash, and ivory in Chapter 13, Taking Care of Fine Art.

3. Don't spill liquids on the keyboard. Organic solvents can damage plastic keys. Water can warp ivory keys and will definitely cause swelling to the key-regulating mechanism and mess up the playing.

4. Do not touch the strings, felts, or any internal parts of the piano with your hands. The oils and acids from your skin will leave a residue and cause damage. Sound familiar?

5. Do not try to repair the piano yourself. Unless you really know what you are doing, the odds are good that you will only make things worse.

6. Keep your piano out of direct sunlight. Direct sunlight will destroy the finish and cause damage to the soundboard and pin block through locally reduced humidity. Place mousetraps and insect traps in the base of the upright. Make sure they are out of the way of the pedal mechanisms.

7. Monitor the interior of the piano frequently for bugs and rodents. Insects love to eat the fabric and paper spacers used in regulating the action, and the action itself is connected by cloth ribbons. Hammers are often made of hard wool felt, a delicacy for some bugs. Mice love to settle in the bases of upright pianos.

8. Dust the interiors very carefully with a soft artist's brush, brushing toward the nozzle of a vacuum cleaner. First, though, cover the nozzle with nylon gauze or something similar to prevent loose pieces from being sucked away.

Piano exteriors: Follow the instructions in "Wood Furniture" in Chapter 8, Preserving Your Furniture.

Harpsichord exteriors: Follow the instructions in "Wood Furniture" in Chapter 8, Preserving Your Furniture.

Decorated harpsichords exterior: Follow the instructions in "Panel Paintings" in Chapter 13, Taking Care of Fine Art.

Don's Rules for Handling and Moving a Piano, Organ, or Harpsichord

1. Pick up the phone and make the call: Have someone else do it.
2. Make sure that someone is a pro who knows what he or she is doing.

Professional piano movers know how to take down, wrap, load, transport, and set up pianos. I know because moving pianos was a steady source of money for me in college.

PRESERVING ORGANS, PUMP ORGANS, AND PLAYER PIANOS

The one rule for all these instruments is the first rule listed near the beginning of the chapter: Keep them in a stable moderate environment, 65 to 75 degrees Fahrenheit and 50 percent humidity. For the most part, with the exception of the player piano, ongoing maintenance is beyond the experience and abilities of most people. The best advice for preserving these is to keep them clean, safe, warm, and dry.

Pipe Organs

Pipe organ preservation relies on recognizing that people are the enemy and that bellows cloth and pneumatic devices wear out and need to be repaired or replaced periodically. Damage is most often caused by housekeeping accidents in the areas surrounding the organ or ill-advised repair attempts by someone who does not know how organs work. A falling ladder

DON'S TIP:
Moving a Piano Yourself: A Recipe for Disaster

A small piano weighs several hundred pounds, and a full upright or grand piano may be close to a half ton. Trust me, you do not want to be around when someone loses his grip on one of those instruments halfway up the stairs. Demolition, disability, and divorce can be the result. The piano crew I worked with was once called to a home where a man and some buddies had tried to move his wife's piano up a half flight of stairs. After the fourth step the two guys on the bottom lost control, and the eight-hundred-pound Victorian beauty began its trek toward earth. These fellows were lucky to have avoided four broken legs. When we arrived several hours later, the piano was stuck halfway through the wall at the bottom of the stairs, and the wife was still screaming at her husband even though she was so hoarse her voice was just a whisper. It had been her great-grandmother's piano, handed down through the generations. I've been in more unpleasant atmospheres, but not often.

or dropped paintbrush, broom, or mop (and the water contained therein) can cause serious damage.

The cleaning and adjustments of pipe organs are better left in the hands of a specialist. Cleaning the insides of a pipe organ is not a job for the uninitiated. Yes, it is true that my daughter helps clean and tune her organ, but she is a very serious amateur on her way to becoming a professional. Unless you devote eons of time to learning about the organ, trying to clean one yourself can result in hundreds of thousands of dollars in repairs. Make sure whoever repairs your organ really knows what he or she is doing. Otherwise, leave the poor thing alone. You (or they) only have to accidentally poke a hole in one cloth bellows to incur thousands of dollars' worth of damage. Knocking off some of the pneumatic tubing that provides the controls for selecting and laying the pipes could result in needing the entire organ control to be completely reworked. Call your broker first.

Pump Organs

In concept, a pump organ is much like a pipe organ except that the sound is not made by a gigantic whistle but by a reed. As such, a pump organ is in some ways more like a woodwind than a pipe organ. Again, cleaning and adjustments are better left in the hands of a specialist. Be extremely careful when removing dust from pump organ reeds. Even the slightest contact can cause a perceptible musical change.

Player Pianos

A player piano is part piano, part robot. Originally, this system was powered by a pair of pump bellows that had to be pedaled by someone. Nowadays almost all old player piano bellows have been replaced by electric air pumps.

Don's Rules for Player Piano Preservation

1. Treat the piano parts just like a piano (see above).
2. Replace the tubing pieces of the player controls as they age and when they break or split.
3. Be sure to keep the tracker bar clean (that's the part over which the perforated rolls run).
4. Lubricate the player mechanisms periodically. Use lightweight ma-

chine oil for metal parts and powdered graphite for everything else that moves.

5. Put mousetraps and insect traps inside the base of the upright piano. Critters love player pianos. Not only do they have fairly large spaces close to the floor, but the bellows offer safe havens that are especially prized by pregnant mice.

Cleaning a Tracker Bar

If the tracker bar gets filled with dirt, the player mechanism will not work. It must be cleaned periodically. To clean this part properly you have to vacuum the small channels using a small tube of rubber, available from the hardware store, hooked to a vacuum cleaner. You will need the following supplies:

Piece of heavy cardboard
Silicone caulk
Vacuum cleaner
¼-inch rubber hose, approximately 36 inches long

1. Cut a piece of heavyweight cardboard slightly larger than the end of the vacuum hose.

2. Punch a hole through the cardboard large enough to fit the rubber tubing.

3. Run a bead of silicone caulk around the opening through which the tube is pushed. You are now done with creating your tracker bar vacuum attachment. When you turn on the vacuum and place the cardboard over the end of the vacuum hose, the suction will hold the cardboard in place and the rubber tube will pick up dust and dirt.

4. With the vacuum on, gently run the small rubber hose over the openings in the tracker bar. The dirt and debris will be vacuumed out.

PRESERVING ACCORDIONS AND OTHER SQUEEZE BOXES

Just as the reed organ is an attempt to mimic the pipe organ, on a smaller, more affordable scale, squeeze boxes are basically a portable version of a pump organ. Most are tough and solidly built, able to withstand the abuse of seafaring and beer halls, while others, accordions in particular, need a more gentle environment. Particular care must be taken not to subject the accordion to extreme environmental conditions.

Don's Rules for Accordion Handling and Use

1. Be careful when placing the accordion in its case. The keyboard goes in first, and be sure to grab it by the handles rather than the keys.

2. Be careful when taking the accordion out of the case. Don't grab or pick it up by the strap alone. The strap has to break only once to really mess up the instrument because the accordion's keys, valves, and bellows can be damaged by even short drops.

3. Never play an accordion near the ocean. Salt mist gets inside and is likely to ruin the instrument forever. All the metal parts will corrode, including (and maybe especially) the reeds.

4. Don't play your accordion in the rain. Expect to kiss your accordion good-bye if you do.

5. In a steam-heated room, it is well to form the habit of placing the accordion as far from the radiator as possible.

6. Guard your accordion from extreme temperature changes. Allow your instrument to warm up slowly to a new room temperature before you take it out of its case. When you change the environment of the accordion, such as taking it into the warm from the cold, the change in temperature will cause condensation in the instrument.

7. Never store your accordion in a very cold environment. The precision with which accordion reed plates are assembled is such that they can be badly damaged by cold-induced shrinkage.

8. Accordions should never be left in the sun or in a hot place such as inside a car in the summer. Not only are the component materials (wood and plastic) damaged, but also the reeds, which are often held in place with wax that will melt. Without the reeds you don't have an accordion—you have an unwieldy fireplace bellows. Heat will also shrink the leather valves covering the reeds, reducing the efficiency of the bellows.

9. Remove any jewelry on your hands or torso that will scratch or gouge the accordion. Also suspenders. I guess the accordion is out for me.

10. Wash your hands before playing or handling.

11. Wash your perspiration off the keys after each use.

12. Always fasten the bellows straps when not playing.

Storing Your Accordion

The long-term preservation of accordions and other squeeze boxes pretty much involves one thing: the storage environment.

An accordion should be stored upright, resting on the bass end (that's the end with the little feet that the instrument is supposed to sit on). If the accordion is not stored with the proper orientation, the internal leather valves (which prevent back flow) may be in the wrong position and cause them to sag open, causing an unpleasant snuffling or rattling sound when the accordion is played. Repairing this problem is complicated, expensive, and unnecessary because it is completely preventable.

Store in a stable environment that is slightly cool and a little on the dry side, such as 60 degrees Fahrenheit and 40 percent relative humidity. As with most composite artifacts composed of both organic and inorganic materials, there is no such thing as a perfect environment for long-term storage of accordions. Storing an accordion in a humid environment is sure to wreak havoc because the moisture will rust the metal reeds. You'll get corrosion on the mechanical parts, the wood parts will swell and warp, and the cardboard and leather of the bellows will degrade. Storing in an overly dry environment will crack the leather and harm the other organic materials.

WIND INSTRUMENTS

In terms of care and preservation, wind instruments fall into two basic categories: those made of metal and those made of wood. Metal instruments are prone to corrosion and can be damaged by denting and bending. Wooden instruments are sensitive to humidity and can crack and distort. You can clean a wooden wind instrument effectively, but cleaning metal wind instruments should be left to experts. That is why I explain how to clean a wooden wind instrument but not a metal one.

Metal Wind Instruments

This category of instrument includes the traditional brasses (trumpets, trombones, tubas, etc.) along with the metal woodwinds (saxophones, flutes, and some clarinets). Some basic truths exist about metal instruments:

With use, metal instruments can become tarnished quite quickly because acids and oils in the skin are transferred to the metal. Also, the breath passing through the instrument condenses inside, encouraging corrosion in places that are not easy to get to. Interior cleaning is difficult to do effectively without special equipment because you often have to take the instrument apart. In general, such work should be left to a metal wind instrument repairer who has the necessary expertise.

Don's Rules for Preserving Metal Wind Instruments

Metal wind instruments that are played daily do occasionally need intensive cleaning and maintenance beyond the scope of this book. Instead, I will focus on instruments played infrequently, where preservation, not performance, is the ultimate goal. The most important factors to remember in caring for your metal wind instruments are cleanliness, lubrication, and storage in a stable, low-humidity environment.

1. Be sure your hands are clean and dry before handling your instrument for playing. Otherwise, handle with clean white cotton gloves.

2. Always clean your instrument thoroughly after use.

3. Never use the same cloth to clean both inside and outside your instrument. The "inside" cloth is full of spit, and the "outside" cloth is full of skin oils and acids.

4. Do not try to oil your instrument with machine or cooking oils. Instrument lubricants are specially formulated, and it is best to stick with them.

DON'S TIP:
Polishing the Brass

In cases where the surface is less than spiffy, make sure it is amenable to polishing. Polishing works only on instruments that are not lacquered. If you are in doubt, check with an instrument repair shop. Once you decide to move forward with polishing, treat the instrument exactly as if it were a giant piece of furniture hardware. See "Cleaning Metal Hardware" in Chapter 8, Preserving Your Furniture.

5. Do not store your instrument against a source of heat such as a radiator.

6. Keep metal wind instruments in dry storage conditions. If they were only metal, I would say keep them bone dry, but there are small but vital components such as leather pads and vegetable reeds that are adversely affected by an atmosphere that is too dry.

7. Keep the instrument in its case. It's the safest place overall.

8. Allow the instrument to acclimate slowly to a new environment, especially if the new one is warmer or more humid than the previous environment.

9. Keep the metal valves lubricated by periodically placing a drop of valve lubricant on the hinge pin of the valve. If you are not playing the instrument frequently, once a year should suffice.

Brass Instrument Preservation

Follow the instructions in "Cleaning Metal Hardware" in Chapter 8, Preserving Your Furniture.

Nickel-Plated Instrument Preservation

Follow the instructions for taking care of silver in Chapter 6, Saving Your Family Treasures.

WOODEN WIND INSTRUMENTS: PRESERVATION

The rules for preservation of woodwind instruments are the same as metal, with one big difference: Wind instruments need a storage environment as close to 65 degrees and 50 percent relative humidity as possible. If there are wide variations in humidity where the instrument will be stored, place it in the case, close it, and place the case in a sealed polyethylene bag. This will buffer the instrument against sudden humidity changes.

In addition, remove the reeds from the instrument whenever it is not being played. Keep them in a clean, enclosed polyethylene container alongside the instrument. Also, keep the instrument disassembled and stored in its case when not played. Be sure the case is in good condition, that the padding is not powdery, and that the lining fabric is not frayed to the point that it snags on the instrument.

Cleaning and Lubricating

Wooden wind instruments include reeded instruments such as clarinets; double-reeded instruments such as the bassoon and oboe; and unreeded instruments such as recorders and flutes. To clean and lubricate these instruments you will need the following supplies:

Soft artist's brush
Nylon screen or gauze
Vacuum cleaner (with nylon or gauze screen attached; see "Don's Rules for Preserving New and Old Upholstery" in Chapter 8, Preserving Your Furniture)
Lint-free cotton cloth
Distilled water
Mild liquid dish detergent
Instrument lubricating oil

1. Clean the wooden parts of wind instruments first by dusting with a soft artist's brush, brushing toward the nozzle of a screened vacuum cleaner.

2. If light brushing fails to remove any accreted dirt and the surface coating on the wood is in good condition, wipe with a clean lint-free cotton rag dampened with a few drops of distilled water.

3. If that is not sufficient, add a few drops of mild detergent to the distilled water before dampening the cleaning cloth.

4. Always clean the instrument after playing, taking special care to get the moisture out of the interior, and let the pads dry.

5. For metal keys, follow the instructions in "Nonremovable Metal Hardware" in Chapter 8, Preserving Your Furniture. It is very important to keep polishing materials away from the wood and out of any crevices. Be sure to protect the surface with a thin plastic film cut to fit around the hardware element.

6. Apply instrument-lubricating oil sparingly to all moving parts with a needle or toothpick to avoid drips or runs onto the wooden surface. Wipe drips immediately with a clean cotton rag or litho pad.

PERCUSSION INSTRUMENTS

Percussion instruments make sounds by being hit. They can be hit with bare hands, such as bongo drums, or with mallets, such as snare drums.

Drums

Basic drum preservation is really as simple as keeping drums, cymbals, and stands clean and in good working condition, and keeping them in a stable environment. This is especially true for drums that employ organic materials such as animal skins or bark.

Clean the drums by dusting them with clean lint-free cotton cloth. If necessary, dampen the cloth with either distilled water or distilled water and mild detergent.

Wooden components: Clean and wax as described in Chapter 8, Preserving Your Furniture.

Metal components (such as bolts, nuts, hinges, and cymbals): Follow the instructions in "Cleaning Metal Hardware" in Chapter 8, Preserving Your Furniture.

Pedals: Lubricate with a little light machine oil as described in "Videotapes and Audiotapes: Cleaning and Equipment Maintenance" in Chapter 10, Preserving Entertainment Memorabilia and Media.

Storing drums: Make sure that the cymbals don't touch each other in storage by placing a piece of clean cotton flannel or acid-free tissue between them. Drape them with cotton dust cloths or polyethylene furniture bags. Store them in the dark at about 70 degrees Fahrenheit and 50 percent relative humidity.

Marimbas and Xylophones

Because of their size and their complexity of structure, handling these instruments properly is critical to their longevity. In every respect the preservation principles of these instruments are the same as furniture pieces of the same size, such as a dining table.

When moving, handle with extreme care because these instruments are easily damaged. Treat them just like a sofa or large piece of furniture as described in "Moving Furniture" in Chapter 8, Preserving Your Furniture. Most damage occurs when the instrument is smashed against a door frame because of carelessness.

Conclusion

The artifacts of our ancestors, both precious and mundane, have reached us through a combination of limited use, accident, benign neglect, and simple good fortune. By applying the preservation principles of careful use and handling, proper maintenance, storage, and environmental controls illustrated in this book, you can improve the chances of your important possessions reaching your descendants intact. I hope you have as much fun preserving stuff as I do!

Saving Stuff

I hope your photos are duplicated,
Your furniture paste-waxed,
Your textiles clean and fumigated,
Your Time Capsule well stashed.

I wish your coin collection well preserved,
Your records stored with care,
Your family trash be a touch absurd,
Your instruments played with flair.

May your books be housed like Pharaoh's treasure,
Your stamps and art not fade,
Your stuffed animals always give you pleasure,
Your scrapbooks be homemade.

May your silver always be polished,
Your sport cards kept from light,
And may none of your stuff be demolished,
By floods, or pets, or blight.

If you follow all the instructions,
If you handle your stuff with care,
Your stuff need not be a worry
'Cause for centuries it will be there.

—Louisa Jaggar

Resources

YOUR *SAVING STUFF* TOOL KIT

A

Abrasive cleaning pad: synthetic steel wool (one is called Scotch-Brite) that can be obtained in a variety of grades ranging from very coarse to very fine. This product is preferable to steel wool because it does not leave tiny steel particles after rubbing. It is good for cleaning the loose rust off iron and steel objects in preparation for hot waxing. Avoid Brillo pads because they are typically coated with pumice (the pink stuff). [1, 2, 3, 7, 9, 11]

Acetone: a sweet-smelling, very volatile (evaporates quickly) organic solvent that cuts through grease and dissolves varnish. Make sure to wear protective gloves, a respirator (see below), and eyewear when using. It is *highly flammable. Use with extreme caution.* [2, 3, 6, 8]

Activated charcoal canisters: used to purify the air. Organic solvent respirator canisters (replaceable filters that are used in painters' face masks) can be purchased from larger paint stores or from auto body paint stores. They come sealed in plastic and do not begin to work until the plastic is removed. Replace the canisters periodically—every six to twelve months for sealed cabinets and every three months for unsealed cabinets. [2, 5, 6, 9, 11]

Ageless® oxygen scavenger: Ageless actually removes the oxygen from the surrounding air. It is usually purchased as sealed packets slightly larger than sugar packets. As soon as the packet is punctured or torn, the reaction begins. You have probably encountered a packet of Ageless inside sealed containers of peanuts, which are especially sensitive to oxygen. [6, 23]

Alcohol (ethanol): also known as pure grain liquor. Used for general cleaning purposes and to remove grease and resinous gunk. Do not substitute rubbing alcohol for alcohol. You may be able to get 190-proof grain alcohol, though any pure grain alcohol will work just fine. Don't use your good bourbon or whiskey because anything other than pure grain alcohol contains too much sugar. Make sure to wear protective gloves, respirator, and eyewear. *Highly flammable. Use with extreme caution.* [6, 8, 10]

Aluminum tacks: fasteners often used because they are corrosion resistant to pollution. [2, 6, 11]

Antistatic devices: reduce static of phonograph records and make them less susceptible to dust deposits. They are typically available online or at Radio Shack. [13]

Antitarnish cloth: impregnated with a tarnish inhibitor that protects the metal objects wrapped inside. These cloths actually slow down the tarnishing process. Fitted antitarnish cloth bags are readily available for many silver objects, at suppliers listed below. Note: Sometimes it is called "Pacific cloth." [4, 6, 24]

Artist's brush: a workhorse in the world of preservation dusting and cleaning. My favorites are $1/2$-inch or larger watercolor brushes made with fine nylon bristles. These are fairly expensive, but unless badly abused, they will last a lifetime. [3, 6]

B

Blotter paper, acid free: made from rag paper or neutralized wood pulp paper, like most of the archival paper products listed in this book, so that it will not contribute to the deterioration of the artifact. [3, 6, 18]

Blue wool fading strips: the standard tool for measuring the potential for damage from light. By following the instructions that come with them, you can determine the risks your collections face from the light levels in your home. [6]

Boxes, archival: storage boxes made from heavyweight, acid-free, buffered, or rag paper board. If you are serious about preserving collections, you will buy and use dozens or hundreds of these. They are a little expensive, but you can often get them tailored for your specific need, and they will last for centuries. [3, 6]

Brass wire: holds the crystal on crystal chandeliers and the like. Hardware store brass wire is fine. If the wire is a little stiff, soften it by heating it. You can heat brass wire by placing it directly on a hot plate at about 400 degrees Fahrenheit for a few hours. Allow to cool off before picking it up to use. [2, 11, 19]

Buffered boards (paper): often used as supports or protection for paper or books. They are made from rag paper or neutralized wood pulp paper so as not to contribute to the deterioration of the artifact. These boards can range in thickness from three or four layers to a hefty $1/4$-inch thick. [3, 6]

Butcher's paper: a useful product for many of the cleaning processes described in this book. Since one side of the paper is coated to prevent meat juices from sopping through, it also works pretty well for containing messy cleaning efforts. [15, 18]

C

Candle, unscented, uncolored: molten candle wax. This is an excellent sealing material, but it's important to use the purest material possible because the colorants or perfumes contained in the candle may cause additional deterioration to the contents of the sealed capsule. [1, 2, 3, 6]

Cardboard: a clean, flat, disposable surface to work on, when cleaning an artifact or making some other mess. Cardboard does the trick. Since it is disposable, almost any type of clean cardboard will do.

Cardboard tube, acid-free: used for rolling textiles or oversized paper artifacts for storage. Acid-free or archival cardboard tubes are made from laminated rag paper or neutralized wood pulp paper, so they will not contribute to the deterioration of the artifact. These can be purchased in virtually every size you might need. [3, 6]

Carpenter's glue: standard wood glue, usually either white or yellow. [1, 2, 3, 6, 11]

Carpenter's level: a tool that tells whether something is level (perfectly parallel to the surface of standing water) or plumb (perpendicular to the surface of standing water). This tool is critical for hanging things straight. [2, 7, 11]

Charcoal: an excellent absorber of organic pollution, especially odors. Use the cheapest charcoal you can find and avoid using Match Light, which is impregnated with paraffin to make it easier to light. The paraffin seals the surface of the charcoal, making it much less efficient as a pollution scavenger. You definitely want Brand X charcoal because it works much better as a pollution scavenger and is so cheap that you feel no guilt when replacing it often. [1, 2]

Clean work surface: a firm, flat surface larger than the dimensions of the object you are working on. It should be large enough that you can safely move or manipulate the object without fear of its falling off. Sometimes this is the hardest resource to find.

Clear plastic bags: large enough to hold children's three-dimensional art. Archival polyethylene bags are especially recommended, but not always possible to find. Sometimes all you have at your disposal is a bag for some other purpose. While black trash bags will do fine from a preservation perspective, when you want to see what's inside, a clean, large plastic bag from the mattress or appliance store or even the dry cleaner is better than the alternative of nothing. [6, 18]

Cloth tape: used alternately as a tie material (wrapping rolled textiles) and an edging material (vacuuming screen). The tape is not permanently in direct contact with the artifact, so any clean unstarched cloth tape from the fabric store will suffice. [3, 4, 6, 12]

Coarse bristle scrub brush: preferably a fairly large (2 inches or more) natural bristle paintbrush with the bristles cut to a 1-inch length. That gives just the right amount of scrubbing and flexibility. You can also use bristle-cleaning brushes. [2, 3, 6, 11]

Coin sleeves: the preferred method of archivally storing collectible coins. They are usually made of paper or plastic film. If you use the former, be sure they are made of archival or acid-free paper, and if the latter, be sure they are archival polyester (Mylar) with as little plasticizer as possible. [3, 6, 17]

Confetti from quality paper: useful as a benign packing material when padding artifacts in cases or boxes. If you have access to a shredder that deals mostly with photocopy paper, which often is wood pulp paper that has been partially neutralized, that should be fine. [3, 18]

Conservation-grade adhesive: particularly important in the preparation of matting and framing for works of art on paper. Conservators choose adhesives and other materials based on their performance, stability, and reversibility (which means it can be removed safely). Most paper conservators prepare their own adhesive from wheat starch paste or rice paste, but the methylcellulose kid's school glue works just fine. This is the gel glue that is typically pale blue or clear. [3, 6, 18]

Cotton cloth: for routine cleaning and polishing. Be sure to wash the cloth before using it to remove any bleach or starch. You can buy this at the fabric store, but I am a big believer in going to the thrift store and buying worn cotton sheets. They are invariably well worn and soft, work perfectly, and are easily disposable and guilt-free. All you need to do is check the label inside to make sure the sheets are cotton. [3, 4, 6, 14]

Cotton gloves, disposable: to protect the surfaces from the oils on your skin. At least a million times in these pages—well, maybe only a half million—I encourage you to handle specific collectibles with clean cotton gloves. Not canvas work gloves but soft gloves made from cotton knit (T-shirt material). They are cheap, easy to make, and should be washed or thrown away as soon as they get contaminated by dirt or your skin. [3, 6, 8, 11, 17, 19]

Cotton swabs: for cleaning intricate surfaces. I recommend buying the extra-long wooden stick swabs because they are easier to work with, but you can use swabs from the medicine cabinet in a pinch. [3, 6, 11]

Cotton webbing tape: sewn onto the Velcro tape used for mounting and hanging textiles and onto the back of the textile. Sometimes larger webbing tape (more than 1 inch) is starched, so be sure to wash it thoroughly before using. [4, 6, 12]

D

Dehumidifier: a critical appliance to have if you have problems with too much moisture in an enclosed space, such as a damp room or basement. A dehumidifier removes moisture from the air and redirects it, thus drying an entire space. Sometimes these can be bought cheaply at yard sales and thrift stores if you do not want to make an expensive investment. Check the appliance before purchasing it by turning it on and watching to see if the coils start "sweating," which means that water appears on the coils. [1, 11, 14]

Dessication (drying) chamber: used to "dry" silica gel. Silica gel is commonly used by conservators to control moisture within a contained space. It absorbs and desorbs excess moisture. Once silica gel has absorbed excess moisture, it needs to be dried in an enclosed space. You can bake it in a disposable baking pan at low temperature, about 150 degrees, for twenty-four hours, but the most convenient desiccating chamber is a Crock-Pot set on high for a full week. *Caution:* Do not use the same Crock-Pot to cook in. [1, 14]

Dishwashing soap, mild liquid: to remove surface dirt and grime. I prefer an anionic detergent such as Triton 100 (listed herein), but a mild liquid dishwashing detergent *without skin conditioners* (any conditioner is just another contaminant as far as I am concerned) is also very useful and acceptable. Ivory and Arm & Hammer are two good choices. Always check the label, and if the word *emollient* or *conditioner* appears, do not use that brand. [1]

Distilled water: for use in any water-based chemical process, including cleaning, because you want the cleanest water possible. Laboratories generally use totally purified water, known as deionized water, but assuming you do not have access to deionized water, grocery store distilled water will work just fine. [1, 2]

Dolly (or dollie): a wheeled platform used to move heavy objects from place to place. These can be purchased from resources listed below, or you can make your own with heavy-duty casters from the hardware store. [2, 11]

Double-stick tape: for sealing polyester envelopes. One method of protecting a paper artifact is to seal it in a polyester envelope, a process known as encapsulation. In our laboratory we have a sonic welder to close the polyester envelope, but you will probably have to use double-stick tape to seal the edges. Make sure to use a good-quality tape, not the cheap stuff from the dollar store. [3, 6]

D rings: attachments that go on the back of frames so the hanging wires can be attached. D rings allow a certain amount of flexibility, which prevents the wire from fraying as quickly. These rings can also be hung directly on screws or bolts in the wall, or wired with picture hanging wire (see the diagrams in Chapter 13). [2, 3, 11]

F

Face peel cleaner: to remove dirt and grime while not scrubbing the surface. Cleaning rough, delicate surfaces is a great challenge, and using a peel-off skin cleaner is one method. A non-emollient face peel from the natural food or department store will do the trick, but be sure that it is hypoallergenic and has no conditioners or emollients. [1]

Felt polishing block: critically needed for abrasive polishing of metals. I use a wedge of felt cut from a solid felt polishing wheel. Be sure to have separate polishing sets (abrasive, cloths, and blocks) for each kind of abrasive you use (pumice, tripoli, whiting, etc.). [2, 7, 11, 19]

Film sleeves, archival: for storing film. Pages of archival polyethylene or acid-free glassine subdivided into partitions exactly the right size for photographic film (you can get them to fit virtually every film size) is perhaps the second most important step you can take for preserving photographic film collections (cold dark storage being the first). [6, 21]

Fine polishing abrasive: to be used instead of sand and pumice, which will clean and polish your prized metal artifacts but are so coarse that they will also destroy their surfaces. A much better option is to use ultrafine polishes developed for other purposes, including jewelry, microscopy, and auto detailing. Polishes used by conservators include jeweler's tripoli, agglomerated micro-alumina normally used for preparing microscopy samples, whiting (precipitated chalk, although I use pulverized limestone from the garden supply or hardware store), ultra-fine auto-polishing compound, or even ground cigarette ashes. [6, 7, 8, 11, 19]

Fine steel wool: can be used with paste wax on lightly rusted steel or iron to stop further corrosion. While I generally prefer synthetic abrasive pads, steel wool will work as well. For heavily corroded brass or copper objects, you can use brass wool for the same purpose. [1, 2, 3, 6, 7, 11]

Fireproof cabinet: for any really valuable collection that can burn. The container should be the same kind you use for your valuable documents, legal papers, cash, and so forth. Louisa and I kept the manuscript of this book in a fireproof file cabinet while we were writing it to ensure its publication even if the house burned down. [6]

Fitted packing: for particularly fragile objects. The best packing provides the exact negative of the space occupied by the object. If your fragile object does not already have its own fitted packing, you can create your own as described on pages 95–96, by sculpting polyethylene or polypropylene foam to fit the object as closely as possible.

Flannel: a clean, soft fabric to polish metals and keep furniture dusted and buffed. Washed cotton flannel is perfect. You can buy it at a local store, but since I tend to wear plaid cotton flannel shirts and wear them until they are rags, my supply of polishing cloths is never farther away than my closet. [4, 6, 14]

Foam core board, archival: required for many preservation applications such as exhibition, storage, and protection. Archival foam core, which is a laminated panel of rigid polyethylene foam faced with noncolored rag, acid-free, or buffered heavyweight paper, comes in thickness ranging from ¹/₄ inch to 1 inch. [3, 6]

Folder, acid-free: for long-term safekeeping of flat artifacts, especially paper artwork, documents, and photographs. Acid-free or archival folders do not contribute to the further deterioration of their contents. [3, 6]

Foot-candle: a term that allows you to understand how much light an object is actually being exposed to. The original old-timey measurement of light intensity was determined by the light of a standard tallow candle from a distance of one foot. From two feet the same candle would provide 1/4 foot-candle (remember your inverse square law when it comes to calculating electromagnetic radiation). Fifty foot-candles of light are the same as fifty standard tallow candles at a distance of one foot, which is a great deal of light.

Frost-free freezer: needs to be part of your preservation lexicon. For photographic film collections especially, putting them in the freezer is the preferred strategy for keeping the collections intact for millennia. [1, 11]

G

Gel glue: a safe, stable, and reversible adhesive for use in matting documents and art on paper. Most gel glue from the department store, marketed as safe for kids' use, is made of methylcellulose, but be sure to read the label. Elmer's Blue Glue is a good brand. [1, 2, 3, 6, 7]

Glassine, archival: a semitransparent, fairly stiff, thin paper frequently used to wrap paper-based artifacts for storage and protection. There are many kinds of glassine, so be sure to use one made from rag, acid-free, or buffered paper. [3, 6]

Glazing: can be glass (from whence comes the term), tempered glass (always preferred), or synthetic polymers such as acrylic (Plexiglas) and polycarbonate (Lexan). Framed art is often protected by a transparent panel at the front, which goes by the general term *glazing*. [2, 3, 6]

Glazing points: small metal pins that hold glazing in its frame. [2, 3]

Graphite powder: a dry lubricant for moving machine parts where oil is not appropriate; for example, when one of the moving parts is not metal, a dry lubricant like powdered graphite can be used. It is a perfectly stable material incapable of deterioration because it is pure carbon. Be very cautious when using graphite powder since it gets everywhere if you are not careful. [2, 6, 11]

H

Hanging wire: several wires braided together for strength and flexibility. Just as stranded rope is stronger than a single mega-thread of cloth, stranded wire is stronger and more flexible than a big single wire. That is the theory behind picture-hanging wire, which is used to hang framed artwork on the wall. [2, 6, 11]

Hook-and-loop attaching system: see **Velcro.**

Hot air gun: for drying out washed and cleaned metal objects, and liquefying wax when coating steel and iron. Nothing works quite so well as a hot air gun designed for shop use (paint-stripping hot air guns set to low are perfect). [2, 3, 6]

Hot plate: can be used to melt a bowl of wax. Make sure you don't turn it so high that if any wax drips on the heating element it ignites. I've heard stories . . . [1, 2, 3, 14]

Hygrometer: used to monitor and control temperature and relative humidity. Measuring them accurately in the old days was done with a very expensive, high-maintenance device called a "recording hygrothermograph," but fortunately for you the electronics revolution has arrived here, too. Inexpensive digital units the size of a small candy bar are widely available to give constant and accurate temperature and humidity readings. [6, 11]

I

Indelible ink pen: to record information about an artifact. For example, you can record on the envelope containing a photograph information that you don't want to fade away. Never, ever record on an artifact except as detailed for photographic artifacts! You might also use a pencil, which will not fade but can be rubbed off. Make sure to write on the envelope before placing the artifact inside it, since ink is a liquid and just might seep through to the other side. [3, 6, 11]

Insect traps: an effective means of controlling insects so they do not get near your collectibles. Use insect traps featuring pheromone attractants (pheromone sticky traps). This is another way of saying the sticky inside of the box/bug trap is baited with something that smells like a hormonal perfume that bugs find irresistible. [6, 25]

J

Japanese tissue paper: a favorite for a wide range of uses in conservation and restoration. Hinges to attach art on paper to a matting system must be made from a very strong, stable, lightweight material, so Japanese tissue paper is the material of choice for most paper conservators. This gauzy paper has an almost unbelievable strength-to-mass ratio. [3, 6]

Jeweler's rouge or tripoli: an excellent polish for copper, brass, bronze, and steel. A commonly used ultrafine metal polish, it is usually a mixture of tripoli, an extremely fine abrasive, and a little wax and petroleum jelly. For silver it is a little too coarse. You can dilute and clean off jeweler's rouge with mineral spirits. [2, 3, 6, 19]

K

Kraft paper: an excellent disposable working surface for a lot of preservation cleaning exercises. Since it is so inexpensive and large, supplying a new, clean piece constantly assures that your efforts will not be compromised by contaminating one surface with the cleaning debris of another. Kraft paper is not a good wrapping paper for direct contact with artifacts because it is an unbuffered wood pulp paper. [1, 2, 3, 6, 11, 18]

L

Large rubber or plastic containers: used for the safe storing of most collectibles in hostile environments. With a little investigation and good consumerism you can identify good-quality, sealable storage containers made from polyethylene and polypropylene, two fairly stable synthetic materials. Rubbermaid and Tupperware are both made from the right types of plastics. [2, 3, 6, 11, 16]

Latex gloves: for those cleaning processes that involve liquids, particularly solvents. It is important to protect your skin as well as your lungs and eyes. Latex gloves work for grimy soap-and-water-type cleaning and are cheap and disposable, ensuring that you do not contaminate one object with the dirt from another. Latex is not impermeable, however, and actually dissolves in many types of organic solvents. My habit is to use chemical-resistant nitrile gloves, which wear and feel a lot like latex. [1, 2, 3, 5, 6, 7, 8, 9, 15, 17, 19, 21]

L bracket: a bent piece of steel screwed or bolted to the wall to support the bottom of a large hanging frame such as a painting or mirror. [2, 11]

L fold polyester sleeve: formed by creasing a sheet of archival polyester into a folder and welding along one of the formerly open edges adjacent to the fold. This enables you to slip paper artifacts easily into and out of the sleeve. You can make your own or buy them by the case in a wide range of sizes. [3, 6]

Lifters: assistance in moving large artifacts in a way that is safe for both the artifact and you. You should have the requisite number of people to help you; for example, one other person for small chairs and so forth, two for sofas, and up to four for really heavy, clunky objects such as a sideboard or a wardrobe.

Light meter: a handy device that measures the intensity of light. It measures the light not at the bulb or at the window but at the place where you hold the meter. By placing the meter adjacent to your artifact, you can get a reading of the foot-candles or lux, which tells you how much light your object is being exposed to. [6]

Linen, coarse: placed over a textile surface as a protective screen during vacuuming. This prevents the textile from being abraded as the vacuum brush is moved over the surface and also prevents textile fragments from being sucked up. Coarse linen fabric as well as a plastic window screen can be used. [3, 4, 6]

Linen or fine rag stationery: made from pulverized and fermented linen fiber pulp and cut into sheets. Because of the materials and processes employed in the making of linen paper, it is among the most stable and permanent man-made materials known to exist. [3, 6, 15, 18]

Linen tape, gummed: used by book and paper conservators for the assembly of matting and framing systems. Gummed linen tape is a strip of linen fabric impregnated with a water-soluble adhesive that can be activated by moisture. [3, 6]

Lint-free cloths (flannel or similar fabric): for polishing metal objects and light cleaning of many other artifacts. A good supply of clean soft lint-free cloths is absolutely necessary. For most of the work I use litho pads (listed below), and for the rest I use new washed cotton flannel from the fabric store or washed worn cotton bedding from the thrift store. Either way, I dispose of them frequently so that I do not harm my stuff with contaminants from whatever else I may have been cleaning. [4, 6, 18, 20]

Litho pads: one of my favorite tools in my preservation tool kit. Litho pads, more accurately called lithography wipes, are small folded squares (about 4 inches by 4 inches) of lint-free cotton felt manufactured for cleaning lithography and other printing plates for the creation of art prints. Clean and easily disposable, they serve as my "go to" tool for virtually every cleaning process described in this book. [6, 18, 20]

Lucite case (also known as Plexiglas): helps keep your stuff safe from pollutants, contaminants, and especially handling. [3, 6, 19]

Lumber: for making both the shadow box and the hanging system for large textiles. A new or at least clean piece of usually clear pine, which actually measures $^3/_4$ inch by $3^3/_4$ inches, is suitable for these tasks. [2]

Lux: a measurement of light intensity. One lux equals 1/10.76th of a foot-candle, or put another way, one foot-candle equals 10.76 lux. (See **Foot-candle**.)

M

Machine oil: for moving parts of machines. A little (or sometimes a lot of) lubricant is usually required to make sure the parts do not wear excessively against one another or fuse together (especially important for long-term storage when items are no longer actively used). A drop placed at a critical location will determine whether an artifact survives as a machine or as a "sculpture" of pieces all rusted together. For delicate machines (tape decks, for example) sewing machine oil will suffice. For industrial machinery use industrial machine oil. [1, 2, 7, 11]

Map case: for the preservation of oversized paper documents such as large-format magazines, newspapers, or prints. A map case is a very large chest of drawers where all the drawers are just an inch or two tall and allow the documents to be stored unfolded and flat. The best map cases are made from metal with fused powder coating or baked enamel paint. [6]

Masking tape: a roll of paper gummed with pressure-sensitive adhesive that will stay put for at least a few years. The adhesive on masking tape will eventually dry out and lose its adhesion and become brittle. It will also stain whatever it is affixed to, so it should never be used in direct contact with any artifact. [1, 2, 3, 6, 7, 9, 11, 15, 18]

Mat board, archival: a heavy laminated paper stock. When preparing flat artworks for display, they are placed in a frame of heavy paperboard called a window mat. Both the window mat and the backing board (the board that goes on the rear of the artwork and to which the artwork is usually attached) are mat boards. Like all other paper-based products recommended for preservation, mat boards should be made from rag paper or other acid-free archival material. [3, 6]

Mat cutter: a razor-blade-type tool used to cut heavy paper stock such as a mat board. [3, 4, 6, 7, 11]

Measuring spoons: invaluable for mixing up solutions or slurries. Do not intermix your cooking utensils with your preservation tools. Buy separate sets for each. [1, 2, 3, 5, 6, 7, 8, 11]

Measuring tapes: necessary for wide-ranging preservation efforts. There are two types: retractable steel or plastic measuring tapes, often called carpenter's tapes, and flexible cloth or plastic measuring tapes, called tailor's tapes or sewing tapes. [2, 3, 4, 6, 7, 11]

Methylcellulose adhesive: an easily used and obtained acceptable adhesive that is available as either children's gel glue or as wallpaper paste. One of the critical factors in preparing paper artifacts for exhibit is the manner in which they are mounted (glued) to supporting boards. Choosing the wrong adhesive can end up destroying the artifact. [1, 2, 3, 4, 6, 7, 11, 18]

Mineral spirits: fairly mild organic solvent especially useful for removing oily, greasy, waxy contaminants from hard surfaces. It is not the same thing as mineral water! Can also be called paint thinner (*not* lacquer thinner) or petroleum benzene (*not* benzene). Make sure to wear protective gloves, respirator, and eyewear when using. *Highly flammable. Use with extreme caution.* [2, 3, 6, 7, 8, 9, 11]

Mixing bowls: for various activities described in the book. I keep a variety of sizes on hand for purposes ranging from mixing my own face peel concoctions to melting and pouring pewter. Consider taking a trip to the thrift store to acquire Pyrex or similar bowls. [1, 2, 3, 11, 14]

Moly bolts: a split hollow cylinder with a threaded rod or bolt through the center. When hanging heavy artwork (or anything else for that matter) from a sheetrock wall, moly bolts are the fasters used to penetrate the wall and provide an anchor for the hanging wire or other mechanism. The cylinder is inserted through a hole drilled in the wall and "mushrooms" on the back side of it when tightened, thus anchoring the threaded bolt to the wall. See the illustration on page 237 for a clearer idea. [2, 3, 11]

Monel staples: for use in a preservation setting because they are both strong and corrosion resistant. Monel is an alloy. [11, 12]

Moth crystals: made from a toxic chemical such as thymol or eugenol and used to protect textiles from moth infestations. Never place them in direct contact with your textile (wrap them in acid-free tissue or clean muslin first). Also, never use them in paper collections because the crystals will redeposit on the paper. Remember that these are toxic materials, so use with caution; wear hand and eye protection, and use in a well-ventilated space. [1, 2, 3, 6]

Mounting board, archival: provides a rigid support on which to mount or attach artifacts for exhibit or display. Always use either acid-free/archival mat board or archival foam core boards. [3, 6]

Movie film paper core: used for storing large-format movie film. It is best to coil it around an archival paper cylinder core designed to store long films with minimal stress and a benign environment. [6]

Mylar: high-density polyester film. You may be most familiar with it as mirroring or shading film for windows. Archival Mylar is a high-density transparent polyester film made with as few unnecessary additives as possible. [1, 2, 3, 6, 11]

N

Nitrile gloves: designed to be impenetrable by common organic chemicals and solvents. Unlike latex gloves, which can allow many chemicals to penetrate them, disposable nitrile gloves really protect your skin! They look pretty much like latex surgical gloves except that they are usually either bright blue or purple and have a smoother, denser texture. Whenever I am in prolonged contact with organic solvents such as acetone, toluene, alcohol, or mineral spirits, not only do I wear a respirator mask, but I always wear nitrile gloves. [5, 6, 11]

Nylon hosiery: used when coating iron and steel artifacts with molten wax because sheer nylon is the best way to wipe them off and buff them up. How you get the nylons, new or used, is up to you. [1]

O

One percent solution: a mixture of 1 percent neutral detergent and 99 percent water. A way to make my favorite aqueous cleaning solution is to take one teaspoon of detergent to a pint of distilled water.

Overhead projector film: a clean, disposable, high-density transparent masking sheet. It is not an archival material, because it is made from cellulose acetate, but transparent projector or photocopying film is extremely useful. For long-term archival stability, you need to use Mylar. [3, 6, 11, 15, 16, 18]

P

Padded hangers: for preserving hanging costumes and clothing. Bugs and light may be the worst enemies of textiles, but creases are bad, too. The hangers must be padded to prevent stress to the fabric that is folded over the hanger. [4, 6]

Paintbrush: for gently removing loose particulate matter, also known as dirt and dust. While any clean soft brush will suffice, I prefer those made from nylon bristles for latex or water paints rather than those made from natural bristles for oil paint and varnishes, and the former is pretty much impervious to mold, insect, and rodent attack. They can also be used for the application of coatings. [1, 2, 3, 6, 11, 15]

Paint-stripping gloves: to protect your hands during long-term exposure to organic solvents. You can use rubberized paint-stripping gloves from the hardware store, but they are bulky and make it hard to maneuver in. If touch and dexterity are important, use disposable nitrile gloves. [2, 3, 5, 7, 8, 9]

Paper envelopes, archival/acid-free: will last for centuries and help prevent deterioration of the artifact inside. Any loose, flat artifact such as photos, prints, and documents should be kept in an archival folder or envelope. They can be obtained in a variety of sizes in both standard paper and glassine. [3, 6]

Paraffin wax, solid/molten: an almost perfect preservation material. Clean paraffin wax, a purified petrochemical, seals and coats, and does not degrade unless it is burned. Microcrystalline wax is one commercial form of paraffin-type wax. Grocery store canning paraffin and uncolored unscented candles are both acceptable sources for paraffin. [1, 2, 3, 6, 11, 15, 19]

Paste wax: stable protective coating applied to furniture and cast iron to protect them from surrounding environment. Make sure to purchase high-quality paste waxes that contain no silicone or toluene (read the label). [1]

Pencil (graphite): the preferred tool for writing around historic artifacts. It eliminates the possibility of ink smudges or marks on the artifact. A medium-hard pencil, such as an HB or 2H, works well, since it can make a clean mark that is not easily smudged. [3, 6, 11]

Penetrating oil: ultralightweight, low-viscosity machine oil. Preserving and restoring mechanical devices depends on keeping moving parts moving. In situations where pieces are stuck, saturating with penetrating oil is sometimes helpful. Two penetrating oils I commonly employ are WD40 and

Marvel Mystery Oil, although I am sure there are many others. [2, 3, 6, 7, 9, 11]

Permanent marker: used for marking artifact housings, such as envelopes, folders, and boxes. It is also better than a pencil for marking directly on the frames of photographic slides. [2, 3, 6, 11, 18]

Photocopier, book duplicating: a special device with a folded glass platen that allows the book to be opened to only 90 degrees to make a copy. It does not require the book to be smashed onto a flat glass plate for the image to be created. To find such a specialized tool, check with any library with a rare book collection, or high-end antiquarian book dealers.

Photographer's compressed air can: to remove loose dust and dirt from the surface of artifacts, a vital part of housekeeping and maintenance. Spray cans of compressed air are the easiest way to blow clean air over the surface in order to remove the loose particulates. [2, 3, 4, 5, 6, 7, 8, 9, 11, 17, 19, 21]

pH strip: used to identify the acidity or alkalinity of an object. The least expensive and most low-tech means of doing this is to use distilled water and disposable paper pH strips that change color according to the acidity present. [5, 6, 8, 11]

Picture wire: see **Hanging wire.**

Polyester batting: used as stuffing and padding for supporting artifacts. [3, 4, 6]

Polyester (Mylar) envelopes: an archival housing for storing flat artifacts for preservation. You can either make them yourself or purchase them from the archival suppliers listed below. [3, 6]

Polyethylene film: made from newly made polyethylene, often referred to as virgin polyethylene, as opposed to recycled polyethylene. Sometimes the most important thing for preserving your prized collectibles is enclosing them in a sealed, chemically stable plastic bag or wrapping them in a sheet of similar film. For the most part, a sealable bag of archival polyethylene is the tool of choice for "not flat" artifacts. Archival polyethylene contains as few additive chemicals as possible, additives such as plasticizers (to increase softness and flexibility) and release agents (to keep it from sticking together). These additives leech out from the plastic as contaminants and are undesirable for preservation, so be sure to check before purchasing. [1, 2, 3, 5, 6, 11, 15, 16, 18]

Polyethylene foam: clean, inert padding material for storing and supporting stuff that is three-dimensional. Polyethylene foam is available in different levels of density, hardness, and thickness (usually 1-inch increments in 2-foot by 8-foot sheets), usually under the brand name Ethafoam. An ultrafine polyethylene foam is known as Volare. [3, 6, 22]

Polyethylene squirt bottles: a squeezable bottle with a small spout. For most chemicals mentioned in this book, a polyethylene bottle will suffice. Water bottles work great. *Make sure you label it properly.* [1, 2, 3, 5, 6, 7, 8, 9, 11, 15, 16]

Polyethylene terephthalate (PET): a high-tech plastic developed primarily for food packaging. It is a stable, oxygen-impermeable moldable plastic that can be formed into jars and containers for foods that are especially oxygen sensitive, such as peanut butter and carbonated beverages. Because of these properties it is a perfect choice for archiving collectibles. A plastic PET jar with a lid is referred to as a time capsule in this book. [3, 5, 6, 8, 11, 15, 16]

Polypropylene foam: much thinner and finer textured than polyethylene foam. It is used when the finer texture of the foam is desired. A common brand name is Nalgene. [6, 11, 16, 22]

Pumice powder: a fairly coarse abrasive that is sometimes appropriate for scouring the surface of a rusty or heavily textured iron surface in concert with a stiff-bristle cleaning brush. [2, 6, 7, 9, 11, 19]

Pyrex saucepan: used for the "wet" cleaning of metal objects, such as furniture hardware. I buy my tough glassy baking pans from the thrift store. [1, 2, 3, 5, 6, 7, 8, 11, 14]

Q

Quake wax: protects objects from falling off tables and other surfaces during an earthquake. It also helps protect the object when someone accidentally bumps into the table or knocks into the cabinet. Attaching stuff (such as figurines, cups, and plates) is accomplished through the application of daubs of this sticky wax, also called museum wax, to the underside of the object and then pressing the object down on the shelf or table. [3, 6]

R

Rag paper: made from pulverized and fermented cotton and linen rags. It is among the most stable and enduring materials ever devised by mankind, with a potential life span of thousands of years. Because of its chemical neutrality, rag paper is a favorite material for many preservation applications. [3, 6, 18]

Razor knife: a heavy-duty keen-edged tool that may come in many forms. It is used to trim heavy paper, paper boards, and support panels such as foam core. [2, 3, 5, 6, 7, 9, 11, 15, 18]

Record sleeves, archival: two U-shaped envelopes, one inside the other. The inner sleeve is glassine, and the outer sleeve is a fine-textured rag or buffered paper. While phonograph records are fairly stable chemically, they should still be stored in paper sleeves made from acid-free or archival paper. [6, 13]

Respirator (organic solvent mask): used to prevent pollution from getting into your body. Whenever I am involved with any task requiring long-term exposure to organic solvents, I wear protective gloves and eyewear and, especially, a protective respirator mask. My favorite is one with replaceable activated charcoal canisters from the auto body supply house. Disposable dust masks impregnated with activated charcoal are better than nothing, but not by much. [2, 5, 6, 7, 8, 9, 11]

Router: an electrical power hand tool with a spinning cutter bit that either cuts contoured edges on wooden boards or, more important for this book, cuts grooves into which backing boards or glazing can be inset. Using a router is not for the uninitiated. [2, 7, 11]

Rubber hose (1/4 inch): used to vacuum tiny spaces. Available from the hardware or auto parts store, it is easily attached to a full-sized vacuum hose. [2, 7, 9, 11, 16]

Rubbing alcohol: a mild cleaning agent that is found in the drugstore and used in specific circumstances. [1, 2, 3, 6, 8, 11]

S

Safety glasses: protective gear that shields the eyes from chemicals, flyaway pieces of stuff, and so on. Many of the activities in this book, while not really hazardous, require safety precautions. For drilling, cutting, and working with open solvent solutions, wear safety glasses with side shields. [1, 2, 3, 5, 6, 7, 8, 9, 11, 15, 16, 19]

Silica gel: collects or gives off moisture in the air. Sold in granular form, silica gel does this efficiently for an infinite number of moisture cycles. You have encountered silica gel if you have ever purchased any small piece of electronic hardware or photographic apparatus. These packages contain a small sugar-pack-size packet of silica gel to control the moisture in the packaging. [3, 5, 6, 8]

Silicone caulk: a rubbery adhesive for gluing and sealing connections. [1, 2, 3, 7, 11]

Soft-bristle brush: for the gentle agitation of the surface of an artifact in order to dislodge loose or nearly loose dirt. I usually prefer soft brushes such as an artist's brush (watercolor brushes are very soft, while oil brushes are a little stiffer) or soft toothbrushes. [1, 2, 3, 6, 7, 11]

Soft cotton string: one of the best tools for getting into the grooves of candlesticks, for example, with the polishing slurry. [1, 2, 3, 4, 5, 6, 7, 8, 9, 11, 15, 18, 19]

Spray filter mask: to protect your lungs when working around dusty artifacts. Also known as an industrial dust mask. [2, 3, 5, 6, 7, 8, 9, 11]

Spray gloss acrylic or cellulose nitrate lacquer: After cleaning and polishing metal artifacts, the effect can be extended by coating the surface completely with a stable coating to prevent dirt and tarnish. No coating material is perfect, but spray acrylic or cellulose nitrate comes as close as anything else on the open market for coating copper, brass, or silver. [1, 2, 3, 6, 9, 11]

Stainless steel mounting pins: heavyweight straight pins, used to mount small textiles to a support backing board. [3, 4, 6, 12]

Stamp sleeves: used for housing and storing stamps and stamp collections. They are usually made from acid-free or buffered glassine. [3, 6, 17]

Staple gun: a mechanical, electrical, or pneumatic heavy-duty staple that can drive staples into solid wood. [1, 2, 3, 6, 7, 11, 15]

Straight pins with ball heads: used to pin together the various elements of a textile hanging assemblage to facilitate the sewing. [3, 4, 11, 12]

Stud finder: an electronic device that when lightly rubbed horizontally over the surface of a standard sheetrock wall will beep or light up as it crosses a wood or steel stud behind the sheetrock. [2, 6, 11]

T

Tapestry needles: required for attaching of Velcro hanging tape to large textiles. [4, 6]

Tissue paper, archival/acid-free: a workhorse of preservation storage. It is used for wrapping, storing, and stuffing artifacts. Conservators use acres of it. [3, 6]

Tripoli: see **Jeweler's rouge.**

Triton 100: A pH-neutral non-ionic detergent that cleans without harming the object if used correctly. A gentle detergent is most often used for routine artifact cleaning, and Triton 100 is my favorite. [6]

T square: used to figure out the axis lines of large flat artworks, especially textiles. Those used most often are carpenter's framing squares and sheetrock hanger's 4-foot T-square. Check the edges of the tools to ensure there are no burrs or anything else to snag on the artifact. If you find anything that would snag, remove it using fine sandpaper. [2, 6, 11]

Tweezers, Teflon-tipped: for handling small, delicate artifacts with big, sweaty, corrosive fingers. Tweezers should never be too far away when handling small stuff. Metal-tipped tweezers can often snag or otherwise damage or contaminate a gentle artifact. On the other hand, tweezers with Teflon tips are smooth and inert. One viable alternative is to use polished bamboo tweezers, but they are not so easy to come by. I make my own, but then I'm a nut about both bamboo and making my own gadgets. [2, 3, 5, 6, 7, 8, 11, 17, 21]

U

Ultraviolet (UV) filter film: polyester or acetate film impregnated with a high concentration of ultraviolet light–absorbing chemicals. Because it absorbs so strongly at the blue end of the light spectrum, it has a faint yellow tinge. UV filter film should be on every window in your house, and sleeves of this film should be around each fluorescent tube. [2, 6, 17]

Utility knife: works well for quick cutting of paper or fabric used in preservation cleaning, wrapping, or storing. It has disposable blades, and I use ½-inch snap-off blades so that I can always have a new cutting edge ready to go. [1, 2, 3, 4, 5, 6, 7, 8, 9, 11, 12, 13, 15, 18]

V

Varnish: an excellent sealant for wood. Whenever wood is used in a closed space with delicate artifacts, the wood should be sealed with a stable coating. Shellac, alkyd, polyurethane, and molten wax are all excellent (although technically wax is not a varnish). [2, 3, 6, 7]

Velcro: a two-part attaching system in which one piece of flannel-like material (the loop) is stuck to a companion material with zillions of tiny plastic barbs (the hook). This system, which is marketed and known widely as Velcro, is used in a thousand different ways, from replacing shoelaces on sneakers to binding rope. In this book Velcro is used to hang textile artworks, and I often use it for attaching minimally intrusive upholstery to seating furniture. [1, 2, 3, 4, 6, 11, 12, 15, 18, 19]

Vinyl window screen: offers excellent protection when vacuuming textiles. Cut a piece about a foot square or so. Wrap the edges with masking tape folded in half lengthwise or cloth tape folded in half lengthwise and sewn around the edge. Place screen directly on the surface of the textile, and pass the vacuum attachment across the screen. This removes loose dirt and dust without damaging the textile. This is a preservation tool that will last for years. [1, 2, 11]

W

Wallpaper paste: an excellent conservation-grade adhesive when made from methylcellulose (see above). It is excellent for mounting paper artifacts in a matting and framing system. [1, 2, 3, 6, 11]

Waxed paper: can be used for many cleaning exercises, such as isolating the area being cleaned from the adjacent surface that is not being cleaned. Ordinary kitchen waxed paper works especially well in specific circumstances described later in the book. [1, 2, 3, 6, 11]

Weights: to weigh down small areas while adhesives dry when mounting a paper artwork into a matting system. In this instance I use small tetrahedral lead fishing weights. To seal them and protect my hands and the artwork from smudges by the soft lead, I coat them with a heavy rubber paint known as "handle grip" or something similar. If I do not want to place the rubber-coated weight directly on the working surface, I first place a small piece of acrylic glazing (with polished edges) on the surface to protect it and then put the weight on top of that. [2, 11]

SUPPLIERS LIST

With only a few exceptions, the supplies needed for preservation are easily obtained from your everyday supermarket or hardware store as long as you know exactly what to ask for. With the above list, now you know. Also included are websites and phone numbers so that you can order the supplies without having to leave your house.

1. Local grocery, pharmacies, and department stores (Sears, Wal-Mart, Target, etc.)
2. Local paint, building supply, and hardware stores
3. Local and mail-order/Internet art and craft supply stores

Dick Blick Art Materials
P. O. Box 1267
Galesburg, IL 61402-1267
(800) 828-4548
www.dickblick.com

Michaels, the Arts and Crafts Store
8000 Bent Branch Drive
Irving, TX 75063
(800) 642-4235
www.michaels.com

Pearl Paint
(800) 221-6845
www.pearlpaint.com

Daniel Smith
P. O. Box 84268
Seattle, WA 98124-5568
(800) 426-6740
www.danielsmith.com

4. Local fabric stores
5. Lab safety suppliers

Lab Safety Supply
P. O. Box 1368
Janesville, WI 53547-1368
(800) 356-0783
www.labsafety.com

6. Conservation/archival suppliers
Recent trips to greeting card and gift stores reveal that many of them are now carrying a wide range of archival and preservation materials such as acid-free tissue, storage boxes, and archival mat boards. For specialty Plexiglas or polycarbonate products, contact a local plastics fabricator (look in the yellow pages under Plexiglas).

Archival Methods
235 Middle Road
Henrietta, NY 14467
(866) 877-7050
www.archivalmethods.com

Archivalware
(800) 442-7576
www.archivalware.com

Conservation Resources
International
5532 Port Royal Road
Springfield, VA 22151
(703) 321-7730; (800)
    634-6932
www.conservationresources
    .com

Conservator's Emporium
100 Standing Rock Circle
Reno, NV 89511
(775) 852-0404
www.consemp.com

Gaylord Brothers
P. O. Box 4901
Syracuse, NY 13221-4901
(800) 448-6160
www.gaylord.com

Hollinger
P. O. Box 6185
3810 S. Four Mile Run
    Drive
Arlington, VA 22206
(703) 671-6600

Light Impressions
P. O. Box 787
Brea, CA 92822-0787
(800) 828-6216
www.lightimpressionsdirect
    .com

Metal Edge Box
337 West Walnut Street
P. O. Box 1488
North Wales, PA 19454
(215) 699-8755
www.metaledge.com/
    metal_edge_boxes/

Talas
568 Broadway
New York, NY 10012
(212) 219-0770
www.talas-nyc.com

University Products
517 Main Street
P. O. Box 101
Holyoke, MA 01041
(800) 628-1912
www.universityproducts.com

7. Specialty and woodworking tool suppliers

Micro-Mark
340 Snyder Avenue
Berkeley Heights, NJ 07922
(800) 225-1066
www.micromark.com

Seven Corners Hardware
216 West 7th Street
Saint Paul, MN 55102
(651) 224-4859
www.7corners.com

Small Parts Inc.
13980 N.W. 58th Court
P. O. Box 4650
Miami Lakes, FL 33014-0650
(800) 220-4242
www.smallparts.com

Tool Crib of the North
www.toolcrib.amazon.com

Woodcraft Supply
(800) 225-1153
www.woodcraft.com

8. Scientific laboratory suppliers

Fisher Scientific
1 Reagent Lane
Fairlawn, NJ 07410
(201) 796-7100
www.fisherscientific.com

Thomas Scientific
P. O. Box 99
Swedesboro, NJ 08085
www.thomasscientific.com

Sigma Chemical
www.sigmaaldrich.com

9. Local auto, auto body, and paint suppliers
10. Local liquor stores (not available in all states)
11. Mail-order/web industrial suppliers

W. W. Grainger
(888) 361-8649
www.grainger.com

McMaster-Carr
P. O. Box 4355
Chicago, IL 60680-4355
www.mcmaster.com

MSC Industrial Supply
28551 Laura Court
Elkhart, IN 46517
(800) 645-7270
www.mscdirect.com

12. Local upholstery suppliers
13. Radio Shack and electronics stores

Radio Shack
www.radioshack.com

14. Local thrift stores
15. Discount warehouse stores

BJ's Wholesale Club
www.bjs.com

Sam's Club
www.samsclub.com

Costco.com
www.costco.com

16. Industrial plastic suppliers

Consolidated Plastics
8181 Darrow Road
Twinsburg, OH 44087
(800) 362-1000
www.consolidatedplastics.com

17. Local or mail-order/Internet coin and stamp stores (there are scores, so make sure to order the archival supplies described in this book)

18. Office, packing, and paper suppliers; in addition to local suppliers you can try:

Office Depot
www.officedepot.com

Staples
www.staples.com

Paper Plus
www.paperplus.com

19. Jewelry craft suppliers

Gesswein
255 Hancock Avenue
P. O. Box 3998
Bridgeport, CT 06605-0936
(203) 366-5400
www.gesswein.com

Shor
20 Parkway West
Mt. Vernon, NY 10552
(914) 667-1100
www.shorinternational.com

Rio Grande
(800) 545-2329
www.riogrande.com

20. Commercial printing suppliers—makers of Litho pads (also known as lithography wipes)

Nensco
(800) 293-0830
www.nensco.com

21. Local or mail-order/web photo supply stores (there are scores; just make sure you purchase archival-grade supplies as described in this book)

22. Specialty packing suppliers (I get my archival foams locally, but you might not be able to)

Advanced Packaging Inc.
Seton Business Park
4818 Seton Drive
Baltimore, MD 21215
(410) 358-9444

All-Foam Products
2546 Live Oak Lane
Buffalo Grove, IL 60089-4609
www.allfoam.com

Foam Design Products
P. O. Box 12178
Lexington, KY 40581
(859) 231-7006, ext. 309
www.foamdesign.com

23. Industrial suppliers of Ageless oxygen scavenger

Mitsubishi Gas Chemical America, Inc.
520 Madison Avenue, 17th Floor
New York, NY 10022
(212) 752-4620; (888) 330-6422
www.mgc-a.com

24. Silver care and maintenance suppliers

Nancy Silver
www.nancysilver.com

25. Suppliers of professional pest control products

Professional Pest Control Products, Inc.
6920 Pine Forest Road
Pensacola, FL 32526
www.pestproducts.com

26. Audiophile suppliers (tape cleaners)

www.tapeonline.com

27. *www.savingstuff.com*—an ongoing information source for readers

Index